D0369060

Conservative
Environmentalism

CONSERVATIVE ENVIRONMENTALISM

Reassessing the Means, Redefining the Ends

James R. Dunn and John E. Kinney

Q

QUORUM BOOKS
Westport, Connecticut
London

Library of Congress Cataloging-in-Publication Data

Dunn, James R. (date)
    Conservative environmentalism : reassessing the means, redefining
the ends / James R. Dunn, John E. Kinney.
      p.   cm.
    Includes bibliographical references and index.
    ISBN 0–89930–993–3 (alk. paper)
    1. Environmentalism. 2. Human ecology. 3. Social ecology.
I. Kinney, John E. II. Title.
GE195.D86   1996
363.7—dc20   96–3620

British Library Cataloguing in Publication Data is available.

Library of Congress Catalog Card Number: 96–3620
ISBN: 0–89930–993–3

First published in 1996

Quorum Books, 88 Post Road West, Westport, CT 06881
An imprint of Greenwood Publishing Group, Inc.

Printed in the United States of America

The paper used in this book complies with the
Permanent Paper Standard issued by the National
Information Standards Organization (Z39.48–1984).

10 9 8 7 6 5 4 3 2 1

Contents

Figures and Tables

FIGURES

TABLES

Preface

We dedicate this book to the environmentally concerned. They are the people who, to the best of their ability, strive to leave a better world for their children. We think that this includes the vast majority of people of all races and of all cultures. We, the authors, include ourselves in this group.

The definition of environmental improvement is relative. It is time-, technology-, and culture-sensitive. For example, predatory animals, starvation, and excessive cold were considerable problems for Paleolithic humans, but these came under acceptable control relatively early in the history of our advanced culture. Gradually agricultural productivity per unit of land increased, and cities and towns developed because a few people could feed many. Production efficiency increased with the Industrial Revolution, and more humans could enjoy a pleasant living environment.

Although there were many gains, the environment still took its toll on humanity as diseases such as cholera, typhoid, tuberculosis, infantile paralysis, malaria, and the plagues flared frequently. In addition, transportation, living at home, and working were all dangerous in comparison with current standards. As late as 1900 American longevity was only 47.3 years. Currently, the populations of only a few Third World nations have such a low average life expectancy. Now, Americans' average longevity is 75.6 years. Currently, such lifestyle choices as smoking, diet, and exercise have major influences on longevity in industrial nations. (Third World people, we note, have few lifestyle choices because they have little control over the environment.)

People of advanced nations have also increasingly cushioned themselves from drought, floods, earthquakes, and crop failures. The cushioning process has not been perfect, so improvements will continue.

Throughout most of civilization's history, humans were preoccupied with protecting themselves from the natural environment. Little thought was given to protecting the natural environment from humans. Still, keen observers in the immediate pre-Christian era saw some effects of human occupation on Earth. In the fifth century B.C. the Spartan general Pausanias related filling of the harbor at Miletus in what is now western Turkey to deforestation along the Meander River. (We show why it took over two thousand years to correct the problem through reforestation.)

The American George Perkins Marsh (1864, 1874) describes the impact of humans on Earth both in history and during his life. (We show why most of the problems he saw are now under control in industrial nations.)

Prior to World War II, America's efforts to protect the environment from people centered around formation of national parks and in some states actions to reduce water pollution. In 1948 Congress endorsed two approaches to clean streams. One was a federal law (PL 80-845) that saw a need for national action and provided limited funding for studies. The law gave no guidelines. The other approach was approval of an eight-state compact establishing the Ohio River Valley Water Sanitation Commission (Orsanco) to protect the quality of the basin's waters. Orsanco was intended to be a model for states with common waterways.

Local leaders initiated the concept and got the compact approved. The guidelines in the compact stated that the commission should counsel with those it would regulate. Orsanco regulations on standards and treatment requirements had the force of law. There were no recognized procedures for counseling. Moreover, there were no agreed-upon techniques for measuring, reducing, or treating waste discharges, particularly from industries. Some twelve organizations published analytical methods. The result depended on the method used. Additionally, states, cities, and industries had their own variations. Under Orsanco leadership a staff of five engineers coordinated a joint effort to provide data as basis for judgment. States, cities, and generic industry groups in the basin, as well as national organizations whose members could be affected by Orsanco conclusions, cooperated. The findings and recommendations were published by Orsanco from 1951 to 1954. John Kinney was committee coordinator in development of the reports. Nationwide demand for the information far exceeded expectations. Interest in decreasing human impact on the environment was obviously considerable.

Industry and political entities were involved. Such research was underway by metal finishing, steel, chemical, oil refining, distillery, bituminous coal, municipal water treatment plants, and aquatic life advisory committees. The groups also funded abstracting toxicity literature for evaluation by Kettering Laboratory in Cincinnati as basis for Orsanco's water quality standards.

Two lessons should have been learned from the 1948 congressional delegations of authority: (1) with competent leadership and opportunity, all users of a natural resource will, in their best self-interest, work toward long-term solutions; and (2) local cooperation can solve environmental problems and have the virtue of sensitivity to local conditions. The lessons were not learned. National legislation resulting in uniform regulations was passed. Some of the consequences of congressional legislation are developed in this book.

Other examples of the environmental awakening exist. For instance, in the late 1940s people reforested the Ducktown Basin in southern Tennessee where sulfur-rich smelter fumes from copper processing had destroyed all vegetation over thousands of acres. Now it is difficult to see any scars in the area.

As people became wealthier, they became less aware of the harshness of nature. They expected a more attractive, cleaner physical world around them, and tended to forget how successful previous generations had been in shielding them from the environment. They were also impatient with the rate of environmental progress. In the 1960s this led to the environmental movement, and because the public demanded laws to protect the environment, the movement had a strong political component. The political Left saw the opportunity to criticize the system so they could move America toward their concept of socialistic utopia. The word "environmentalist" was coined.

The political Left was very successful at making the public aware of environmental problems. They galvanized public opinion, leading to increasingly stringent environmental laws. Although air and water quality had been improving for decades, the Left helped to accelerate the process.

We frequently quote leaders of the political Left. Limited space prevents us from summarizing all the Left's ideas. Readers can learn them elsewhere. This is not too difficult. For over thirty years, the views of the Left have been covered by the major media. Additionally, many books have been published. However, an informed person thoroughly familiar with reports from the major media and with best-selling books by the political Left would still have significant information gaps. To be truly informed is difficult. Although the environmental literature is vast, it is largely indigestible. The average person does not have the time or will to sift through it, to check inconsistencies, or to evaluate it. Many summaries of environmental data exist, but often these are slanted to support politically inspired preconceptions. Additionally, much literature contains serious errors, some possibly the result of political orientation, some possibly the result of ignorance.

Setting the record straight involves correcting errors as well as pointing out missing information. It also extends to forecasts of possible consequences based on available experience so there is a basis for decision making that promotes environmental improvement, both locally and globally.

It will be apparent that our effort is primarily anthropocentric: we regard the world first in terms of human needs. This stance contrasts with that of those who are biocentric and more interested in maintaining the natural ecosystems. However, we do not ignore nature. We show how the environment for both people and nature can be improved at minimum economic and social costs.

Many express the attitude we are "stewards of the Earth"; we "must protect and enhance the environment." We concur. However, many programs to improve the Earth deny an enhanced way of life for the world's poor. As now promoted by many who seek disuse of natural resources rather than responsible use, even the affluent will eventually be disadvantaged.

Seeking the environmental truth, therefore, we examine the impacts of First and Third World nations on the world's environment. Our references date from George Perkins Marsh to more recent information from the American government, the United Nations, peer-reviewed scientific sources, and books. We attempt to alert Third World nations to unworkable First World standards. Third World environmental problems are vastly different from ours. Enough is now known in science and engineering to permit real improvement. We describe how First World dictates to Third World nations commit them to perpetual poverty as well as effectively causing a quiet form of genocide.

To help systematic analysis, we balance two views of the environment: a liability and an asset side of an "environmental ledger." The liability side is the negative view of the environment stressed by environmental leaders and the media; the asset side is the good news about the environment. Much good news is available but not well covered by popular media, government agencies, or the educational system. Awareness of good news is essential if humans are to learn from past experience, experience that has an upside as well as a downside.

We do not cover the entire field of "the environment." This work would then be encyclopedic. For example, under agriculture we do not discuss possible short- or long-term specific effects of fertilizers or pesticides, which are of great concern to many. We do, however, describe the nature of the evidence basic to evaluation and regulation of such chemicals. We do not discuss most sociologic and economic aspects of agriculture. Such discussions might make the presentation seem more balanced, but it diverts attention from the theme of this book. Our major subjects are: (1) the impact of humans on the natural environment, including forests, wildlife, water quality (as related to human bodily wastes) and quantity, and soil; and (2) the impact of nature and humans on human health. Most of the data pertain to the United States although we discuss other nations for comparison purposes.

We then relate all data to wealth and the wealth-creating process. There are four sources of income: extractive industries (agriculture, mining, timbering, energy, water development), manufacturing (to convert extracted materials into marketable products), tourism, and service (includes government). Only the first two produce new wealth; the other two redistribute wealth.

While we see the environmental benefit industry brings to our world, we are critical of some activities of industry. Similarly, while we find no fault with some ideals expressed by environmental leaders, we are critical of much of the current direction of environmentalism.

We are cautiously optimistic that humanity can greatly improve both the world's natural and human environments for all nations. We derive a model for this from our data on which we build a framework of activities that would make the world a better place for humans while simultaneously improving the natural world. We consider the model to be consistent with conservative perspectives although conservatives do not now follow the model. The activities do not involve major restructuring of world order or major sacrifices for First World nations.

Finally, some of our conclusions may surprise readers. Some surprised us. When information is collected and systematically integrated, conclusions often become obvious. We state these conclusions although we realize they may be unsettling to many people. We now begin an adventure to see where facts and a positive attitude can lead us.

We gratefully acknowledge the help we have received from the many state experts in forest and wildlife management who answered our written requests for information. In particular, Gordon Batcheller, a wildlife specialist and editor of the *Furbearer Management Newsletter,* New York State Department of Environmental Conservation, has patiently answered many questions and supplied much published data. We are grateful to a dear friend, without whom our book could not have been written. She prefers anonymity. We are also grateful to Joan J. LaFleur of Write Source, whose editing was invaluable. She made us toe the line. We thank Susan Smyth, who collected valuable data about nutrients and human health. We also much appreciate the help and heroic patience of our wives.

CHAPTER 1

Introduction

Few subjects create such emotion and polarize public opinion more than "the environment." Government regulatory decisions regarding the environment are made in the arena of advocates. Public perceptions are often less related to the real world than to the latest image on television. While every picture the public sees can be accurate and every fact correct, all the public's conclusions can be wrong. This is the world of the anecdotal, the world of the negative. In such an atmosphere mistakes are common and monetary resources are easily squandered. More often than not, environmental priorities are upside down.

As people who are very concerned about the world's natural and human environments, in this book we discuss renewable and nonrenewable resource sustainability, soil, forests, wildlife, biodiversity, water, and atmospheric resources. We address the nature of human resources, including longevity, health, urbanization, and population. We interconnect these with the common thread of wealth and human productive efficiency. Finally, we show that the present direction of general environmental thought has led to needlessly expensive remedies. Worse, the bottom-line results of these remedies, carried out to their logical conclusions, will be massively counterproductive in their own explicit and implicit terms. We suggest an alternate approach to solving environmental problems. Our approach is not coercive, cruel, or expensive. It will not require major cultural dislocations in First or Second World nations. Although most readers may be surprised at our major conclusions and recommendations, by the time we summarize them in the final chapters, the previous data will make our thinking perfectly good sense to readers.

And so we write this book to help put our environmental priorities in order. This first chapter describes the book, gives a brief summary of environmental perspectives, and describes our own environmental orientation and philosophy.

We divide the book into four unequal parts, each preceded by its major conclusions. Part 1 pertains to the natural and human environments, showing how they got the way they are and how they interrelate. Part 2 compares the environmental perspectives of Third World nations with those of the wealthy nations. We show quantitatively how wealth influences the human and natural environments. Then, we discuss the concept of sustainability and how it relates to growth and wealth. The first two parts are summaries of environmental facts from standard sources. The facts are largely "good news." We feel that more of this is needed as an antidote to the steady diet of bad news emanating from major informational sources. This balance is critical as a sort of "confidence builder" for the conscientious, hard-working people who are responsible for the greatest environmental gains in human history. In later chapters we show that to a remarkable degree the environmentally concerned—to whom this book is dedicated—have accepted the environmental evaluations of their implacable enemies. The first two parts are meant to be apolitical, and only the most obvious conclusions are drawn. We fully realize, however, that those who consider virtually everything to be political may disagree. Even some of our most obvious conclusions will be considered controversial in some quarters.

The last two parts of the book are frankly political. The answers to improving the world's environments—natural and human—lie in political activities. We would like to believe that the environment is far too important to be influenced by politics. Unfortunately, both knowledge about the environment and laws and regulations pertaining to it have been influenced by political partisanship. We show how many regulations supposedly meant to improve human health or nature are really political statements. Too often they are environmentally counterproductive. Once people understand this, they will be in a position to make the world a better place.

Part 3 is a description of the political conflict between the current leaders of the environmental establishment and the free market establishment. Although industry (i.e., the producers of wealth) is a major subject of the conflict, it is generally not significant in the debate. We know of no important works critical of environmentalism that have originated from the private industrial sector. In fact, about half of the funding for environmental organizations is from industry. We show why industry has been under attack by major environmental organizations. We describe the long-term environmental implications of political philosophies and regulations. Have we gone too far? Part 4 summarizes the perspectives and activities that are needed to improve all environments of the world. Readers may be surprised by the recommendations. We hope they share our optimism.

Now, a disclaimer. Our data are largely directional because we discuss only those subjects that lead to our recommendations pertaining to improving our world. Thus, we say little about industrial contaminants of air and water of First World nations. We concur with Easterbrook (1995), who concludes that industrial contamination of air (p. 182) and water (p. 646) is mostly under control. The most significant health hazards from bad air and water are to be found in industry-poor Third World nations. In addition, we stress environmental gains, largely because they are so often ignored or little understood by major communications media. As longtime participants in the environmental field, we are perfectly aware of many downside effects. However, we will omit detailed discussion of them here, including them instead in a general way in chapters 10, 11, and 12, where we analyze the nature of current environmental regulations and thought.

ENVIRONMENTAL THOUGHT—THE LEADERSHIP

In the early days of the environmental movement, environmentalists[1] could point to contaminated water and air as potential health hazards. America's rivers were receptacles for raw sewage and industrial wastes; smoke and dust clouded the air in too many places. Beginning in the 1960s many leaders of the environmental movement were from the political Left and used the environment as a way to discredit free enterprise as well as the industry and technologies that thrive in an open political system. They had a point: *we could have done better.* However, thoughts of environmental leaders have evolved throughout the years into some rather surprising philosophies. Many environmental leaders from the political Left owe their orientation to writings and philosophies of Karl Marx. From Marx, they got hatred of free enterprise along with skepticism about the ability of individuals to make decisions beneficial to the societies in which they live.

Then in 1962 Rachel Carson published *Silent Spring.* It gave the political Left background data to discredit free enterprise, industry, and the chemicals required to make the system work. Carson, more than anyone else, helped create the fear that much of the public still has of manufactured chemicals (except, perhaps, those used in medicine).

Ten years later Meadows et al. published *The Limits to Growth.* Using computer programs, they showed that all mineral resources are finite, and hence, they concluded, economic growth is not sustainable in industrial societies that rely heavily on mineral resources. (The many reasons to question their thesis are summarized in chapter 8.) We analyze in the current context some implications of the works of these environmental pioneers.

Common Environmentalist Perspectives on Industry and Modern Civilization

For many decades, leaders of the environmental movement have called industry, especially that within the democracies, the major environmental culprit. A few quotations by some prominent environmentalists demonstrate this orientation.

Al Gore: "industrial civilizations' terrible onslaught against the natural world" (Gore 1992, 282).

Dr. Barry Commoner, 1980 candidate for president of the leftist Citizens Party: "Our present system of technology is not merely consuming this capital, but threatening— probably within the next 50 years—to destroy it irreparably" (Efron 1984, 36). Commoner also recommended that "we must go back to the spinning wheel, returning to a beatific state of endless drudge labor, six days a week, and exhaustion on Sunday" (Ray 1993, 77).

Maurice Strong, secretary general, 1992 UN Conference on Environment and Development: "It is clear that current lifestyles and consumption patterns of the affluent middle-class . . . involving high meat intake, consumption of large amounts of frozen and 'convenience' foods, ownership of motor vehicles, numerous electronic household appliances, home and work place air conditioning, suburban housing, is not sustainable. . . . The United States is clearly the greatest risk" (Jasper 1992, 36).

Professor Paul Ehrlich of Stanford: "There is no, I repeat, no conceivable technological solution to the problems we face" (Efron 1984, 35).

Ted Turner: "The indigenous people were the ones that were right! I mean they had their own religion, their own ethics, and their own technology. We just went down the wrong road" (Ray 1993, 80).

Ralph Nader: "the carcinogenic century," "historic abuse" of the environment by corporations, and "corporate cancer" (Efron 1984, 22).

National Education Association: "Every elimination of habitat or species, every introduction of a new artificial chemical, every increase in the demand we are already making on the environment represents an increased risk of unknowingly crossing some threshold that will cause the system to collapse" (London 1984, 38).

Margaret Mead: "our technologically inventive and irresponsible age" (Efron 1984, 28).

Chellis Glendinning, author of the Neo-Luddita Manifesto: "We favor the dismantling of the following destructive technologies: nuclear technologies, chemical technologies, genetic engineering technologies, television, electromagnetic technologies, computer technologies" (Glendinning 1990).

Jeremy Rifkin: "[Cold fusion] is the worst thing that could happen to our planet" (Ciotti 1989, 1).

Professor Paul Ehrlich of Stanford: "[Cold fusion is] like giving a machine gun to an idiot child" (Ciotti 1989, 1).

In this book, we show that the above statements and perspectives are not only incorrect, but basing government policy on them will ultimately lead to destruction of both the human and natural environments as we know them.

Common Environmentalist Perspectives On Humanity and Nature

Although some of the public might agree with the above prominent environmentalists, it is hard to believe that the same public would also agree with the following statements by environmental leaders:

David Foreman, co-founder of Earth First!: "We must . . . reclaim the roads and the plowed land, halt dam construction, tear down existing dams, free shackled rivers and return to the wilderness millions and tens of millions of (acres of) presently settled land" (Ray 1990, 166).

Pentti Linkola: "Everything we have developed over the last 100 years should be destroyed" (Milbank 1994, A1).

Stewart Brand, *Whole Earth Catalogue:* "We have wished, we eco-freaks, for a disaster or for a social change to come and bomb us into the Stone Age, where we might live like Indians in our valley" (Fumento 1993, 335).

Prince Phillip of England: "If I could be reincarnated, I would return as a killer virus to lower human population levels" (McManus 1992, 30).

David Foreman, Earth First!: "We advocate biodiversity for biodiversity sake. It may take our extinction to set things straight" (Bidinotto 1990, 417).

Earth First! Newsletter: "If radical environmentalists were to invent a disease to bring human populations back to sanity, it would probably be something like AIDS. It has the potential to end industrialism, which is the main force behind the environmental crisis" (Ray 1990, 168).

Environmentalist Dr. Van den Bosch, University of California, chided others about their concern for "all those little brown people in poor countries" who might be saved if DDT was used (Ray 1993, 77).

David Graber, biologist, National Park Service: "Human happiness, and certainly human fecundity, is not as important as a wild and healthy planet. . . . Some of us can only hope for the right virus to come along" (Graber 1989, 9).

Charles Wurster, chief scientist, Environmental Defense Fund, speaking to a reporter about the number of people who might die if DDT is not used to control insect vectors: "There are too many people and this is as good a way to get rid of them as any." Later in congressional testimony in 1971 Wurster said that the use of more poisonous organophosphate insecticides "only kills farm workers, and most of them are Mexicans and Negroes" (Ray 1993, 77).

Dr. Paul W. Taylor, CUNY professor of philosophy: "Given the total, absolute, and final disappearance of *Homo sapiens*—not only would the Earth's Community of Life continue to exist but—the ending of the human epoch on Earth would be greeted with a hearty 'good riddance' " (Sanford 1992, 4).

A chilling quotation attributed to the UN's Maurice Strong (Ray 1993, 11) pertains to a novel he would like to write:

> What if a small group of world leaders were to conclude that the principal risk to the Earth comes from the actions of the rich countries? And if the world is to survive, those rich countries would have to sign an agreement reducing their impact on the environment. Will they do it? The group's conclusion is "no." The rich countries won't do it. They won't change. So, in order to save the planet, the group decides: Isn't the *only* hope for the planet that the industrialized civilizations collapse? Isn't it our responsibility to bring that about? This group of world leaders form a secret society to bring about an economic collapse.

The above leaders of the environmental movement see little in industry, modern technology, or humanity that benefits the natural environment. We show that prominent environmentalists reach their conclusions by consistently looking at the anecdotal or often invented downside of industry and technology.

The stated purposes of the above leaders vary from destruction of all humanity, to destruction of industry or modern society, to various forms of socioeconomic tinkering. All appear to place the environment foremost in their order of priorities. The above leaders might be considered mere eco-freaks or radicals. Perhaps some people may see them as a reincarnation of the Luddites, who from 1811 to 1816 tried to reverse industrial progress by destroying machinery. (Their leader, Ned Ludd, feared the loss of jobs because of mechanization.) The environmental leaders represent enormous wealth, power, and political influence. It is from them that news media seek interviews and that legislators get testimony. Their views and motives cannot be lightly dismissed.

Some questions we answer are:

- Is there a common thread, other than the environment, which ties the above people together?
- To what extent have these leaders influenced environmental legislation and regulations?
- If they are ultimately successful, what would be the impacts on the human and the natural environments?

We suggest that the article "Fear of Fusion" in the *Los Angeles Times* (Ciotti 1989) gives us clues about the common thread: motivation. Quoted are the usual environmental experts sought by the media. They include Ralph Nader, Paul Ehrlich, and Jeremy Rifkin. Uniformly, they are against cold fusion because it could result in the world having a source of abundant, cheap energy. But suppose that the *lack* of abundant, cheap energy is a major cause of destruction of the world's forest (see chapter 3) and the wildlife therein (see chapter 4)? Another clue, perhaps, can be obtained by noting that about a third of the quotes from environmental experts see destruction of all or part of humanity (especially poor people of nonwhite races) as the answer to many problems. Thus, saving human life does not seem to be a primary motivation.

We can conclude that if they are not really motivated by desire to improve the world's environments or the lot of the world's people, they must have other motives. We thoroughly analyze those motives, because understanding them is absolutely critical to improving Earth for both humans and nature. A clue to the real motives of prominent environmental leaders comes from the 1992 United Nation's Environment and Development Conference in Rio de Janiero. The protocol was based on the international Socialist Party's platform, according to Norway's prime minister, Gro Harlem Brundtland (Ray 1993, 5). We analyze this question: Is politics actually more critical to environmental leaders than nature or human welfare? Incidentally, Al Gore, who later became America's vice president, approved the Rio activities, America's Senate ratified the Rio Declaration, and President George Bush signed it (Ray 1993, 9).

We show that if the world continues to follow policies emanating from leaders of the political Left much of the world's forests and wildlife will be destroyed along with much of humanity. Yet a significant segment of the public in America continues to vote for politicians who follow the stated aims of the environmental Left. We suggest that the Left political establishment has been able to disguise its purposes and persuade the public that somehow their environmental motives are not really the same as those of the leading environmentalists.

PUBLIC PERSPECTIVES

In 1990, 66 percent of the American public believed the environment was getting worse (*Wall Street Journal* and NBC poll, April 1990). Additionally, all environmental problems of concern to them, they believed, were caused by industry. Clearly, much of the public shares at least some of the views of the environmental leaders.

But, if most people were given a vote in such matters, would they actually vote against automobiles, home appliances, and air conditioning? Would most people favor reducing the human population through AIDS, other diseases, starvation, or mass sterilization? Would most people agree that all dams and plowed fields should be destroyed, or that modern civilization should return to some prior state when humans were "more in harmony" with nature, or when there were no humans at all? All these alternatives imply massive human misery and undoubtedly are not what most people truly want. Hatred of humans and, by implication, hatred of humanity's great accomplishments—music, art, architecture, literature, engineering works, great medical and scientific discoveries—is almost certainly not shared by the general public.

In the following chapters, we show that the current negative views about industry held by environmental leaders and much of the public are overwhelmingly incorrect. Although we certainly do not hold industry environmentally blameless, the impacts of industry (and wealth, technology, and the free enterprise system in which industry thrives) on the environment have been strongly positive in both human and natural terms. Positive impacts, however, were not planned by industry; they were inadvertent spin-offs. McKibben (1995) calls them "accidental." We show that most great environmental benefits are the inevitable results of industrialization and the wealth it creates.

SCIENTISTS' PERSPECTIVES

To a large extent, scientists sat on the sidelines during the early years of the environmental movement. Most scientists are relatively reclusive, preferring to do pure research, often in an "ivory tower." Many times, practical spin-offs are only incidental to the purpose of the original research. According to this view, scientific knowledge is accumulated for its own sake, and many scientists would be horrified to have a peer suggest that their work might have some practical value. Given this orientation, most scientists have long remained aloof from the environmental fray.

Starting in the 1960s another type of scientist evolved: the politically oriented scientist for whom the political impact of his or her work was often more important than its accuracy. Whereas mainstream scientists had an almost pathological fear of making a scientific error, the new scientists could be repeatedly wrong and rarely, if ever, have any misgivings—provided the conclusions had the desired impact on public opinion. Mainstream scientists had trouble adjusting to the newcomers because the mainstream tended to believe in the basic honesty of most scientific work. Thus, for example, they often accepted, at least tentatively, much politically oriented epidemiologic research into the causes of cancer.

As time passed, many scientists became increasingly dismayed at the poor quality of much environmental research and even more dismayed that politically oriented scientists see no problem with making claims about the environment to the news media, often *before* their research is published in peer-reviewed journals. Mainstream scientists abhorred such publicity because most considered peer-reviewed articles in scientific journals to be the only acceptable outlets for their research. Now, many mainstream scientists see politically oriented scientists for what they really are: a threat to science itself. Often, hearing the debate between mainstream and politically oriented scientists, the public brushes off the conflict as merely an argument among scientists. Clearly, the public is not sufficiently educated to distinguish between propaganda and true science.

In the late 1980s and early 1990s mainstream scientists started to fight back, first in the scientific literature and then in the media. A major step was the Heidelberg Appeal (1992), in which politically oriented science was deplored. Over four thousand world leaders, mostly scientists and including seventy-five Nobel Prize winners, signed this document (for the full text, see chapter 11).

In an editorial in *Science,* Abelson (1993, 1859) reviewed two books—*Toxic Terror* by Elizabeth Whelan (1993) and *Phantom Risks* edited by Huber, Foster, and Bernstein (1992)—and said, "The public has long been subjected to a one-sided portrayal of risks of environmental hazards, particularly industrial chemicals. . . . Reviews of the accumulated history of the utterances of the doomsayers reveal their lack of judgment, respect for facts and honesty. Their assertions are not a sound basis for wasting trillions of dollars on phantom risks."

Abelson stated well the current views of mainstream scientists.

OUR PERSPECTIVE

According to various polls, the public wants to see an improved environment and is willing to pay for it. The American public (largely indirectly) has already spent trillions of dollars to improve the environment. Have these trillions been well spent? How much of this expenditure has actually improved the environment?

In looking for some answers to these questions, we examine relationships among resources, sustainability, industry, wealth, regulations, and the environment. We admit to having some preconceptions, but we do not automatically take the side of either industry or environmentalist. In fact, we agree heartily with some in industry and with some in the environmental movement.

In this volume we show how the world's environment can be made truly green and how the human condition can be improved worldwide. We are very concerned with the environmental condition of much of the world, in both human and natural terms. At the same time, we do not want to be called "environmentalists." That would imply we might be members of what has been called "the environmental cult or religion" with all its accompanying irrationality.

We believe any effort to improve the world's environment must begin with facts that survive statistical or scientific analysis. Unfortunately for the world, the opposite, the anecdotal approach, can be used to prove virtually anything and, even worse, has led to silly laws and counterproductive regulations.

Nature

We do not idealize nature. We recognize that nature is cruel. We know that natural death is usually very hard. It comes from starvation, disease, or predators. Sudden death is a blessing. Predators often play with their prey, such as a cat with a mouse or a killer whale with a wounded sea lion. And predators often eat their prey alive: a cobra swallows a duck, lions eat a live eland, a baboon feasts on a monkey while it screams its life away. Such violent events are more the rule than the exception in nature.

Nature is cruel in other ways. Weather, for example, does not discriminate. Severe winters decimate herds of deer. New York's conservationists have concluded, for example, that the major damage to deer herds in New York's Adirondacks is the result of severe winters. Droughts destroy duck habitats and forest fires may decimate wildlife.

When people venture into nature's domain, they do so at their own risk. Nature can punish the stupid, such as the person who goes into a desert with insufficient water or inappropriate clothing; the person who drinks stream water contaminated with beaver feces; or the person who hikes without proper footwear. But nature does not discriminate; it can also punish the unlucky, regardless of that person's competence. The media often report stories of a sprained ankle, a broken leg, or a sudden illness in the wild that leads to death or an attack by a mountain lion or a bear; or a boat lost at sea, even though captained by the most knowledgeable.

Civilizations and Nature

Similarly, we do not idealize primitive people (people "more in harmony with nature"). Although we find little statistical information, we surmise that societies closest to nature, the most primitive, are generally the cruelest in terms of how they treat each other. Certainly, the abysmal human rights records of many nations in Africa and Southeast Asia bear this out. For example, of the world's 17 million refugees, 80 percent are from developing nations of Africa and Southeast Asia. Conversely, the ten nations officially accepting the most refugees are all major industrial democracies, those nations with populations most protected from nature.

European civilizations in early days were certainly cruel by modern standards as a look at any castle's torture chamber will show. Yet, as civilizations became evermore sheltered from nature, as they created wealth and the "good life," they became—guess what?—more civilized. Certainly, inhumanity still exists in developed nations, but it is relatively minor. Although few people can look with total pride at the record of all modern people, statistically, democratic, high-tech, wealthy civilizations are relatively benign, very probably the most benign civilizations of all human history. Asmus (1993) puts it clearly: "It is a plain historical fact that the treatment of man by man became conspicuously more humane side by side with the rise of capitalism."

Many people in modern civilizations have an opposite problem: they have been so sheltered from nature, from primitive cultures, and from their own history that they exaggerate the "inhumanity" they find in modern societies. They glorify nature and primitive cultures. Theirs is the world of the idealist. Unfortunately, many idealists finding imperfections in the modern world often reject it all. We will show that this latter group may be incredibly dangerous for the environments of the world.

Dispersed Effects

We use the concept of dispersed effects of various human activities throughout this volume (see Dunn 1983). To a large extent, environmentalists ignore dispersed effects, even though they can be the most important results of an activity. What do we mean by dispersed effects? The following are some examples:

- In the late 1980s Westchester County, New York, closed a landfill. Soon after, highways in the county became littered with debris. Solving the landfill problem created a widespread, dispersed, largely uncontrollable effect: highway litter.

- In 1991 some Saratoga residents sought to close one of two adjacent quarries in Upstate New York. Dunn Corporation, an environmental firm, showed the dispersed effects of such a closure would be an added cost of over $3 million per year to the residents of a large area, a cost the people could not afford.

Without competition, the remaining quarry could radically increase the price of its crushed stone products because its nearest competitor would be over thirty miles away (i.e., several dollars of haul cost per ton).

• A third example is well documented in chapter 3. Mining of coal and development of oil from relatively small areas contribute to the widespread, dispersed effect of expanded forests. Because people use coal and oil for fuel, less wood is needed for energy, thus taking pressure off forests.

Frequently, the dispersed effects of human activities are overwhelmingly large. Yet too often these effects are not considered in environmental equations. One reason is that dispersed effects are often subtle, widespread, and difficult to relate to what may be an obvious local condition. Another reason is that the people conducting an activity often do not do so for the dispersed reasons; that is, coal miners or quarrymen are trying to make a profit, not expand forests or keep local prices down. *The dispersed effects are, therefore, usually inadvertent results of activities.* Throughout this book, we show that dispersed effects of human activities should never be ignored.

It is, perhaps, paradoxical that local problems created by industry are often counterbalanced by enormous dispersed benefits (see also Dunn 1978, 1992). Conversely, Friedman (1993, 812) sees government as creating "concentrated benefits and diffused costs," those costs looming as a very large problem for the nation. Government, supposedly acting for the benefit of the public, could destroy the economy and much of the nation's human and natural environment. We suggest that industry (private enterprise in general) acting on its own behalf is doing far more for the benefit of the nation than those whose job is to help the nation. The nation will continue to improve economically and environmentally so long as the dispersed benefits from industry are larger than the dispersed costs created by government. How close are we to this threshold?

Statistics

In this book, we base most conclusions on statistical data. Statistics are the only sensible basis for logical environmental decisions. We use statistics from the United Nations, national and state agencies, and peer-reviewed scientific articles. Because statistics can be misleading, information has been cross-checked where possible and necessary. America's forest and wildlife statistics have been extensively cross-checked because of major misconceptions held by the public and many environmentalists. In a few cases, contradictory data have been included without any attempt to evaluate which is more accurate.

The Environmental Ledger

We introduce the concept of the environmental ledger and use it extensively throughout the book. Ledgers have a liability side and an asset side. Businesses base economic decisions on their analysis of both sides of the ledger. Any other approach leads to failure. Civilizations have advanced proportionately to their ability to protect themselves from nature's vagaries and cruelties. Their success in such endeavors is in the asset column. However, the act of adjusting the environment to make life safer for people has often been destructive of many components of that environment. The destructive aspects are the liability side of the environmental ledger.

People living close to the survival level are rarely concerned with environmental liabilities. Or they simply may not understand the environmental implications of their activities. Thus, growing and fattening cattle in North Africa may improve the human environment by providing food. However, if overgrazing and desertification are long-term effects, the liability side of the environmental ledger may, in time, consume the asset side. In a more modern context, smeltering metal sulfide ores may produce economic assets, but unprocessed stack fumes will kill vegetation downwind—the liability side.

We show that the public has been massively and consistently misinformed about environmental matters. Major media and environmental leaders have consistently shown the liability side of the ledger, often exaggerating it or even creating it. The bleak view of the environment currently held by many people is not based on reality. The negativity people see in the media is rarely balanced with reports of such major assets as new forests, expanded wildlife, and better soil, even though these benefits are all around us. Making environmental decisions based only on the bleak picture promulgated by environmental leaders is like a business making decisions based only on the liability side of its ledger. However, in our own effort to balance the downside of the environment, which is what the public sees, we are guilty of stressing the upside, the asset side of the environmental ledger. Because we have both worked in the environmental field for many years, we are very much aware of downside problems. We chose not to stress them. In this, we are consistent with Wattenberg (1984) and Easterbrook (1992, 1994, 1995).

We see two cultures in conflict—the Liability Culture and the Asset Culture. The leaders of the Liability Culture gain economically, politically, or philosophically by stressing the liability side of the environmental ledger. The Asset Culture consists of builders and workers in general; their leaders are free market-oriented. We are in the Asset Culture.

When people focus on the liability side of the environmental ledger, regulations seem to be the answer to environmental improvement. When people focus on the asset side of the ledger, building and development are seen as solutions to environmental problems.

Stressing the downside causes us to lose sight of major environmental gains. To a remarkable degree, the people of the West's Asset Culture, who are responsible for the greatest environmental improvements in human history, have accepted the politically inspired environmental criticisms of their enemies—the environmental Left. Further, acting on the Left's downside "data"—often exaggerated or invented—leads to topsy-turvy priorities in which we spend vast wealth on small problems while we virtually ignore major environmental problems in the United States and elsewhere (Whelan 1992, 1993; Easterbrook 1994, 1995; and chapter 12).

Will the United States be able to solve or be prepared for the inevitable huge natural environmental problems? Scientists studying hurricanes, floods, and volcanic eruptions tell us that such events are inevitable and potentially catastrophic. A huge environmental problem will be the "big one," a major earthquake on the San Andreas fault in California. When such an earthquake occurs (and it is inevitable), will we wish we had used more of our limited wealth for reinforcing bridges and buildings? Will we wish we had spent less on the environment?

And for the world, many scientists believe that the greatest environmental problem of all is the Earth possibly being struck by a large extraterrestrial object. Such occurrences are inevitable, though rare. Many scientists attribute most of the world's great extinctions of life to impacts of extraterrestrial objects. If we are able to foresee such an event, will we have sufficient wealth to produce the means to divert or neutralize such an object?

Finally, will the world be a greener, better place because of the environmental activities of the United Nations, our government, and our environmentalists? Will humanity be better off? Will nature be improved? We think not—*if* we continue in our current direction.

People have ways to solve or minimize all major environmental problems. The single most critical factor is wealth. We must create wealth. Without wealth, neither the human nor the natural environment can improve. Compare the sights in a wealthy suburb with those of a poor one. Or compare the average landscape of North America or Europe with that of nations such as Ethiopia, Haiti, or the Philippines. And compare the health of people in wealthy nations with that of people in poor nations. Clearly, both human and natural environments are superior where there is wealth.

However, wealth is voraciously consumed by environmental regulations. We show that this consumption is inevitable, given current laws and their implementation. The reason is quite clear and should always have been obvious: the laws are open-ended. We know of no case in which an environmental cutoff for a law has been defined. As a nation, we failed to say when we will be satisfied, when we have gone far enough. Thus, regulating less and less at ever greater expense ad infinitum is *absolutely inevitable.* There will always be an increment to remove for any contaminant. Under current conditions the end point will be defined by economics, not environmental considerations. When we run out of money, we will be forced to stop regulating. When will this end point occur? Will our environmental gains reverse because we have already consumed too much of our wealth? Are we too late?

NOTE

1. When we refer to environmentalists, we generally are speaking of the high-visibility leaders of the environmental movement. Many people who are concerned with the environment and contribute to the environmental movement are not from the political Left and probably do not really subscribe to many of the beliefs of their leaders. We feel that the rank and file have been massively deceived by their leaders.

REFERENCES

Abelson, P. H. 1993. Pathological growth of regulations. *Science* 260: 1859.

Anon. 1992. Heidelberg Appeal to heads of state and governments. *Projections* 7/8: 121–22.

Asmus, B. 1993. Private sector solutions to public sector problems. *Imprimis.* 22(10).

Bast, J. L., P. J. Hill, and R. C. Rue. 1994. *Eco-Sanity.* Lanham, Md.: Madison Books.

Bidinotto, R. J. 1990. Environmentalism: Freedom's foe for the 90s. *The Freeman,* November.

Carson, R. 1962. *Silent Spring.* New York: Houghton Mifflin.

Ciotti, P. 1989. Fear of fusion: What if it works? *Los Angeles Times,* April 19, sect. 5, 1.

Dunn, J. R. 1978. Back to the land: Environmental suicide. *Reason* (March): 16–20.

———. 1983. The dispersed benefit riddle. 18th Forum on Geology of Industrial Minerals, occasional paper 37, Indiana Geologic Survey.

———. 1992. America the beautiful. *National Review,* June 6, 4–5.

Easterbrook, G. 1992. Hiding good news. *Chicago Tribune,* June 25.

———. 1994. Forget PCB's, radon, Alar (the world's greatest dangers are dung, smoke and dirty water). *New York Times Magazine,* September 11, 60–63.

———. 1995. *A Moment on the Earth.* New York: Penguin.

Efron, E. 1984. *The Apocalyptics.* New York: Simon and Schuster.

Friedman, M. 1993. Why government is the problem. Hoover Institute on War, Revolution and Peace, Stanford University.

Fumento, M. 1993. *Science under Siege.* New York: William Morrow.

Glendinning, C. 1990. Notes toward a Neo-Luddite Manifesto. *Utne Reader,* March–April.

Gore, A. 1992. *Earth in the Balance.* New York: Houghton Mifflin.

Graber, D. M. 1989. Mother Nature as a hothouse flower. *Los Angeles Times,* Book Review, October 22, 9.

Grigg, W. N. 1992. Their authoritarian agenda. *The New American* (special report, *The Resilient Earth*) 8, no. 11 (June): 31–32.

Huber, P., K. Foster, and D. Bernstein, eds. 1992. *Phantom Risks.* MID Press.

Jasper, W. F. 1992. Rio and beyond. *The New American* (special report, *The Resilient Earth*) 8, no. 11 (June): 35–38.

London, H. I. 1984. *Why Are They Lying to Our Children?* Briarcliff Manor, N.Y.: Stein and Day.

McKibben, W. 1995. An explosion of green. *Atlantic Monthly,* April, 61–83.

McManus, J. F. 1992. Environmental paganism. *The New American* (special report, *The Resilient Earth*) 8, no. 11 (June): 7, 8.

Meadows, D. H., D. L. Meadows, J. Randers, W. W. Behrens, II. 1972. *The Limits to Growth.* New York: Universe Books.

Milbank, D. 1994. In his solitude, a Finnish thinker posits cataclysms. *Wall Street Journal,* May 20, A1.

Ray, D. L., with L. R. Guzzo. 1990. *Trashing the Planet.* Washington, D.C.: Regnery Gateway.

————. 1993. *Environmental Overkill.* Washington, D.C.: Regnery Gateway.

Sanford, R. F. 1992. The nature of environmentalism. *Society of Exploration Geophysicists Newsletter* 9: 4.

Wattenberg, B. J. 1984. *The Good News Is the Bad News Is Wrong.* New York: Simon and Schuster.

Whelan, E. M. 1985. *Toxic Terror.* Ottawa, Ill.: Jameson Books.

————. 1992. America's inverted health priorities. *Priorities* (Fall): 11–13.

————. 1993. *Toxic Terror: The Truth behind the Cancer Scares.* Buffalo, N.Y.: Prometheus Books.

PART I

The Natural and Human Environments

Conclusions

- Of all the world's civilizations, only industrial nations during the past seven decades have successfully reversed the degradation of the natural environment that has characterized most human habitation.

- In the United States, average agricultural yield per acre since 1910 has exceeded the rate of population growth by almost 560 percent.

- Since 1920 the United States has gained over 140 million acres of forest. This new forest is larger than all the land area of Vermont, Massachusetts, Rhode Island, New York, Pennsylvania, New Jersey, Maryland, Virginia, and North Carolina.

- The expansion of forests is largely the result of technology. This has created many new industrial chemicals, new forms of energy, the internal combustion engine, an efficient transportation network, and improved methods of food production, handling, and preservation. Abundant, affordable energy and efficient agriculture are most responsible for the improvement in the natural environment.

- If America's current agricultural yields per acre were the same as those during the late 1930s, the equivalent of all the land east of the Mississippi River plus Michigan would have to be used for agriculture. America's new forests and all the contained wildlife would not exist.

- The fear that pesticides would cause a decrease in the population of many common birds was never valid. In fact, without pesticides many bird populations would be far lower. Pesticides are largely responsible for America's high per acre agricultural yields. Thus, America needs less land for agriculture. The unneeded land is the locale for America's 140 million acres of new forest and all the related wildlife.

- Per acre agricultural productivity throughout the world should increase as the carbon dioxide level in the atmosphere increases. Both humanity and nature would benefit.

- Wildlife are most diversified and abundant in a complex mix of habitats. Each habitat favors a different fauna. Thus, in the eastern United States where habitats vary from cities to open fields to old forests, we find a flourishing and diverse fauna. The florally complex suburban areas may encourage the greatest faunal diversity.

- In the eastern two-thirds of the nation, deer and other wildlife are more abundant than when Indians were the only human inhabitants. The need now is for competent wildlife management.

- Modern industrial societies are far less of a threat to faunal species than current Third World nations. Primitive cultures, such as the Polynesians, the American Indians, and early European tribes, caused extinction of far more species of fauna than any modern industrial societies. The early cultures of Polynesia and Micronesia in the Central and South Pacific probably caused the extinction of over 1,500 species of wildlife.

- Looking at the geologic record of all species of plants, animals, and other forms of life, evolution and extinction of species is the norm.

- Industrial nations multiply natural resources.

- Third World nations are consuming their natural environments and only slowly improving their human environments.

- The creation of wealth is critical to improving both the natural and human environments. Without wealth and the resultant markets for agricultural products, efficient agriculture is not possible.

- Starting somewhat before the improvements in the natural environment, the human environment in terms of health and longevity greatly improved in the industrial nations.

- Environmental changes in other First World nations are similar to those in America.

- Among industrial nations, democracies have the best environmental record.

- Inefficient, environmentally insensitive industrialization, as occurred in the early days of Western nations and more recently in communist eastern Europe, actually improves both the natural environment and the human environment. For example, expansion of forests and wildlife, decreased soil erosion, and improved human health characterize all industrial nations, democratic or communist.

- In terms of cost in human lives, the world's most dangerous air pollution is indoor smoke particulates from heating and cooking fires fueled with biomass in the Third World. The most dangerous water pollution is by human feces in Third World nations. The most dangerous disease vectors are insects in Third World nations.

- People in First World nations largely control their environment. People in Third World nations are largely controlled by their environment.
- The momentum of environmental change in America is still positive.
- America's forests and most wildlife should continue to expand at least to the year 2030. The human environment should also continue to improve.
- We caution, however, that the environmental future is contingent on political factors.

CHAPTER 2

Agriculture and Soil

No human activity so profoundly influences the world's natural and human environments in terms of natural resources and human health as the production and handling of food. How well we are doing is controversial. For example, from the negative side, Albrecht (1971, 397) says: "While exploiting his soils, man is destroying his host and slowly accomplishing his own death." Gore (1992, 3) says: "Unfortunately, little has changed: even now, about eight acres' worth of prime topsoil floats past Memphis every hour."[1] Believed, the bleak views of these and like-minded authors lead to fear for humanity's future.

There is another perspective, one shared by the U.S. Department of Agriculture (USDA). They conclude that erosion is steadily decreasing and that food production per acre of agricultural land has never been higher. And they believe that both parameters of agricultural efficiency will continue to improve.

To determine whether the negative or the positive view is correct, we evaluate agricultural efficiency in terms of the amount of land required to put a unit of food on the dinner table. We show that this is a multifaceted function, dependent on agricultural production efficiency and mechanization, transportation, food handling, and food preservation. We show that food delivered per acre of soil for industrial nations has far more than kept up with population growth. This has resulted in much agricultural land becoming available for other uses. As stress on soil resources in industrial nations is declining, stress on soil resources in most Third World nations is increasing.

Understanding the factors that influence agricultural efficiency is critical to understanding how to improve the natural and human environments of the world. Thus, this book starts with a discussion of agriculture and soil.

AGRICULTURE AND SOIL—A HISTORIC VIEW

The history of agriculture has been one of improving efficiency in terms of energy input, human labor, and food output per unit of land used. Currently, production from large areas of ancient agricultural lands, which have been cultivated for thousands of years, has never been higher and promises to improve even more.

But the road has not been easy. Civilizations have made many mistakes, and people continue to repeat those mistakes. Ruins of ancient cities surrounded by barren land, such as the tells in the deserts of the Middle East, abandoned agricultural terraces and farmlands, ancient cities now covered with jungle in Asia and Latin America, cliff dwellings in western America abandoned after a few decades, and sediment-clogged irrigation canals and harbors are silent monuments to human failure to properly use soil resources. Even now, practices that created these problems continue in large areas of the world.

To lay a base for our conclusions, we briefly review humanity's efforts to obtain food.

Stone Age Cultures

Originally, humans were hunters and gatherers. Obtaining food by such means left little time or energy for anything else. Such cultures are rare in the modern world. One example of this stone age culture is the Sirionos, who number about two thousand and occupy about two hundred square miles of northeastern Bolivia. Such societies are largely preagricultural and have had little impact on the environment. Because they have little control of their environment, they are at its mercy. Characteristically, hunter-gatherer populations have been thinly spread over the land.

Early Agriculture—Shifting Cultivation

Shifting cultivation or slash-and-burn cultivation of forested areas occurs largely in late Stone Age cultures and was almost ubiquitous in ancient forested areas. People cut sections of forests, burned the downed vegetation, and planted crops. Soil fertility lasted from one to three years. When the soil wore out, the people repeated the procedure elsewhere. Currently, slash-and-burn agriculture exists in some tropical areas of South America, Africa, and the Pacific Oceanic islands. American Indians of the eastern third of North America also grew food in this manner. Although a step up from hunting and gathering, the practice is not efficient. About twenty calories of forest are burned to produce one calorie of food (Evans 1980, 389).

Slash-and-burn agriculture has little impact on the environment except that the new growth that appears after each patch of land is abandoned is favorable for much wildlife (see chapter 4). The eastern American Indians were well aware of this and found former agricultural clearings to be excellent places to hunt for game.

Subsistence Agriculture

This type of agriculture is more permanent than slash-and-burn methods, and is typified by villages whose inhabitants till the surrounding land with or without supplementary livestock. This form of agriculture is currently dominant in much of the Orient, Africa, and Latin America and was the main form of agriculture in Europe after the fall of Rome. Each family grows its own food and very little is grown for others. The influence on the land is often severe, particularly in areas of rugged terrain where people till excessively steep slopes. Soil losses during heavy rains often vary from severe to catastrophic.

Commercial Agriculture

The type of agriculture whereby the agricultural community grows food not only for itself but for sale to others is most common in our world today. During the Bronze Age, commercial agriculture allowed cities to develop in ancient North Africa, the Middle East, and Asia. With the commercialization of agriculture, many people were released from the need to produce food, and written language, art, science, engineering, medicine, philosophy, and mathematics developed.

AGRICULTURAL PRODUCTIVITY AND LAND USE

In industrial nations, the cumulative effect of all aspects of agriculture is that production per acre has continuously increased. Some increases are startling. For example, compare an Indian cornfield, small hills of stalks sparsely spaced five feet apart, with a typical lush corn crop in the central United States. The productivity of modern agriculture is extraordinary.

- Wheat crop yields in Britain increased from about 0.4 metric tonnes per hectare (mt per ha) in A.D. 1200 to 5.4 mt per ha in 1980, an increase of about 1250 percent. As shown in figure 2.1 it took 700 years for the first 425 percent increase but only 80 years for the last 825 percent. Evans (1980) shows a similar increase in the rice yield in Japan.

- Wheat crop yields in the United States during the 1938–40 period were 14.2 bushels per acre (Barrons 1975), but yields in 1992 were 39.4 bushels per acre, up 177 percent (Agricultural Statistics Board 1993).

- Potato crop yields in the United States averaged 67 hundredweight (cwt) per acre in the 1930s and 275 cwt from the early- to mid-1890s, an increase of 310 percent (Barrons 1988, 5).

- Improved efficiency in terms of production continues for most crops. Of 26 crops monitored in 1992, 54 percent had all-time per acre production records (Agricultural Statistics Board 1993). In some cases, the 1992 per acre production records are startling. Corn used for grain was 11.2 percent higher than the pre-

Figure 2.1
Wheat Production in England, 1250–1980

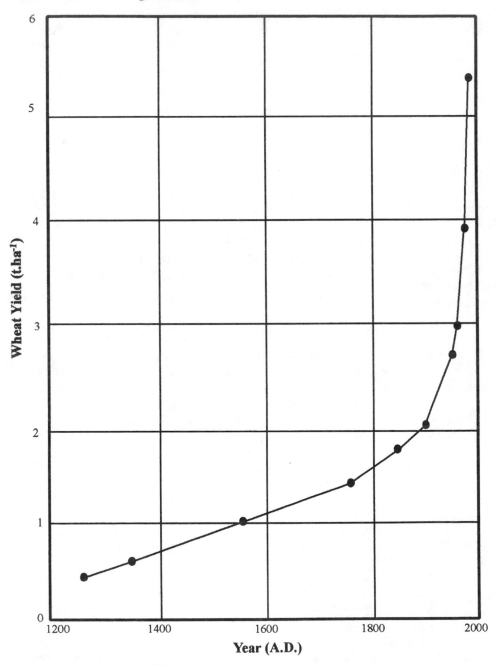

Source: Adapted from Evans, 1980

vious best; soybeans used for grain were up 9.9 percent. High per acre production allowed the total farm acreage to drop 197 million acres from 1960 to 1992, a 17 percent decrease (Wright 1994, 220).

- About 3.5 acres of cropland were required to feed one person in the United States in 1910, whereas about a third of an acre is needed now (Borlaug 1993, x). This is a 950 percent increase in overall production efficiency in 82 years. During this interval, the U.S. population grew about 170 percent. Agricultural production efficiency grew 5.59 times faster than the population.

The profound impact of agricultural efficiency on America's soil resources is summarized by Borlaug (1993), who says: "Had the yields of 1935–40 persisted, to have produced the 1978–80 harvest, it would have been necessary either to have plowed up approximately 73 percent of America's pasture and grazing lands or to have converted 61 percent of the forest and woodland to cropland." And further, "Were this to have happened, land for many other uses—including recreation, wildlife, forestry, and urbanization—would have been lost." Borlaug notes that the added area required would have been 437 million acres, equivalent of all of the land area east of the Mississippi River plus the area of Michigan. The current 140 million acres of new forest in the United States would have been nonexistent, along with the related wildlife within that forest (see chapters 3 and 4).

Farm population figures show further evidence of production efficiency. Coinciding with the increased per acre productivity cited above, the farm population decreased. The farm population was 41.9 percent of America's population in 1880; in 1992 it was 1.9 percent. Coinciding with the population shift has been a reduction of agriculture's share of the gross domestic product (GDP): 3 percent in 1970, 2 percent in 1990 (Wright 1994).

In a sense, by retiring land from agriculture, the soil resource is multiplied. For example, a 100 percent increase in per acre production efficiency is the equivalent of doubling the amount of agricultural land. The U.S. Department of Agriculture (1989) sees a probable continuation of these favorable trends. They predict a 57 percent reduction in erosion of agricultural land between 1990 and 2000, and that the amount of farmland required by the United States will be further reduced by up to 160 million acres in the interval between 1989 and 2030 (p. 141).

CAUSES OF AGRICULTURAL EFFICIENCY

Optimism that the acreage of land required to feed America will steadily decrease is the result of agricultural efficiency. We define agricultural efficiency as all factors that contribute to the reduction of land required to put a unit of food on the dining table. Components contributing to this efficiency include agricultural chemistry, plant and animal genetic changes, farm equipment, food transportation, food handling, and food preservation.

Bioengineering

Humans have always "bioengineered" plants and animals to increase food production. Early bioengineering was largely inadvertent and consisted of selecting seeds from the best plants for the next year's crop or of breeding the best animals.

Selective Breeding of Plants. Food crops used even in ancient times often bore little resemblance to the original wild plants. For example, no natural plant resembles corn, even the types of corn grown by the Indians of the Americas. By selecting seeds from the best plants over hundreds or thousands of years, humans change the nature of the plants. In a sense, the plants adjusted to human need (Anderson 1956). Plants, thus, become more prolific, more resistant to various diseases and pests, and more compatible with climatic conditions. In areas of extreme variations in climate and elevation, the number of varieties can be enormous. For example, the Incas in the Andes grew about three thousand varieties of potatoes.

As we have learned more about genetics, we have tailored plants for specific characteristics. Pioneer horticulturist Luther Burbank (1849–1926) created sixty varieties of plums and prunes, plus various berries, apples, potatoes, tomatoes, squashes, asparagus, and many flowers. Much of his work was trial and error. Although he rejected tens of thousands of his new creations, he created hundreds of plants that are still being used.

Today humans grow over 6,500 varieties of apples (Rupp 1990), over 3,000 types of roses (Mackey et al. 1991), and over 350 cultivars of tomatoes (Hendrickson 1977) or, perhaps, 2,000 to 3,000 varieties (Walters 1995). An ever increasing number of new cultivars of vegetables and flowers appear annually. This process is most rapid in industrial nations and promises to accelerate as new bioengineering techniques become available.

Humans also created biodiversity by redistributing useful plants. Dating back at least to the Greco-Roman empires (Sauer 1956), humans redistributed agricultural vegetation over the world. Gore's "genetic treasure map" (1992, 134–35) shows the sources of useful agricultural plants that have been distributed in this way.

Selective Breeding of Animals. As humans changed the nature of plants, for similar reasons, they also changed animals. Initially, changes were more or less inadvertent. Historians credit Robert Bakerwell of Leicestershire, England, with first selectively breeding animals in the mid-1700s for high meat weight per unit of feed. He bred his Leicester sheep to be fit for market in two years instead of the customary three to four. Based on Bakerwell's principles of breeding, many domestic animals were changed. In 1710 average beef cattle weighed 370 pounds; calves, 50 pounds; sheep, 28 pounds; and lambs, 18 pounds. By 1795 the weights were 800 pounds, 148 pounds, 80 pounds, and 50 pounds, respectively. This was an improvement of over 130 percent in 85 years.

Modern Bioengineering of Animals. Changes are rapidly occurring, increasing food productivity through bioengineering. For example, on November 5, 1993, the Food and Drug Administration (FDA) approved the use of bovine somatotropin (bST), a hormone naturally produced by cows. Increasing its use increases the quantity of milk per cow by 10 percent to 15 percent with no measurable difference in quality. It also decreases the amount of feed per unit of milk by some 12 percent (Etherton 1994). Reduction of feed and pasture requirements potentially releases a significant amount of agricultural land to be used for other purposes. This could be roughly 12 percent of the land currently needed for pasturage and silage to sustain milk production.

Similarly, the use of porcine somatotropin (pST)—not yet approved—could reduce feed requirements for pigs by 15 percent to 35 percent per unit of body weight. And the body weight will consist of up to 80 percent less fat (Etherton 1994). As with bST, the use of pST will significantly reduce the amount of land required for food production.

Chemical Technology in Agriculture

The major single influence on per acre crop yields has been chemical technology. Chemical technology:

- improves soil fertility
- controls pests and disease during growth
- controls weeds
- controls pests and fungi after harvesting

Without farm chemicals, Knutson et al. (1990) conclude that corn yields in America would drop 53 percent; wheat yields, 38 percent; cotton yields, 62 percent; and rice yields, 63 percent. The environmental implications of such a reduction are staggering. America would have to return tens of millions of acres of forestland back to farming.

Fertilizers and Lime. To varying degrees, humans have long understood the need for various supplements to increase agricultural productivity. Primitive peoples, including the American Indians, understood that fish, manure, ash, and marl (lime) added to the soil improved crop production. Green manuring with legumes, testing soil for acidity, neutralizing lime, rotation with alfalfa and clover, animal manures, and composting were all used by the Romans as early as 200 to 300 B.C.

Although they understood the value of various additives and technologies, it was not until humans began to understand chemistry that control of soil productivity became scientific. Early technologies were inefficient, often using too much of one constituent and too little of another.

The first chemical fertilizer was used in 1660, when Sir Kenelm Digby showed the value of saltpeter (potassium nitrate) for plant growth. In the early nineteenth century chemists learned that plants derived their carbon dioxide and oxygen from air and nitrogen and other constituents from soil. In the mid-1800s the value of phosphate, ammonium sulfate, and potash salts was demonstrated, and the first mixed mineral fertilizers were used. Gradually, the importance of minor trace elements such as magnesium, copper, cobalt, boron, and manganese were understood and used as supplements as required.

Protection from Insects, Nematodes, Viruses, Weeds, and Other Pests. Almost as important as fertilizers and lime for maintaining high agricultural production is the myriad of chemicals for controlling pests, diseases, and weeds. We make no attempt to enumerate them. Any list constantly changes with better understanding of the nature of plants and pests and as chemical technology advances.

Agricultural chemicals tend to be more and more selective, targeting specific problems or insects and having little influence on others. Also, agricultural chemicals tend to be less toxic to humans. For example, early pesticides and fungicides containing lead, arsenic, or copper have largely been replaced by more sophisticated chemicals that target specific characteristics of pests' life cycles.

Knutson et al. (1993) show that without pesticides, potatoes could not be grown in Maine; tomatoes and sweet corn could not be grown in Florida; peaches could not be grown in Georgia; apples could not be grown in Washington and Michigan; and only one percent of grapes could be grown in California.

Knutson et al. (1993) conclude that without pesticides, corn yields would fall 32 percent; wheat, 24 percent; cotton, 39 percent; and rice, 57 percent.

Knutson et al. (1990, 1993) also show that not using various farm chemicals would result in increased costs to consumers of several hundred dollars per year, depending on which chemicals are not used. Additionally, the public would not have access to many healthful fruits and vegetables that are now available throughout the year.

Agricultural chemicals also contribute greatly to the release of tens of millions of acres of agricultural land to other uses.

Agricultural Mechanization

The effect of mechanization of farming has been similar to that of improved agricultural production. Although mechanization does not necessarily improve per acre productivity, two things that are environmentally beneficial have occurred because of it: (1) land necessarily devoted to pasture for draft animals for virtually every single farm was released to other uses; and (2) land needed for barns for animals and for living quarters for farm hands could be put to other uses.

For example, according to the 1945 *Census of Agriculture,* from 1920 to 1940 the number of tractors on New York farms rose 1144 percent while the number of draft animals decreased 58 percent. The area of pastureland dropped 8 percent, the relatively small drop occurring because dairy herds used the newly available pastureland. During the 1920 to 1940 interval America's farm population dropped about 5 percent, from a little over 32 million to about 30.6 million. Since 1940 the farm population decreased 85 percent, from 30.6 million to 4.6 million (1991). Land no longer needed becomes available for crops, cattle, or new woods.

Food Handling, Processing, and Preservation

A very important and often forgotten component of agricultural efficiency is food handling. Because of more efficient ways of handling food, amounts of waste food have steadily decreased. Canning, drying, freezing, and refrigerating, along with rapid transportation, have contributed to agricultural efficiency. And irradiation of food increases shelf life of meats and vegetables and significantly reduces spoilage. Less spoilage means less land is required for food production. Additionally, because of these factors, America's agriculture and food processing has "provided us with the safest, most varied and plentiful food supply in the world" (Case 1993, 6).

In contrast, in the former Soviet Union and in most Third World nations, inefficient food handling, including lack of rural roads, proper vehicles, refrigeration, and other preservation techniques coupled with losses because of rodents and molds, often result in the loss of over 50 percent of food produced. In such nations, improved food handling alone could allow about half of the agricultural land currently in use to be retired. This would be an enormous environmental benefit because retired land could return to a natural state (see chapters 3 and 4).

Wealth

Often overlooked is the importance of a population wealthy enough to buy efficiently produced agricultural products. For example, Haiti's people primarily survive by subsistence agriculture. The stress on the land caused by tilling steep slopes is enormous. Per acre productivity for such subsistence farming is low because farm chemicals are too expensive for people who earn only $200 a year. But suppose Haiti industrialized, and most of the people had sufficient wealth to buy their food? Now, with a market for agricultural products, farmers could afford to purchase agricultural chemicals, to terrace steep slopes, and to use other conservation practices. Per acre productivity would greatly increase and many steep slopes would be abandoned. Additionally, with more money, wood would no longer be needed for fuel and forests could be restored. Wealth is a requirement for efficient agriculture and land use.

Water and Agriculture

Efficient agriculture can save water. Knutson et al. (1993) point out that if agricultural pesticides were not used, the land required for growing fruits and vegetables in the United States would increase from 5.83 million acres to between 8.16 and 8.75 million acres. The extra land would be required to compensate for crop losses due to pests. Much of the new land would require more water for irrigation. In addition, if herbicides were not used, weeds would compete for available water so cash crops would require additional water.

The Carbon Dioxide Bonus

Carbon dioxide is plant food. The increase in carbon dioxide is already showing up as increased tree growth rates over the world. Thousands of experiments demonstrate that increased carbon dioxide will increase crop yields (Robinson 1995, 4). In some cases, the increase could be up to 50 percent. Thus, the forests and wildlife of the world can do even better as less land is required for agriculture. Finally, according to a documentary film by Archives Ltd., increased atmospheric carbon dioxide could increase crop yields and further decrease water requirements.

Politics and Agriculture

We have taken a rather optimistic view about the future of America's agriculture and soil. This optimism must be tempered by the potential impacts of sociopolitical realities. Part 3 describes the relationship between politics and resources. What ultimately happens will largely be determined by who wins the current political conflicts. The mind of man will determine the future of both humanity and the natural environment.

AGRICULTURE AND SOIL IN OTHER INDUSTRIALIZED NATIONS

Because of similar technology, other industrial nations have similar agricultural efficiency. Throughout Europe most agriculture is limited to relatively flat land because steep slopes are no longer needed. Many difficult-to-maintain agricultural terraces have been abandoned. Revegetation of abandoned steep areas has greatly reduced soil loss and aided water retention. For example, the flash flooding and enormous erosion in southern France described by Marsh (1874) have been greatly reduced because of reforestation of the lower French Alps.

Much land throughout European and Asian industrialized nations has been tilled or used for agricultural purposes for two thousand to five thousand years. For most land, productivity has never been better. For example, despite past soil abuses (including salination and water logging), the Tigris–Euphrates basin now supports 139 persons per square kilometer whereas ancient Mesopotamia at its peak in 1900 B.C. supported a maximum of only 11.4 persons per square kilometer (Simmons 1993). With modern farming methods, there is no reason to believe successful use of these lands will not continue. This is beyond "sustainability," a true multiplication of resources.

AGRICULTURE AND SOIL IN THIRD WORLD NATIONS

Agriculture in most developing nations is very inefficient largely because of insufficient use of mineral fertilizers and other agricultural chemicals. Pests alone cause an average crop loss of 50 percent in tropical areas. Harden (1990), and an anonymous author describe the inefficiencies of food production in developing nations. Not surprisingly, the average worldwide increase in agricultural productivity relative to population growth is nowhere near as impressive as in the United States. Richards (1990) estimates that the world's cropland increased 466.5 percent from 1700 to 1980, while the world's population increased about 750 percent during that same interval. Thus, overall agricultural production efficiency relative to the world's total population increased only about 60 percent ($466.5/750 \times 100$) over 280 years, whereas America's increased almost 460 percent over population growth in just 82 years. Agricultural land area in America has actually been decreasing for over seven decades. Clearly, most of the world's agriculture does not share America's efficiency.

As previously noted, lack of food preservation techniques and a very inadequate transportation infrastructure cause additional losses with estimates as high as 50 percent of production of grains and produce and as high as 70 percent for meat. Improved agricultural production and food preservation and handling practices in developing nations would result in much less pressure on the land resource.

SUMMARY

Environmental leaders have expressed considerable pessimism about the future of agricultural productivity. They have not considered all the relevant facts. Specifically, the USDA (1989) concludes that erosion will decrease and agricultural productivity per unit of land will increase well after the year 2000. The amount of food delivered to the dining table per unit of agricultural land has increased rapidly. In America, from 1910 to 1992, the amount of food produced per acre increased 5.59 times faster than the population growth rate. Had America's agricultural production per acre remained constant at 1935–1940 levels we would have to use all the land east of the Mississippi River plus Michigan to feed the population. The USDA predicts a release of up to about 4 million acres per year to the year 2030; that is, improved food technology should continue. Agricultural land is, thus, being continuously released to other purposes, including forests, wildlife, swamps, urbanization, and recreation. Less land requirement for agriculture also reduces pressure on water resources.

Reasons for this efficiency start with high per acre productivity. This is the result of modern breeding of food crops and animals and of using synthetic hormones, agricultural chemicals, and machinery. The efficient transportation, handling, and preservation of food also contribute significantly to reducing the need for agricultural land. Increasing atmospheric carbon dioxide should further improve productivity.

Whereas improvements in America are matched by improvements in other industrialized nations, agricultural efficiency in Third World nations is generally where America's was in the 1800s. Far more land is needed per person for food than in industrialized nations. Inefficient food handling alone causes losses of over 50 percent of the food produced in many developing nations. Agriculturally, some Third World nations are actually sliding backward. The increase in atmospheric carbon dioxide (plant food) could partially reverse some of the agricultural inefficiency.

NOTE

1. Gore does not say what "eight acres' worth of prime topsoil" is because he gives no depth or volume. If we assume a generous foot of topsoil on Gore's eight acres, then the total annual topsoil loss appears to be about 0.006 inch per year if the Mississippi River above Memphis drains 740 million acres. An average annual loss of 0.006 inch does not seem to be excessive. Further, in large wooded areas of the eastern two-thirds of America, topsoil is being created faster than it is being lost.

REFERENCES

Albrecht, W. A. 1971. Physical, chemical and biochemical changes in the soil community. In *Man's Impact on the Environment,* edited by T. R. Detwyler. New York: McGraw-Hill.

Anderson, E. 1956. Man as a maker of new plants and new plant communities. In *Man's Role in Changing the Face of the Earth,* edited by W. L. Thomas. Chicago: University of Chicago Press.

Anon. 1990. Why they still starve. *The Economist,* October 20, 50–52.

Barrons, K. C. 1975. *The Food in Your Future.* New York: Van Nostrand Reinhold.

———. 1981. *Are Pesticides Really Necessary?* Chicago: Regnery Gateway.

———. 1988. *The Positive Side of Pesticides.* Louisville, Ky.: National Council for Environmental Balance.

Borlaug, N. E. 1993. Foreword in *Toxic Terror: The Truth behind the Cancer Scare,* edited by E. M. Whelan, xii–xvii. Buffalo, N.Y.: Prometheus Books.

Case, A. G. 1993. Editor's introduction. *Priorities* (Spring): 6.

Detwyler, T. R., ed. 1971. *Man's Impact on the Environment.* New York: McGraw-Hill.

Etherton, T. D. 1994. The efficacy, safety and benefits of bovine somatotropin and porcine somatotropin. New York: American Council on Science and Health.

Evans, L. T. 1980. The natural history of crop yields. *American Scientist* 68: 388–97.

Gore, A. 1992. *Earth in the Balance.* New York: Houghton Mifflin.

Harden, B. 1990. Africa's great black hope. *World Monitor,* August, 31–44.

Hendrickson, R. 1977. *The Great American Tomato Book.* Garden City, N.Y.: Double-day.

Knutson, R. D., C. R. Taylor, J. B. Penson, and E. G. Smith. 1990. Economic impacts of reduced chemical use. American Farm Bureau Research Foundation, Park Ridge, Ill.

Knutson, R. D., C. R. Hall, E. G. Smith, S. D. Cotner, and J. W. Miller. 1993. Economic impact of reduced pesticide use on fruits and vegetables. American Farm Bureau Research Foundation, Park Ridge, Ill.

Mackey, B., A. Reilly, B. R. Rogers, B. Pleasant, D. Bilderback, and B. Brooke. 1991. *The Gardeners Home Companion.* New York: Macmillan.

Marsh, G. P. 1874. *The Earth as Modified by Human Action.* New York: Scribner, Armstrong.

Robinson, A. B. 1995. *Access to Energy,* December.

Rupp, R. 1990. *Red Oaks and Black Birches: The Science and Lore of Trees.* Troy, N.Y.: Gardenway.

Simmons, I. G. 1993. *Environmental History.* Oxford: Blackwell.

Sauer, C. O. 1956. The agency of man on the Earth. In *Man's Role in Changing the Face of the Earth,* edited by W. L. Thomas, 49–69. Chicago: University of Chicago Press.

U.S. Department of Agriculture. 1989. *The Second RCA Appraisal.* Washington, D.C.: U.S. Government Printing Office.

Walters, J. F. 1995. Something for the tomato-growing crowd. The Associated Press.

Whelan, E. M. 1993. *Toxic Terror: The Truth behind the Cancer Scare.* Buffalo, N.Y.: Prometheus Books.

Wright, J. W. 1994. *The Universal Almanac.* Kansas City: Andrews and McMeel.

CHAPTER 3

Forests, Trees, and Floral Diversity

Americans usually perceive acreage of forests and trees incorrectly. They vastly underestimate the quantity. Gore (1992, 120) writes: "The developed nations . . . have massive deforestation problems." And Lester Brown (1990, 31), president of the Worldwatch Institute, in his *State of the World* says: "Surveys show that Europe and Japan are the only parts of the world currently increasing their total forest area." He attributes deforestation in industrial nations to "development." Matschke et al. (1984) deplore the loss of forestland to development in America because it reduces the deer population (see chapter 4). Lowe (1994, 83) talks about "car-oriented sprawl" in the United States causing "loss of valuable farmland and the disappearance of plants and animals as forests and other natural areas shrink." Brown, Gore, Matschke, and Lowe are apparently not aware of the huge and continuing expansion of forests in the United States as well as in all other industrialized nations. Unfortunately, government often bases public policy on such misconceptions.

In this chapter we describe the state of the forests in major regions of the world. We also show how human activities cause changes in forest areas.

WORLD FORESTS—ANCIENT DEFORESTATION

Deforestation is an ancient process. Sumerians and contemporaneous cultures largely deforested the Zagros and Taurus mountains of the Middle East by 3000 B.C. (Eckholm 1976). By the Christian era most forests of the Middle East were gone. It is probably no coincidence that forests and wood are mentioned frequently in the Old Testament but not at all in the New Testament. The remaining Mediterranean area was stripped by about A.D. 500, and most of the rest of western Europe and the British Isles shortly afterward (Davis 1956).

In Asia, over a period of 5,500 years, China developed a huge appetite for wood. Once deforested, the land was used for agriculture. Its forests declined from covering about 50 percent of the nation to about 8 percent by the mid-1970s (Eckholm 1976). Deforestation in China resulted in enormously eroded landscapes and devastating floods, particularly in the Yellow River Valley.

AMERICAN FORESTS—THEIR ANCIENT HISTORY

At the end of the last glacial age about ten thousand years ago, North America was largely forested. There was desert in the West and Southwest, some park-like wooded grasslands adjacent to the deserts, and barren areas above mountain timberlines. The rest of the land was covered with trees. "Dry" lightning storms periodically caused extensive forest fires in the western mountains, mostly in old forests in which dry, dead wood was abundant. Lightning-caused fires were rare in the Midwest and East, and those that did occur were generally of limited extent.

Then humans arrived. They moved quickly throughout the Americas. Their impact on the environment, primarily by using fire, was enormous considering their small population. Mitchell (1981, 84) calls the Indians "the oldest established permanent free floating arsonists in the world." His description may be somewhat overdrawn because virtually all primitive cultures have burned woodlands and prairies (see McNeely et al., 1990; and Simmons, 1993). However, there is little doubt the Indians used fire extensively to improve their lot. Salomon (1984) describes how Indians in New York State burned woods along the Hudson and Mohawk rivers. Stewart (1956) extensively documents the use of fire by Indians to create much of the grasslands of North America. And Anderson et al. (1990) conclude that the central plains of the United States were forested until about five thousand years ago. Stewart (1956, 128) minimizes the likelihood of most prairie fires being started by lightning: "I have been able to discover no authentic record of any grass fire ever being ignited by lightning." Later (p. 129), he concludes: "The unrestricted burning of vegetation appears to be a universal culture trait among historic primitive people." Thus, he concurs with Marsh (1864, 129): "The data on grasslands of the tropical and temperate zones of the world support the view that they have been formed and undoubtedly maintained by man by means of fire." Chadwick (1993, 116) describes how fire "set deliberately" at modern prairie set-asides in the Midwest is needed to have a "natural prairie" because fire "kills shrubs and trees."

AMERICAN FORESTS—MODERN CHANGES

When the Europeans arrived in North America, the contiguous forty-eight United States had about 950 million acres of forest (Frederick and Sedjo 1991). These settlers, like the Indians, saw the forest as an obstacle to food production, so they cleared large areas. They downed so many trees that a series of articles appearing between 1900 and 1909 in the *New York Times* predicted that the nation's forests would soon disappear (Maurice and Smithson 1984). (Inciden-

Table 3.1
U.S. Forest Cover and Population Growth

Date	Forest Cover, Acres	Approximate Population
1492	950,000,000[1]	500,000
1850	838,500,000[1]	23,192,000
1920	600,000,000 (low)[1]	106,022,000
1960s (early)	650,000,000[2]	180,000,000
1987	728,000,000[1]	242,060,000
1990	733,000,000[3]	248,710,000
1992	737,000,000[4]	254,000,000
1994	740,000,000[5]	256,000,000

[1]Sedjo 1991.
[2]U.S. Department of Agriculture 1980.
[3]U.S. Department of Agriculture 1991b.
[4]Powell et al. 1993.
[5]Authors' conservative estimate. World Resources Institute (1980) estimates that the United States added 4 million acres of new forest annually during the 1980s. The average annual increase from 1920 to 1987 was 1.9 million acres per year. Mangold (1990) places the area of trees planted annually in recent years at about 3,000,000 acres. From these figures an estimate of the total forest land for the end of 1994 of about 740,000,000 acres appears conservative.

tally, Mitchell [1981] voiced a similar concern about New England forests in the early 1980s. However, with the return of low energy prices, the pressure on the forests dropped.)

The view from New York, however, was not the same as the view from the Midwest. Peripheral to the central prairie afforestation occurred on a large scale. With the prairies no longer burned by the Indians, many areas that were not cultivated became wooded. The change was subtle yet extensive. The amount of such afforestation has not been measured, but with 75 million acres of new mesquite forest in Texas and Oklahoma alone, the total new forest may have been well over 100 million acres. (See also the discussion about Canada prairie under Industrial Nations heading.)

Overall, however, America was losing forests, primarily in the East. Deforestation continued until about 1920, when the area of forested land dropped to a low of about 600 million acres (see table 3.1). Even though the population was increasing, the area covered by forests started to expand. New trees increased in size so that by 1940 the volume of wood grown was about equal to the volume of wood cut. Sedjo (Federick and Sedjo 1991) estimates forest cover for 1987 at about 728 million acres. Powell et al. (1993) estimate forest cover at 737 million acres. Our own check of forest cover data for New England, New York, Florida, Missouri, Iowa, Michigan, Wisconsin, and Minnesota suggest that the Forest Service's figure is now probably conservative. The rate of new forest growth from 1920 to the early 1960s was about 1.2 million acres per year; from the early 1960s to 1990, the rate increased to 2.9 million acres per year. The World Resources Institute estimates that the increase in the 1980s averaged over 4 million acres annually, which shows the rate of increase further accelerating. This is consistent with the data for farmland—59 million fewer acres from 1980 through 1992 (Famighetti 1994), an average reduction of 4.9 million acres per year. Further, volume of wood growth in the United States for 1989 exceeded removal by 37 percent (Haynes 1990). Finally, for the eastern two-thirds of the United States, nearly all record deer harvests have occurred in the past two to three years (see chapter 4). Deer habitats are thus still expanding as woods expand.

From several perspectives, we see that America's forests have continued to expand since their low in 1920. America's forest cover is now probably well over 740 million acres. The added 140 million-plus acres of forest exceed the combined land area of all of Vermont, Massachusetts, Rhode Island, New York, Pennsylvania, New Jersey, Maryland, Virginia, and North Carolina. By the year 2030, the total tree-covered area in the United States may even approach the original 950 million acres present when Europeans first arrived.

Table 3.2 is a summary of forest and tree cover for some specific areas of the United States and of areas of the industrial world.

Discrepancies—U.S. Forest Statistics

The state of a nation's forests, whether expanding or contracting, is very important for environmental assessment. Forests act as a barometer measuring the impact of a culture on the natural environment.

However, misconceptions are fostered by such inconsistent reports as that of Williams (1990). He states that between 1910 and 1979 in the United States 239,000 square kilometers (59,033,000 acres) of farmland reverted to forest. In the same report, however, he says that between 1940 and 1982 total forest area declined from 2.43 million square kilometers (600,210,000 acres) to 2.29 million square kilometers (565,630,000 acres), a loss of 0.14 million square kilometers (34,580,000 acres). Peterson (1992) also reports a decline since 1920. Brown et al. (1990, 31) say: "Even in Canada and the United States, forests are shrinking, largely due to the spread of land-intensive suburban and commercial development." If so much farmland reverted to forests, how can this be? (Brown et al. might have noticed this discrepancy, as their 1990 statement does not appear in the 1994 edition of *State of the World.*)

Conversely, Sedjo (Frederick and Sedjo 1991), as previously noted, states that new forestland in the United States from 1920 to 1987 increased by some 128 million acres and that net forest growth in cubic feet rose 267 percent in that interval. Similarly, Mangold et al. (1991) show that the area planted in trees in the United States increased about 2000 percent from 1930 to 1991. Other ex-

Table 3.2
Trees, United States and Other Industrial Nations

Item	Area	When	Change/Reference
Forest land	NYS	1900–1993[*]	Up 147% to 61%[**] (Anon. 1989b; Stanton 1992)
Forest land	MI,WI, MN	1869–1988	Up 40,257,000 acres (+380%) (Marsh 1874; Wright 1993)
Forest land	US	1920–1987	128 million acres of new forest (Frederick & Sedjo 1991)
Forest land	US	1920–1993	140,000,000 (this report)
Net forest growth, cubic feet	US	1920–1987	Up 267% (Frederick & Sedjo 1991)
Mesquite	Panhandle area, Oklahoma to Mexico	1492–early 1900s	75 million acres of new mesquite (Stewart 1956)
Area planted in trees	US	1930–1991	Up 2000% (Mangold 1991)
Trees	Central US	1492–1991	More than in 1492 (this report)
Trees	Oregon and Washington	1920–1991	More than in 1920 (Hatfield 1991)
Forest land	Canada	1976/77– 1988	Up 28% (Canadian Minister, Supply & Service 1978 & 1988)
Forest land	Canada	1980s	Up 720,000 hectares a year (World Resources 1990)
Forest growing stock	Western Europe	1950–1991	Up 143% (Kaupi et al. 1992)
Forest growing stock	Mediterranean Europe	1950–1991	Up 87% (Kaupi et al. 1992)
Forest growing stock	Eastern Europe	1950–1991	Up 38% (Kaupi et al. 1992)

Table 3.2 (Continued)

Item	Area	When	Change/Reference
Forests	Australia, Israel Japan, New Zealand South Korea, Taiwan	1958–1980	Expanded by larger average per- cent than US (UN FAO and Hsu Ho 1991 etc.)
Forest land	USSR	1980s	Up 4,540,000 hectares a year (World Resources 1990)
Forest land	Turkey	1980s	Up 82,000 hectares a year (World Resources 1990)
Forest land	South Africa	1980s	Up 63,000 hectares a year (World Resources 1990)

†Current estimate, 70 percent for 1994, is a figure obtained by extrapolation of the trend that forests are still expanding and that 1992 had the record official deer take for New York.

**Note particularly that forests have expanded in all major industrialized nations according to Kaupi et al. 1991, and according to United Nations sources.

amples from the U.S. Forest Service are: Brand and Walkowiske (1990) writing about Iowa; Considine and Frieswyk (1982), New York; Haynes (1990), United States; USDA (1991a), United States; Leatherberry (1990), Missouri's Ozarks; Miles (1990), Missouri's Ozarks; Smith (1990), northwest Ozarks; Remington and Sendak (1989), New York and New England; Sheffield and Bechtold (1981), South Florida; Sheffield and Craver (1981), Virginia; and Spencer and Hahn (1984), Michigan. All these references indicate an increase in America's forests both for individual states and for the nation as a whole. In addition, the World Resources Institute (1990) shows expanding forests in both the United States and Canada.

Two other lines of evidence indicate that forests are expanding in many areas. First, the record increase of the white-tailed deer population over so much of the United States is largely the result of expanded forests (see chapter 4). Second, the continued reduction in the amount of farmland means that more land can go to forest. That process will continue. The USDA (1989) anticipates that America's major cropland may drop by as much as 50 percent (160 million acres) by the year 2030.

If so much evidence exists for expanding forests, how can some authors conclude otherwise? Part of the reason lies in the definition of "timberland." It was defined by Alig et al. (1990, 1) as "forest land that can produce 20 cubic feet of timber per acre per year and is not reserved for other uses." This excluded from "timberland" such forested areas as national parks, state parks, wilderness areas, young immature woods, and privately held forests unavailable for timbering. Huge, newly designated wilderness areas of Alaska and the West were removed from the timberland inventory. Thus, although America's forests are greatly expanding, "timberland" (i.e., forests available for commercial logging) may be declining.

In addition, environmentalists are much more likely to believe there are environmental problems than benefits. Thus, they more readily accept, without checking, data about forests that indicate that forests are in trouble (for more about environmental perspectives, see chapters 10, 11, 12, and 13).

CAUSES OF FOREST EXPANSION

Data show that the greatest expansion of forest cover occurs in industrialized democratic nations. The following analysis centers primarily on the United States, but much of the discussion is applicable to other industrial nations as well.

Reduced Fuel Pressure

In early America the only source of heat energy was wood. The need for fuel wood depleted forests around urban areas throughout the eastern United States. Coal and oil were discovered and developed in the early to mid-1800s. America's transportation infrastructure improved and industrialization produced enough wealth for people to buy the newly available fuels. Pressure on the nation's forests declined. By 1890 about 50 percent of America's thermal energy was from wood. Thermoelectric and hydroelectric power were later produced and distributed throughout the United States. Although the production of such energy may be at the expense of local forestland, the overall impact has been to take pressure off a much larger area of forest elsewhere. During the energy crisis of the 1970s, America again used over 50 percent of the wood cut for fuel. Currently, about 23 percent of America's cut wood is used for energy (Conservation Foundation 1984). Current fuel pressure on forests is negligible.

Agricultural Efficiency

Along with alternate fuels, an efficient agricultural sector bears much responsibility for America's new forests. Most of the 140 million-plus acres of new forestland had been used for agricultural purposes (see chapter 2). Much of the 160 million acres of agricultural land that could be released by the year 2030 will also go to forestland. An efficient agricultural sector is an enormous conservation plus for America.

We stress a point made in chapter 2. When people leave the land, they go predominantly to more urban areas. Concentration of people in towns and cities contributes to reforestation because people have left the land. Brown et al. (1990, 3), blaming loss of forests on suburban and urban development, are thus wrong on two counts: (1) America's forests are actually expanding; and (2) urbanization actually *contributes* to reforestation and afforestation. When people leave land for the cities, the abandoned land tends to return to a more natural state.

Mineral Products for Construction

Initially, most construction material in America's homes, commercial buildings, bridges, and many road surfaces was wood. Piled stone was used for foundations but could not be piled very high without strong mortar. Lime mortars were available, but were slow to set, and construction with stone required expensive tight joints. The pozzolanic cements used by early Romans were very strong. However, the required raw materials, limestone and volcanic glass or volcanic ash, did not occur close enough together to be economical in most of the United States. Until the late 1800s, therefore, construction with stone was too expensive for many purposes.

The discovery of portland cement technology in England in 1824 and the manufacture of portland cement in the United States starting in 1890 in Pennsylvania radically changed construction practices in America. Tall buildings of stone and reinforced concrete became economical, and cities no longer required so much wood for construction.

This use of mineral products for most major buildings further reduced pressure on America's forests. An immediate result in New York State was that the forest of its Adirondack Mountains, which was stripped by the late 1800s for construction wood, could return. Not only was wood less important for construction; tall buildings meant that urbanization required far less land. If New York City's buildings had to be built of wood, millions more acres of land would be needed. The small area used by the construction mineral industry, in effect, contributed greatly to the widespread, dispersed benefit of renewed forests.

Wood Preservation Technology

Making wood in buildings last longer by painting the wood, using wood preservatives, aerating dead spaces, and using pesticides to control termites and carpenter ants reduces the pressure on forests. According to Barrons (1981, 60), were wood preservatives not used, a forest twice the size of New England would be required to replace rotted wood in the United States on a sustained basis. (For the U.S. Environmental Protection Administration's [EPA] view on wood preservatives, see chapter 12.)

Tree Planting

Although forests were destroyed in America by the early European settlers, tree planting around homes and along streets also occurred. At first, the net result of both activities was a loss of trees. Then, as other forms of energy became available and agriculture and food handling became more efficient, new trees, including those planted, outnumbered those cut.

Large-Scale Planting. Mangold et al. (1991) summarize information about the total trees planted in the United States for fiscal 1990 as follows: 2,862,207 acres were planted. About 41.5 percent were planted by the forest industry, and 39.7 percent were planted by the nonindustrial private sector. The total acreage in 1990 was about 2000 percent higher than in 1930. The number of commercial seedlings was about 1.9 billion.

Small-Scale Urban "Forests." Flying out of Chicago and looking at a low angle at old suburbs west of the city, you can see many areas where homes are completely hidden by the trees planted around them and along the streets. Many suburbs throughout the United States are like this. Although these areas are not considered forests and the trees are not included in forest statistics, the amount of tree cover is considerable and the equivalent of a natural parkland.

Farm-Related Trees—Midwest. The central Midwest was a dreary place when the first white settlers arrived. In vast prairie areas, there were no trees. New settlers soon began planting trees around their farm homes, in their villages, and in woodlots. Later, they planted trees along boundaries of fields. Now, planted trees number in the billions in the Midwest. In a sense, the increase in the number of trees in the Midwest was the result of the "coming of the plow."

Afforestation has also greatly increased the number of trees, particularly at the periphery of the Midwest prairie where the land was not farmed and prairie fires no longer raged. Stewart (1956) shows a 60 percent decrease in the size of Wisconsin's prairies because of afforestation between 1829 and 1854. He describes Illinois barrens that were converted to forest "as by magic" when fires that maintained the grasslands were no longer set. Additionally, parts of Tennessee, Kentucky, Ohio, Indiana, Virginia, and Michigan around the central prairie were afforested starting in the mid-1800s. To the west, aspen forests moved hundreds of miles into the northern prairie. Texas, south of the Panhandle area of Oklahoma, and some adjacent areas saw a regrowth of mesquite in the late 1800s covering some 75 million acres of former prairie.

People and Vegetative Diversity

"The loss of diversity is the most important process of environmental change—because it is the only process that is wholly irreversible" (Wilson, quoted in Chivian 1993, 193). Most of the loss of vegetative biodiversity, however, is in tropical jungle areas (Chivian 1993, 195). By contrast, along with forest expansion, the industrial nations have maintained species diversity of trees and other vegetation and have greatly increased diversity in many areas. The amount of such change is greatest in wealthy nations.

In part, humans also increase the biodiversity of areas by planting exotic trees. Some common examples seen in the United States are Russian olive, Colorado blue spruce, Scotch pine, Norway spruce, Austrian pine, eucalyptus (Australian), and Chinese chestnut.

OTHER NATIONS' FORESTS

Industrial Nations

The Food and Agriculture Organization (1990) states that some confusion exists about timber trends in Canada. As in the United States, reclassification has resulted in discrepancies. Statistics from the Canadian Minister of Supply and Services (1978, 1988) show that Canada, with 10 percent of the world's total forest, has increased its forest from 341,700,000 hectares (844,341,000 acres) in 1976–77 to 436,400,000 hectares (1,078,344,000 acres) in 1988, an increase of 28 percent (see table 3.2). Williams (1990) says that in the 1980s Canada averaged 7,200 km² (1,779,096 acres) of reforested land per year. In addition, Canada since 1500 has gained 163,000,000 acres of new, largely aspen, forests in former prairie areas (Krug 1991). As in the United States, when the prairies were no longer burned, aspen forests returned to many areas. Canada uses only 4 percent of the wood it cuts as fuel wood (World Resources Institute 1990) and shares America's agricultural efficiency. It should, therefore, keep its new forests.

The factors responsible for North America's new forests have also operated in Europe (see table 3.2) to produce the dispersed effect of expanded forests. But an additional cause of forest expansion in Europe is its greater use of stone, brick, and concrete as construction materials, particularly for homes. When forests were largely depleted centuries ago, people had to turn to these materials for shelter. This effectively reduced stress on forests. The Minoan civilization (pre-1500 B.C.) made columns for temples and other structures largely of wood. But with depletion of forests, the later Egyptian, Nubian, Greek, and Roman civilizations built major structures mostly of stone. Extensive construction using mined materials started in the pre-Christian and early Christian eras in Europe and the Middle East, and it continues to this day. Mining has helped take pressure off forests in many areas. Therefore, mining has had the dispersed effect in these areas of contributing to the expansion of forests.

As in the United States, the use of fuels other than wood has also reduced pressure on forests. The average consumption of fuel wood is 16 percent of wood cut for the fourteen wealthiest European nations (World Resources Institute 1990), thus holding energy pressures on forests to a minimum. Only Albania, Italy, and Greece use over 50 percent of their wood cut for fuel.

England's productive forest cover doubled from 1920 to 1978 (Francis 1978).

Kauppi et al. (1992) found that the forest growing stock increased in western Europe by 143 percent from 1950 to 1991 and in Mediterranean Europe by 87 percent. Even eastern Europe increased its growing stock by 38 percent during this interval although it lost somewhat less than 0.5 percent of the total potential forest to smelter fumes.

Industrialized nations of the western Pacific region have also increased their forest cover in the past three to four decades. From an analysis of data from Food and Agriculture Organization (1961, 1976, 1993), World Resources Institute (1992), and Hsu-Hu (1991), Australia, New Zealand, Japan, South Korea, and Taiwan all have expanded forest cover. The change varies from an increase of 16 percent for Japan to 64 percent for New Zealand. This should not be surprising as these are industrialized nations with efficient agriculture. They also use little wood for fuel. Australia uses 16 percent of the wood it harvests for fuel; New Zealand, less than one percent; Japan, 2 percent; and South Korea, 72 percent. The high figure for South Korea is probably incorrect now because the country has a very successful reforestation program. It is characteristic of industrial nations, even those industrializing inefficiently as in eastern Europe, to be able to reforest their lands.

The ability to expand wooded areas is absolutely dependent on availability of alternatives to wood as sources of energy, on high agricultural efficiency, and on populations wealthy enough to buy the energy sources and the agricultural products. This is true whether expansion of forests is an inadvertent spin-off from industrialization or is intentional as in the case of tree planting.

Third World Nations

In contrast to First World nations, the situation in most developing nations is grim. Forests are being lost at perhaps the greatest rate in history.

The Council on Environmental Quality (1980) estimates that the growing stock of wood in Third World nations is 57 cubic meters per capita as compared to 142 cubic meters for industrial countries. They report the disparity as rapidly increasing. The Food and Agriculture Organization (1993) also shows that the disparity continues to increase.

McNeely et al. (1990) place the rate of deforestation of 64 tropical nations at 0.6 percent per year. More recent data from the United Nations (1993) for 90 tropical countries state that the average annual rate of deforestation was 0.8 percent for the interval 1981–1990. They say the rate of deforestation is accelerating. Tropical Africa for the 1981–1990 interval was deforesting at an annual rate of 0.7 percent; Asia and Pacific, 1.2 percent; and Latin America and Caribbean[1], 0.8 percent. Aldhous (1993) gives slightly higher but similar annual losses. The annual rate of deforestation for all tropical countries from 1961–1965 to 1986–1990 has increased about 60 percent (modified from United Nations (1993). The forests of the Third World would appear to be in trouble, particularly the tropical rainforests. Certainly, humans have depleted the forests of some nations such as Ethiopia and Haiti.

Richards (1990) says that the total loss of forests in the world was 4.0 percent in 1700 and 18.7 percent in 1980. Considering that the forests of Europe, the Middle East, eastern North America, and China were largely gone in 1700, the 4 percent figure seems low.

Bast et al. (1994, 84, 85) conclude that environmentalists have exaggerated the picture about tropical rainforests. They question the accuracy of the estimates of deforestation statistics, especially for the Amazon Basin. They suggest the rate of tropical forest loss may be as low as a tenth of a percent a year. Easterbrook (1995, 596) arrived at similar conclusions. Their conclusions are not surprising considering the tendency for environmentalists to exaggerate dangers (see chapters 10, 11, and 12).

According to Eckholm (1976) and Pardo (1978), the primary cause of forest loss in developing countries is the use of wood for energy. They estimate that as much as 90 percent of the wood cut was used for energy. The maximum use of firewood in the 1970s was in Africa, where about 97 percent of the total wood cut was used for fuel (United Nations Food and Agriculture Organization 1967) or about 58 percent of their total consumed energy (International Union for Conservation of Nature and Natural Resources 1980). More recent data summarized by the World Resources Institute (1990, their table 18.2) shows the average use of fuel wood in Africa (omitting South Africa) to be 81 percent of the wood cut, an apparent improvement. For Central America (omitting Barbados, Jamaica, Trinidad, and Tobago), 88 percent of the wood cut is used for fuel; for South America, 60 percent; and for Asia, 80 percent. Much energy for India is from dried dung, hardly an improvement over wood as failing to return dung to the soil reduces soil quality.

Ranking with the need for wood for fuel as a cause for forest loss in developing nations is the inefficient use of land for agriculture (described in chapter 2).

According to the World Resources Institute (1990, 71), "a substantial proportion (of deforestation) takes place spontaneously and without control." The current deforestation of developing world nations has two contributing causes:

- They do not produce enough wealth for most people to afford energy sources other than wood, dried dung, or crop residues. The Food and Agriculture Organization (1967) states that the annual fuel wood consumption per one thousand inhabitants in sub-Saharan Africa was 680 cubic meters, more than twice as high as the estimated world average. This problem is exacerbated by high OPEC oil prices. As Eckholm (1976, 111) says: "The long-term interest in preserving the productive capacity of the earth and in maximizing the welfare for the greatest number of people might argue for lower prices and a rapid *increase,* not a halt, in the adoption of kerosene and natural gas in the homes of the poor." (We show in chapter 13 that Eckholm's wisdom has largely been ignored by the environmental community.)

- High birthrates, particularly in Africa, combined with low agricultural productivity (actually decreasing in parts of Africa south of the Sahara Desert), put additional pressure on forests because cleared land is often needed for food production. Stopping all export of timber would have little effect on deforestation. For example, the volume of timber exported from sub-Saharan Africa was only 0.001 percent of the wood cut in the 1960s (United Nations and Food and Agriculture Organization 1967).

A surprising Third World exception is India, which had an 18 percent increase in forest cover between 1987 and 1990 (United Nations 1993). Another exception in the developing world may be China, which added 4,552,000 hectares (11,248,000 acres) of forest during the 1980s. Both India and China were major beneficiaries of the "green revolution." They were able to greatly improve agricultural efficiency in terms of food produced per acre (thanks largely to the work of Ernest Borlaug, a winner of the Nobel Prize for Peace). Improved agricultural productivity is certainly a major reason for increased forest cover in these nations.

Whether India and China can continue to be agriculturally independent and to expand their forests will probably be determined by their ability to control their populations. The 1990 birthrate minus deathrate figure for India is twenty-one per one thousand per year; for China, fourteen per one thousand. Although their birthrates are not high in comparison to some Third World nations, Indian and Chinese birthrates may still be on a collision course with their improving natural environments. For comparison, birthrate minus deathrate for Japan is four; for Europe, two; for the United States and Canada, five (data from Wright 1994).

SUMMARY

The extent of afforestation and reforestation in industrialized nations in recent decades is striking; in fact, such large-scale expansion of forests has no equal in recorded history. The only forest expansion that is in the same category is the nearly 300 million acre afforestation that occurred peripherally to the American and Canadian prairies after the white man settled in the mid- to late 1800s. Forests of the industrial nations now comprise about 50 percent of the world's forests. The expansion has occurred for the following reasons:

- Wood is no longer the major fuel.
- Agricultural efficiency is high in terms of yield per unit area largely because of use of agricultural chemicals.
- Mechanized equipment eliminates the need for pastureland for draft animals.
- Refrigeration and various preservation techniques reduce food losses.
- Efficient transportation contributes to getting perishable food to consumers before it spoils.

- Modern construction techniques and chemicals make wood last longer in fencing and construction.

- Mined products replace wood as building construction materials.

- Mined products allow the construction of tall buildings, so human living space and working space occupy smaller land surface areas.

Industrial nations have all expanded their floral biodiversity by importing hundreds of species of shrubs, grasses, and trees for food, decorative purposes, or wildlife enhancement.

In the related areas of agricultural production and forests, America has evolved well beyond balancing the availability of resources with resource use (sustainability) because these resources are being multiplied. The multiplication should continue. The USDA (1989) predicts that improved agricultural efficiencies will allow up to 160 million more acres of farmland to be released from agricultural use by the year 2030. Recent record crops are consistent with the USDA's predictions. Political factors to be discussed in later chapters will determine the extent to which the USDA's predictions come true.

The facts about forests in developed regions of the world make the conclusions of such environmentalists as Brown, Gore, Krimsky, and Matachke quoted in the first paragraph of this chapter highly questionable at best. The industrialization and development they deplore have obviously enormously improved our world. Industrialization even improved the forest, wildlife, and soil erosion conditions in the very inefficient communist nations of eastern Europe.

In contrast to industrial nations, Third World nations are consuming their forest resources. This deforestation will continue until these developing nations reach a minimal degree of industrialization as reflected in GNP per capita per year (see chapter 8). Reforestation is generally not possible until nations achieve Second World status. Since many nations of sub-Saharan Africa and the new nations of the former Soviet bloc have a declining per capita income, according to Wright (1995), the chance of significant continued increases in forest may be reduced in all these nations.

NOTE

1. However, the people of the major Indian civilizations of Honduras, Belize, and Mexico from about A.D. 800 to 1000 had less forest than today.

REFERENCES

Aldhous, P. 1993. Tropical deforestation: Not just a problem in Amazonia. *Science* 259: 1390.

Alig, R. J., W. G. Hohenstein, B. Murray, and R. G. Haight. 1990. *Changes in Type of Timberland in the United States, 1952–2040, By Ownership, Forest Type and*

State. U.S. Department of Agriculture, Forest Service, General Technical Report SE-64.

Anderson R. C., E. L. Collins, and L. L. Wallace. 1990. The historic role of fire in the North American grassland. In *Fire in North American Tallgrass Prairies,* edited by S. L. Collins and L. L. Wallace. Norman: University of Oklahoma Press.

Anon. 1993. Are we running out of trees? *Reader's Digest,* November, 125.

Bandow, D., and I. Vasquez, eds. 1994. *Perpetuating Poverty.* Washington, D.C.: Cato Institute.

Barrons, K. C. 1981. *Are Pesticides Really Necessary?* Chicago: Regnery Gateway.

Bast, J. L., P. J. Hill, and R. C. Rue. 1994. *Eco-Sanity.* Lanham, Md.: Madison Books.

Brand, G. J., and J. T. Walkowishe. 1990. *Forest Statistics, Iowa.* U.S. Department of Agriculture, Forest Service, Resource Bulletin NC 136.

Brown, L., et al., ed. 1990. *The State of the World 1990.* New York: W. W. Norton.

———. 1994. *The State of the World 1994.* New York: W. W. Norton.

Ministry of Supply and Service. 1980. *Canadian Forestry Statistics, 1978.* Ottawa: Canadian Government Publishing Centre.

———. 1988. *Canadian Forestry Statistics, 1985.* Ottawa: Canadian Government Publishing Centre.

Chadwick, D. H. 1993. The American prairie, roots of the sky. *National Geographic,* October, 91–119.

Chivian, E., ed. 1993. *Critical Condition.* Cambridge, Mass.: MIT Press.

Collins, S. L., and L. L. Wallace, eds. 1990. *Fire in North American Tallgrass Prairies.* Norman: University of Oklahoma Press.

Conservation Foundation. 1984. *The State of the Environment.* Washington, D.C.: The Conservation Foundation.

Considine, T. J., Jr., and T. S. Frieswyk. 1982. *Forest Statistics for New York, 1980.* U.S. Department of Agriculture, Forest Service, General Technical Report NE-11.

Council on Environmental Quality. 1980. *Global 2000 Report.* Washington, D.C.: U.S. Government Printing Office.

Davis, J. H. 1956. Influences of man upon coast lines. In *Man's Role in Changing the Face of the Earth,* edited by W. L. Thomas. Chicago: University of Chicago Press.

Easterbrook, G. 1995. *A Moment on the Earth: The Coming Age of Environmental Optimism.* New York: Viking Penguin.

Eckholm, E. P. 1976. *Losing Ground.* New York: W. W. Norton.

Famighetti, R. 1994. *The World Almanac and Book of Facts.* Mahwah, N.J.: Funk and Wagnall.

Food and Agriculture Organization. 1961. *Timber Trends and Prospects in the Asia-Pacific Region.* Geneva: United Nations.

———. 1967. *Timber Trends and Prospects in Africa.* Rome: United Nations.

———. 1976. *Forest Resources in the Asia and Far East Region.* Rome: United Nations.

———. 1990. *Timber Trends and Prospects for North America.* Rome: United Nations.

———. 1993. *Forest Resources Assessment 1990, Tropical Countries.* Rome: United Nations.

Francis, G. J. 1978. *Need for the Continuous Quantitative and Qualitative Assessment of the Forest Resource Base and Its Accessibility.* Edinburgh: Forestry Commission.

Frederick, K. D., and R. A. Sedjo. 1991. *America's Renewable Resources.* Washington, D.C.: Resources for the Future.

Gore, A. 1992. *Earth in the Balance.* New York: Houghton Mifflin.

Halls, L. K., ed. 1984. *White Tailed Deer, Ecology and Management.* Harrisburg, Pa.: Stackpole Books.

Hatfield, M. 1991. *Old Growth and the Media: A Lawmaker's Perspective.* Washington, D.C.: Freedom Forum Media Studies Center, Island Press.

Haynes, R. W. 1990. *An Analysis of the Timber Situation in the United States: 1989–2040.* U.S. Department of Agriculture, Forest Service, General Technical Report RM-199.

Hsu-Hu, C. 1991. *Forestry Administration and Forestry Technology.* Council of Agriculture, Taipei, June.

International Union for Conservation of Nature and Natural Resources. 1980. *World Conservation Strategy.* Gland, Switzerland: IUCN.

Kauppi, P. E., K. Mielikainen, and K. Kuusela. 1992. Biomass and carbon budget of European forests, 1971 to 1990. *Science* 256:70–74.

Krug, E. C. 1994. Yet another nail in the green utopia's coffin: Canadian pre-settlement forest. *Environment Betrayed,* November 3.

Leatherberry, E. C. 1990. Timber resource of Missouri's Eastern Ozarks, 1989. North Central Forest Experiment Station, St. Paul, Minn., April

Lowe, M. D. 1994. Reinventing transport. In *The State of the World,* edited by L. Brown et al. New York: W. W. Norton.

Mangold, R. D., et al. 1991. Tree planting in the United States. U.S. Department of Agriculture, Forest Service, March.

Marsh, G. P. 1864. *Man and Nature; or Physical Geography as Modified by Human Action.* New York: Scribners.

Matschke, G. H., et al. 1984. Population influences. In *White Tailed Deer, Ecology and Management,* edited by L. K. Halls. Harrisburg, Pa.: Stackpole Books.

Maurice, C., and C. U. Smithson. 1984. *The Doomsday Myth.* Stanford: Hoover Institution Press.

McNeely, J. A., K. R. Miller, W. V. Reid, R. A. Mittermeier, and T. B. Werner. 1990. *Conserving the World's Biological Diversity.* Washington, D.C.: World Bank.

Mellor, J. W., and R. H. Adams, Jr. 1984. Feeding the underdeveloped world. *Chemical and Engineering News,* April 23, 32–39.

Miles, P. D. 1990. Timber resources of Missouri's Southwest Ozarks, 1989. St. Paul, Minn.: North Central Forest Experiment Station, April.

Mitchell, V. G. 1981. Whither the Yankee forest. *Audubon,* November–December, 78–99.

Pardo, R. 1978. Forestry as if people mattered (editorial). *American Forests,* August, 4.

Peterson, J. 1992. About America's forests. *Evergreen* (Special Bonus Issue): 2–5.

Powell, D. S., et al. 1993. *Forest Resources of the United States, 1992.* U.S. Department of Agriculture, Forest Service, Rocky Mountain Forest and Range Experiment Station, General Technical Report RM-234.

Remington, S. B., and P. E. Sendak. 1989. *New England and New York's timber economy.* U.S. Department of Agriculture, Forest Service, Northeastern area.

Richards, J. F. 1990. Land transformation. In *The Earth as Transformed by Human Activity,* edited by B. L. Turner III et al. Cambridge: Cambridge University Press.

Robbins, C. S., D. Bystrak, and P. H. Geissler. 1986. *The Breeding Bird Survey: Its First Fifteen Years, 1965–1979.* U.S. Department of Interior, Resource Publication 157.

Roberts, P. C. 1994. Development planning in Latin America: The lifeblood of the mercantilist state. In *Perpetuating Poverty,* edited by D. Bandow and I. Vasquez. Washington, D.C.: Cato Institute.

Rodgers, R. 1992. *Small game hunter activity survey for June 1, 1991 to May 31, 1992.* Kansas Department of Wildlife and Parks.

Rogich, D. G. 1991. The future of materials: Plastic component is growing. *Minerals Today,* June, 30–32.

Rubenstein, E. 1994. Dire states? *National Review,* January, 15.

Rubin, C. T. 1994. Environmentalism as "everythingism." *PERC Reports* 12(4):4–5.

Ruff, H. 1994. *The Ruff Times* 2.

Rupp, R. 1990. *Red Oaks and Black Birches: The Science and Lore of Trees.* Troy, N.Y.: Gardenway.

Salomon, J. H. 1984. Indians that set the woods on fire. *The Conservationist,* March–April, New York State Department of Environmental Conservation, 34–39.

Sheffield, R. M., and W. Bechtold. 1981. *Forest statistics for South Florida.* Ashville, N.C.: Southeastern Forest Experiment Station, July.

Sheffield, R. M., and G. C. Craver. 1981. *Virginia's pine resource: An interim assessment.* Ashville, N. C.: Southeastern Forest Experiment Station, August.

Simmons, I. G. 1993. *Environmental History.* Oxford: Blackwell.

Smith, W. B. 1990. *Timber resources of Missouri's Northwest Ozarks, 1989.* North Central Forest Experiment Station, St. Paul, Minn., April.

Spencer, J. S., Jr., and J. T. Hahn. 1984. Michigan's fourth forest inventory: Timber volumes and projections of timber supply. North Central Forest Experiment Station, St. Paul, Minn., June.

Stanton, B. F. 1992. The changing landscape of New York agriculture in the twentieth century. Department of Agricultural Economics, New York State College of Agriculture and Life Science, Cornell University.

Stewart, O. C. 1956. Fire as a first great force employed by man. In *Man's Role in Changing the Face of the Earth,* edited by W. L. Thomas. Chicago: University of Chicago Press.

Sumner, D. A., and R. Allen. 1993. *Annual Crop Summary.* Washington, D.C.: Agricultural Statistics Board.

Thomas, W. L., ed. 1956. *Man's Role in Changing the Face of the Earth.* Chicago: University of Chicago Press.

Turner, B. L., III, et al., eds. 1990. *The Earth as Transformed by Human Activity.* Cambridge: Cambridge University Press.

United Nations. 1993. *Forest Resources Assessment.*

U.S. Department of Agriculture. 1980. *Assessment of the Forest and Range Situation.* Forest Service, January.

———. 1989. *The Second RCA Appraisal* (Soil, Water and Related Resources on Nonfederal Land in the United States).

————. 1989. *An Analysis of the Land Base Situation in the United States: 1989–2040,* Forest Service, General Technology Report RM-181, October.

————. 1991a. Farms and land in farms, 1979–1987, final estimates by state.

————. 1991b. The conditions and trends of U.S. forests. Forest Service.

————. 1992. The conditions and trends of U.S. forests. Forest Service.

Williams, M. 1990. Forests. In *The Earth as Transformed by Human Activity,* edited by B. L. Turner III et al. Cambridge: Cambridge University Press.

Wilson, R. 1979. Analyzing the daily risks of life. *Technology Review,* February, 45.

World Resources Institute. 1990. *World Resources.* New York: World Resources Institute and the International Institute for Environment and Development, Basic Books.

————. 1992. *World Resources.* New York: Oxford University Press.

Wright, J. W. 1993. *The Universal Almanac.* Kansas City: Andrews and McMeel.

————. 1994. *The Universal Almanac.* Kansas City: Andrews and McMeel.

————. 1995. *The Universal Almanac.* Kansas City: Andrews and McMeel.

CHAPTER 4

Wildlife

Endangered species frequently make headline news, but changes occurring in many more common wildlife populations seldom do. People, therefore, tend to know about endangered species, but not much about the status of other wildlife populations. What they do hear may very well be misleading and even incorrect. For example, Al Gore (1992), who says little about wildlife in general, deplores a developer near Washington, D.C., "bulldozing the last hundred acres of untouched forest in the entire area." This activity, he says, displaced pheasants and deer. The impression the reader gets is that development is a major problem for wildlife and forests. Yet deer are at an all-time record level in Maryland and Virginia adjacent to Washington, D.C. (and in Gore's home state, Tennessee) and forests of the eastern third of America have vastly expanded in the past seven decades.

Similarly, Peters and Lovejoy (1990) say incorrectly: "Despite a precedent-setting system of national parks and reserves, degradation of habitat continues both within and outside of protected areas. . . . The overall result of habitat destruction, hunting pressure, and, to a lesser extent, effects of exotic species and pollutants has been a dramatic decrease in populations of many species."

Lilienfeld and Rathje (1995) say: "Certainly industry has played a significant role in destroying habitats" and "Habitats are being destroyed. Biodiversity is declining." The statements are curious in an article debunking components of environmentalism.

Are they correct? In this chapter we describe factors influencing wildlife populations and how they have fared in the United States and, to some extent, elsewhere. Our information comes from government sources and shows that Gore, Peters and Lovejoy, and Lilienfeld and Rathje are incorrect. In America, nearly all species of birds and animals that require trees or forests as habitat have enormously expanded populations, *an entirely predictable result* given the data in chapters 2 and 3.

NATURAL FACTORS INFLUENCING WILDLIFE POPULATIONS

Wildlife populations rise and fall for many natural reasons. Wildlife are constantly exposed to the vagaries of nature. In the natural world, wildlife lead short lives. Most deaths are painful and violent. Changes in conditions can be profound enough to cause species to vanish, to change, or to proliferate. At any point in geologic history some species of life thrived and expanded, other species declined; most evolved. Almost all species of birds, animals, and insects that ever populated Earth have become extinct; that is, *species extinction is the norm.* Nature has always been dynamic. (We leave to others discussion of the mass extinctions that probably resulted from the Earth being struck by large extraterrestrial objects.)

Disease

Like humans, wildlife may get sick from viral, fungal, bacterial, or parasitic diseases. Sicknesses often reach epidemic proportions. Wildlife populations can be depleted temporarily because of epidemics. Such diseases as rabies can attack many species. Conversely, duck herpes is most devastating to black ducks. The introduction of the woodland caribou into Maine has largely been unsuccessful because a parasite carried by deer (but doing them no harm) attacks the brains of the caribou and kills them. Generally, epidemics cause blips on the megatrend population curves, and affected species recover after the diseases have run their courses. In the case of the current rabies epidemic in the northeastern United States, wildlife managers estimate raccoon populations will be cut to 15 percent before the epidemic ends. Because of the excellent habitat for raccoons, their population will rapidly recover. (A side effect of fewer raccoons is an increase in the turkey population—raccoons eat turkey eggs.)

Weather

Weather may also cause short-term blips on population curves. Severe winters, for example, can deplete by starvation nonmigratory species of wildlife such as deer. Severity of Adirondack winters in New York State has had more impact on the Adirondack deer population than have human activities (Severinghaus and Brown 1956). Unusually low numbers of wintering diving ducks (redhead, common goldeneye, and merganser) in New York are attributed to the very mild winter of 1990–1991, causing them to arrive from the north after the January 2–8, 1992 survey date. A later survey would have reported higher populations. The decrease in the duck population in the Midwest has, in part, been the result of drought that dried up prairie potholes in which ducks breed.

Just as severe winters can deplete wildlife populations, mild winters can cause increased populations. A contributing cause of the record deer population in

Michigan in recent years is a series of relatively mild winters (Michigan Department of Natural Resources n.d.).

Predation

Increased numbers of predators influence wildlife populations in many areas. Dogs and the eastern coyote, for example, are responsible for the death of many deer—up to 4 percent in New Brunswick. And Franklin's ground squirrel, fox, badger, and skunk eat eggs of breeding ducks. They are partially responsible for the low 5 percent to 15 percent breeding success in the Midwest. At least 20 percent is required to sustain the population.

Fires

Forest fires started by lightning are natural in the semiarid western United States. After the initial fire trauma, the new growth greatly improves habitats for much wildlife, including deer, elk, and many birds. Skovlin (1982, 372), writing about elk habitats in the West, says: "Natural post fire succession provides an immediate surge and subsequent rapid decline of forbs and grasses in the herbaceous layer, a somewhat slower but prolonged shift in the shrub layer, and a slow but steady return of the forest that eventually dominates the plant community." The new grasses, forbs, and brush, which are dominant for about twenty-five to thirty years, support abundant wildlife.

Fires also influence fish and other water life. A burned area erodes rapidly, and silt, clay, and ash wash into streams. Water runoff increases. Stream waters become more alkaline, upsetting their chemical balance. Depending on the size of the burned area, the nature of the local streams, and precipitation amounts, the influence on water life varies from trivial to catastrophic.

HUMAN INFLUENCES

Humans have mixed effects on wildlife populations, decreasing some, expanding others. Probably all wildlife populations have been influenced to some degree by people.

Habitat Changes, Unmanaged

The greatest influence of humans on wildlife populations is via alteration of habitats. This influence, intentional or inadvertent, can increase or decrease populations. Generally, the data show that human influences tend to increase wildlife populations in industrial nations and to decrease them in Third World nations. The new forests of the industrial nations have, of course, been enormously beneficial to the wildlife that require trees for habitat. In America, the record increases in so many wildlife populations is the direct result of expanding forests.

The practice of stripping forests for fuel or agricultural purposes is probably as old as the human race. The effects on wildlife are usually devastating when the demand for land or fuel is so strong that forests cannot return. Early in human history wildlife populations in the Middle East, large sections of Africa, and Europe were radically changed. Steadman (1995) describes the deforestation by ancient Polynesians of Easter Island and the resulting extinction of all but one of the original thirty species of birds that nested on the island.

Yet deforestation is not necessarily bad, provided a forest is allowed to return after human use. McNeely et al. (1990, 51), writing for the United Nations about biological diversity, quotes Lugo as concluding that "environmental change and disturbance may be required to maintain species-rich tropical landscapes." Similarly, speaking of the Amazon rainforest, Miranda (1994, 163) says that human disturbance (provided the forest is allowed to return) favors faunal diversity.

McNeely and Miranda are writing about primitive societies, but their conclusions can be applied to the eastern and midwestern United States as well. Human disturbance has caused some wildlife to be both more abundant and more diversified than before the arrival of the white man. The mix of farmland, open fields, naturally afforesting fields, and old forests favors maximum diversity and abundance of wildlife. The total wildlife per acre in highly developed New York State is undoubtedly far greater than in more pristine Alaska, which is largely covered with old forest.

Protecting old forests from fire may help some rare wildlife, but the far more common wildlife, such as deer and elk, thrive on new plant life that springs up in burned-over areas. Deer and elk populations in the West would probably be far larger if forest fires were allowed to burn. According to Skovlin (1982, 371), 4,623,746 acres of western forest were burned from 1910 through 1919, by 1950 through 1959, the area burned dropped to 36,364 acres. The diminished burned-over acreage "has reduced the diversity of elk habitat drastically." Skovlin might have added—along with much other wildlife. Of course, the Indians knew this very well, and, hence, they burned forest areas to increase wildlife populations.

The vegetative diversity of suburban areas and the immediately adjacent rural areas may greatly improve habitats for many birds. Goudie (1990, 100–101), speaking of birds in the Helsinki area, says: "Altogether, human civilization appeared to have brought about a very significant increase of diversity in the whole area: there were thirty-seven species in city and rural areas that were not found in the forest." And for suburban west-central California, "residential areas were found to support a larger number of both species and individuals. Horticultural activities appear to provide more luxuriant and more diverse habitats than do presuburban environments." In more rural agricultural areas people have increased the diversity of wildlife by planting trees around fields and farm houses and in towns.

Conversely, the decline of some songbird populations in the United States has been related to loss of habitat in the Caribbean, Central America, and South America, where they migrate in the winter (Line 1993).

Wildlife Management

People, in response to popular causes, may try to control habitats in order to expand or maintain the population of a single species. However, improving the habitat for one creature is always at the expense of others. Thus, at its simplest, improving an area for pronghorn antelope is at the expense of deer because the open plains and sagebrush favoring the pronghorn antelope are not suitable for deer. Making conditions ideal for killer whales is at the expense of sea lions and seals, but helping sea lions and seals is at the expense of steelhead trout. Expanding old forests, which are said to be ideal for spotted owls, is at the expense of a much larger volume of wildlife, including deer, elk, and turkeys, which thrive in a habitat of mixed clearings, new plant cover, and young woods. The improvement of habitat for squirrels, woodpeckers, deer, moose, elk, and turkeys is at the expense of pheasants, meadowlarks, prairie chickens, song sparrows, and field sparrows, which prefer open fields.

Professional wildlife managers know that nature is dynamic and that wildlife populations respond accordingly. This has always occurred and will continue to occur. Changes in habitats are enormous and wrenching when forest and prairie fires rage unchecked. Dust and ash storms and accelerated erosion are additional results of such fires. Some disruption of fish populations is inevitable. However, wildlife managers know that in the long run the fires benefit much wildlife.

Because people can have such an enormous influence on wildlife habitats, wildlife managers must be very sensitive to human activities, but realize that they cannot be all things to all wildlife. Wildlife specialists can only manage so much. They can contribute to management of habitats in areas of expanding forests. In wealthy nations, they can control game harvesting. However, they have little control over markets or poaching by the poor, nor can they have much influence over macroeconomic conditions that so alter forest conditions.

Wildlife professionals know that with less burned-over areas, the best practical way to maintain vegetative diversity is to log old timber. The following quotation from the Michigan Department of Natural Resources (MDNR) is instructive about the impacts of logging on the white-tailed deer: ''After the white pine logging, many forest openings produced hardwood regrowth along with shrubs and grasses. Deer population increased rapidly on this abundant food supply.'' Like the Indians, the MDNR now creates openings in the forests of northern Michigan to improve deer habitat. Michigan has the second highest per-square-mile deer population of those states surveyed.

Keller (1982, 35) says: ''a conscious effort can be made to create successional mosaics that benefit both game and non-game species. . . . Such habitat manipulation can be made within the framework of periodic timber harvests.'' Keller describes for New York State a five-stage progression of vegetative cover from open field to old forest; each stage is characterized by certain birds and other wildlife. It is axiomatic that a habitat favorable for one group of wildlife species is virtually *always at the expense* of another mix of species.

When natural predators are not present, professionals control populations of such wildlife as deer, elk, and beaver through regulated hunting and trapping. Management of big game harvests throughout the United States has generally been successful. Unfortunately, in some instances trapping is no longer effective. With hardly any demand for beaver pelts, for example, beavers have proliferated in much of the United States. This creates a problem for much other wildlife because beavers cut down trees and change forested areas into swamps. In New York alone some two hundred thousand acres of forest were recently lost to beavers. New York's fur-bearer managers have concluded that the trend will continue. The 1992–1993 beaver harvest was about 67 percent below the optimum level (Batcheller 1994).

Management of game by professional game managers who balance the size of animal and bird populations by controlling game harvests, food supply, and habitats has been outstandingly successful for most big game and turkeys. As a result, the size of most big game and turkey harvests in recent years has greatly increased over most of the United States.

Even people who are not professional wildlife managers may intentionally expand wildlife populations by planting trees or shrubs to attract wildlife or by erecting birdhouses or feeders. The effect of birdhouses can be significant. For example, the largest colonies (up to two hundred pairs) of purple martin are found in large birdhouses (Bull and Farrand 1977). People have assured the survival of the eastern bluebird (the state bird) in New York State by erecting many bluebird houses.

Wildlife managers in the past have caused intentional depletion of some predatory species such as coyotes, wolves, and eagles by placing bounties on them. Restoration of some depleted species can be as simple as removing the bounty.

OTHER FACTORS INFLUENCING WILDLIFE POPULATIONS

Pesticides

Starting with Carson (1962), much concern has been expressed about the influences of pesticides on wildlife, particularly birds. Of course, pesticides are poisons and if wildlife or people ingest excessive amounts they may become sick or die. Carelessly used insecticides, like any poison, can be dangerous. Examples of careless use can be found. However, Carson's concern about DDT's poisoning robins ("on the verge of extinction") was in the face of a 1138 percent *increase* in the robin population in the twenty years before the publication of her book (according to the Audubon Society's Christmas bird counts). Easterbrook (1995, 80–82) describes the rise in population of most common birds Carson considered endangered. The fact is, *the overall impact of pesticides on wildlife has been enormously beneficial.* By increasing agricultural productivity, pesticides bear a large responsibility for America's new forests and the wildlife therein (see chapters 2 and 3; see also Avery 1995). In addition, Barrons (1981, 60) said that without pesticides and wood preservation chemicals, America would need a forest twice the size of New England to replace rotted wood. Clearly, a major impact of pesticides is to enormously increase forest size and, hence, forest bird populations. Thus, Carson's major thesis was exactly 180 degrees in error. She should have lauded pesticides.

Uncontrolled Hunting and Trapping

Uncontrolled hunting of game animals or birds by humans can have a profound influence, and can result in extinction of species. Humans caused the extinction of wild ox, wolves, and bears in Great Britain, and the lion in Asia Minor, Syria, Greece, and Sicily. American Indians may have caused the extinction of many postglacial species of large animals such as the giant sloth and the mastodon.

Poaching can also have a profound influence on wildlife populations, leading, potentially, to extinction of species. Pressures on populations of elephant, rhinoceros, panda, and Siberian tigers, for example, are almost wholly caused by poaching. Poachers can often sell parts of animals for their purported aphrodisiac properties. The problem is most severe in Third World nations. However, grizzly bear, bighorn sheep, and moose populations in America's West are apparently being stressed by poachers, who sell parts of the animals largely to Asian markets. Considering the high quality of the habitats for bighorn sheep, moose, and grizzly bear, the relatively small harvests in some of the West may be a function of poaching. The international poaching business totaled almost $3 billion in 1995 (Anon. 1995). In addition, hunters poach worldwide to obtain meat for the table. In New York State counties peripheral to the Adirondacks usually produce lower official deer takes than anticipated, considering the quality of the habitat. This is probably the result of poaching by local inhabitants (Severinghaus and Brown 1956).

Poaching, in virtually all cases, is a byproduct of poverty. In New York, the income of people in the peripheral Adirondack areas is lower than in most of the state. For many of these people, the trouble of finding, killing, and butchering a deer compared to potential trouble with the law is often worth the risk—if it produces meat for the table. Poaching in poor nations for food and for animal parts is endemic. Wherever it occurs, poverty puts pressure on wildlife. A poorer world would be a world with increasingly depleted wildlife.

Market Forces

Changes in demand for animal products can have a profound influence on wildlife populations. Marsh (1874) describes how beavers introduced into

France had almost become extinct because of the popularity of their pelts for hats. Then, a Parisian manufacturer invented the silk hat, demand for beaver pelts declined, and the beaver population increased.

More recently, decrease in demand for furs largely because of "animal rights" concerns has caused detrimental increases in some fur-bearing species. Populations of nutria in the Southeast, beavers over much of the United States, and the furry opossum in New Zealand were kept in check because they were trapped for pelts. Now, populations are greatly expanding to the detriment of local vegetation and habitats of other species (Anon. 1993b).

Most often poaching is a result of market forces. For example, a widely publicized example of a market putting stress on a species is the current pressure on the rhinoceros in Africa. Asians pay much for rhinoceros' horns because of their reputed aphrodisiac benefits.

Sale of game for food, as well as for fur or horn, can have significant influence on wildlife populations. For example, demand for meat in cities in the northern Midwest reduced the deer population in Michigan almost to the vanishing point by 1900. Taking "10–15 deer a day with snares, dogs, traps and guns" was not uncommon (Michigan Department of Natural Resources n.d.). Wildlife populations in Africa are also stressed because much of the protein consumed by sub-Saharan Africans is from game animals.

Road Kills

A significant number of animals and birds are killed on roads each year, but accurate numbers are usually not determinable. According to official records, for example, about 10,000 white-tailed deer were killed by automobiles in New York State in 1993, the number increasing about 15 percent per year over the past several years. The actual number could be up to 6 times greater. The official number of road kills of deer in Pennsylvania is about 60,000 annually. For New York, 10,000 deer killed by cars represent about 4 percent as much as the official deer harvest. For Pennsylvania, deer road kill is about 18 percent of the deer harvest. Gotie (1995), based on an admittedly small sample, estimated that 2.6 million wild animals died on New York roads from April 1993 to April 1994. He attributes the high number to the state's abundant wildlife.

Introduced Birds and Animals, Faunal Diversity

Humans have always moved birds and animals all over the world. Many species, such as the pheasant, have been beneficial to the area to which they were moved. However, when some species such as goats or donkeys revert to the wild, local environmental problems may develop. Introduction of some species of wildlife, such as the mongoose into Hawaii, the nutria into the Southeast (inadvertently), and the starling and house sparrow into the United States, has created problems. Steadman (1995) attributes much of the loss of species of birds in Polynesia, Micronesia, and other island groups in the Pacific to the introduction by humans of pigs, rats, and dogs. As many as 1,600 species of birds disappeared within the first few centuries of the arrival of humans. This was well before the arrival of Captain James Cook, the first European, in the mid-1700s. Past human errors suggest that ecologic analysis is warranted before any new species are introduced.

U.S. WILDLIFE POPULATIONS

Early History to Pre-1920

At the end of glaciation about ten thousand years ago, such animals as ground sloths, horses, camels, and mammoths lived in the United States. These animals shared North America with the early Indians, and archaeological evidence clearly shows that these beasts were hunted by the Indians. Then these animals became extinct. Although reasons for extinction are not clear, there is much evidence that points to overhunting (Long et al. 1974; Martin and Klein 1984).

Conversely, the population of bison may have peaked just before the white man appeared in the prairie areas. Indians continuously maintained and expanded the prairie by fire and such management favored bison.

With the coming of Europeans and changing land-use patterns in North America, the quantity and distribution of wildlife changed enormously. Some results are obvious. For example, the millions of buffalo that roamed the plains until the mid-1800s were reduced to a few small herds. Other prairie wildlife such as prairie dogs and prairie chickens now have sharply reduced populations. As noted in chapter 3, the maximum clearing of forest in the United States occurred about 1920, at which time wildlife that required trees for habitat were at a low for the eastern third of the United States.

Changes in New York State

Changes in wildlife in highly developed and populous New York State are typical of the eastern United States. In the 1920s white-tailed deer were down to two small herds, one in the Catskill Mountains and one in the Adirondacks. Official hunting statistics kept since 1927 give a clear picture of changes in the deer population (Severinghaus and Brown 1956; New York State Department of Environmental Conservation [NYSDEC] 1985 to 1992). From the mid-1800s through 1930 there were virtually no deer in such populous counties as Albany, Monroe (Rochester), Onondaga (Syracuse), and Westchester (contiguous to New York City), and therefore no hunting was allowed until the 1940s. However, deer taken in Essex and Hamilton counties in the Adirondacks were 949 and 1,743, respectively, in 1927, the first year in which modern statistics were kept. Both counties, typical of the Adirondacks, have consistently produced moderate official deer takes since then.

In the 1940s afforestation of abandoned farmland in the more densely populated counties of the state allowed deer to return. Perhaps coincidentally, these changes occurred when the volume of forest growth in the United States as a whole was starting to recover. In 1950 the total official deer harvest in Albany, Monroe, Onondaga, and Westchester counties was 872.

In the 1992 hunting season, the official deer take in these four counties was 11,484 (4.21 deer harvested per square mile), a record for all four counties. Meanwhile, the official deer take for Essex and Hamilton counties in the Adirondacks was only 2,477 (0.74 deer per square mile), somewhat down from the 1960 high of 2,818. The official deer take for New York State since 1927 is up 2618 percent and probably up nearly 5000 percent since 1900 (from Severinghaus and Brown 1956; New York State Department of Environmental Conservation 1993).

Changes that occurred in the deer population are mirrored in other wildlife populations as well (see table 4.1). Turkeys, for example, were extinct in New York in the mid-1800s, but are now abundant enough to be hunted throughout the state. Also, coyotes, once extinct, have returned naturally and are now trapped for pelts.

Populations of such woods animals as squirrels, foxes, opossums, beavers, bears, and raccoons[1] are all on the rise. Even moose, once extirpated, are returning to the state, as demonstrated by four moose–car accidents in New York in 1992 and 1993. The NYSDEC is considering importing additional moose into the state because of improved habitat. Along with the woods animals, woods birds such as grouse, chickadees, titmice, woodpeckers, and raptorial birds such as hawks and owls are increasing.

Additionally, according to a NYSDEC news release (Anon. 1991), most species of ducks are on the rise, and wintering Canada geese have increased 2600 percent from the average of the years 1949–1968 to the average of 1981–1990. All these changes in wildlife populations have occurred in the highly developed, second most populous state in the United States.

Changes in the United States

Most of the eastern third of the United States has seen changes in wildlife populations similar to those of New York State. Some changes are striking. Table 4.2 summarizes some changes in wildlife populations in certain local areas and in the United States as a whole. Statistics are most accurate for the white-tailed deer, because it is the major game animal of the eastern two-thirds of the United States. The best estimate is that its numbers have increased by about 5000 percent since 1900 (Anon. 1992b; Flather and Hoekstra 1989). Conway (1992) suggests that there are more white-tailed deer now than in 1492. However, McCabe and McCabe (1984, 60) suggest that the pre-Columbian white-tailed deer population might have been far larger before 1500 than today. They all agree that there has been great expansion since 1900. In our opinion, the old forests of so much of the East and the prairies of so much of the Midwest were

Table 4.1
Wildlife Increases, New York State

Wildlife	Area	When	Change	Reference
Official white-tailed deer take	Albany Co., NY	1940–1992	None to 2948	NYSDEC 1993; Severinghaus and Brown 1956
Official white-tailed deer take	NYS	1900–1992	Up about 5000%	NYSDEC stats; Severinghaus and Brown 1956
Ruffed grouse	NYS	1880–1987	Almost extirpated, now near historic highs	Andrle & Carroll 1988
22 wintering water birds	NYS	1981–1991	Most on rise*	Anon. 1991b (NYSDEC)
Mallard	NYS	1900–1988	Virtually absent, now common	Andrle and Carroll 1988
Coyote	NYS	Present	Extirpated to about 1970, now trapped through much of state	NYSDEC; Nelson 1992b
Cormorant	Little Galloo Island, NY	1976–1982	Up 650%	Anon. 1993a
Wintering Canada geese	NYS	(1949–1968) to (1981–1990)	+2600%	Anon. 1991b
Canada geese	NYS	1940–1987	+183%	Andrle & Carroll 1988
Turkey	NYS	1843–1900 to present	Were extirpated, now hunted everywhere	Conway 1992
	NYS	1991, 1992, 1993	Consecutive record harvest years	Nelson 1994
Beaver	NYS	1900–1992	15 to 70,000	Bishop et al. 1992
Bear	NYS	1992	22% above 10-year average	Anon. 1993c
Moose	NYS	1900–present	Extirpated, now returning	Hicks & McGowan 1992

*The 1991 NYSDEC results of the wintering water birds survey of 22 species including two species of geese, two species of swans, the Atlantic grout, the American coot, and sixteen species of ducks show a net gain of 9% over the average of the previous ten years (1981–1990). This appears to be at odds with those who see a declining population in the U.S. (U.S. Fish and Wildlife Service Waterfowl Status Reports) but is consistent with data gathered by Robbins et al. (1986).

Table 4.2
Wildlife Increases, United States

Wildlife	Area	When	Change[1]	Reference
White-tailed deer	E.U.S.	1900–1990	+ 5100%	Anon. 1992b
	E.U.S.	1900–1987	+ 4700%	Flather & Hoekstra 1989
	E.U.S.	1492–1992	Higher now	Conway 1992
	U.S.	1930–1990	+ 700%	Peterson 1991
Total deer	U.S.	1965–1990	+ 100%	Frederick and Sedjo 1991
Beaver	Rocky Mts.	Present	6-12 million	Anon. 1992a
Small animals, deer, turkey	Central U.S.	1492–present	Most much higher now	Conclusion, this report
Elk	BLM Lands[2]	1965–1992	+ 372%	U.S. BLM, Public Land Statistics
	U.S.	1900–1990	+1783%	Anon. 1992b
	U.S.	1930–1990	+ 657%	Peterson 1991
Javelina	BLM lands	1965–1992	+ 366%	U.S. BLM, Public Land Statistics
Bison	U.S.	1900–present	+2900%	Anon. 1992b
Pronghorn antelope	U.S.	1940–1990	+8233%	Anon. 1992b
	U.S.	1920–1985	+4515%	Flather & Hoekstra 1989
	U.S.	1965–1990	+ 300%	Frederick and Sedjo 1991
	U.S.	1930–1990	+ 817%	Peterson 1992
Crow, housefinch, boblink, field sparrow, bob-white, prairie warbler, & other birds	U.S.	1492–mid-1970s	More abundant in 1970s	Bull and Farrand 1977
Water birds	U.S.	1965–1985	Increasing	Robbins et al. 1986
Birds	Central U.S.	1492–present	Many absent in 1492, now abundant	Welsch 1992; Bull & Farrand 1977
Robins	U.S.	1941–1960 (Max. DDT use)	Up 1138%	Audubon Society's Christmas Bird Count
Woods animals and birds	E.U.S.	1920–present	Enormous increase	This report; Robbins et al. 1986; Flather & Hoekstra 1989
Trumpeter swan	U.S.	1933–1990	66 to 10,000	Frederick and Sedjo 1991

Table 4.2 (Continued)

Wildlife	Area	When	Change[1]	Reference
Canada geese	U.S.	1966–1990	Up 100%	Frederick and Sedjo 1991
Turkey	U.S.	1900–1990	+1783%	Anon. 1992b
	U.S.	1492–1991	More widespread now	Conway 1992
	U.S.	1930–1990	Up 760%	Peterson 1992
Raptorial birds	U.S.	1965–1985	Most on rise	Robbins et al. 1986
Gulls	U.S.	1965–1985	Most on rise	Robbins et al. 1986
Birds, general, sample of 410 species	U.S.	1968–1981	73% even 16% up 11% down	Flather & Hoekstra 1986

[1]Some statistics from different sources are not consistent. They are included without comment to show the range of estimates.
[2]Bureau of Land Management (BLM).

such unfavorable habitats for deer that Conway's conclusion is much more likely to be correct (see "Natural Factors Influencing Wildlife Populations").

State Game Harvests—Data Check. Because of the negativity of Peters and Lovejoy and others (quoted at the beginning of this chapter), we checked national data about wildlife in table 4.2 by obtaining statistics on game harvests from individual states. We contacted all states of the United States and about half responded. We compiled data from respondents (tables 4.3–4.4). In some cases, the last year of record was 1992; in others, 1993. We made no attempt to get 1993 or later data because the trends are amply demonstrated without the update.

Harvest data are often good indicators of some game populations. They are particularly valid for deer where, by plan, the magnitude of harvests reflects the population. However, for small game other factors influence the data. In some cases the amount of game taken is a function of the number of hunters rather than the amount of the game. Fur-bearers, for example, are not now sought as much because of a decline in the market for furs. The number of squirrels and opossums taken appears to be largely a function of hunter interest. Populations of ducks, on the other hand, especially in the Midwest, are actually declining, and the decline in duck harvest in that area is truly related to the number of ducks. (Ducks in the East appear to be increasing.)

Table 4.3 relates, for each state, the total deer harvest to human population density and to the number of deer harvested per square mile. Harvest per square

Table 4.3
Deer Harvest and Human Population Density Data, Selected States

State	Latest Data, 1992 or 1993 Deer Harvest	Human Population per Square Mile	Deer Harvest[1] per Square Mile	Years of Record Harvest
PA	388,015	243	7.94	90,89,91
MI	426,142	166	7.48	89,90,91
WV	169,014	74	7.01	92,90,93
NJ	49,941	1042	6.69	93,89,90
MS	277,714	54	5.88	92,91,87
AL	293,100	80	5.77	87,86,91
MD	51,098	499	5.19	92,91,90
VA	200,446	156	5.05	93,92,91
GA	285,640 (4-yr. av)	116	4.92	92,91,93
LA	214,900	96	4.83	92,91,90
NY	220,000	380	4.64	92,91,90
TN	125,915	74	3.06	93,92,91
OH	108,750	265	2.65	92,91,88
IL	83,639	158	2.33	92,91,90
KY	78,482	95	1.99	91,93,92
TX	468,893	65	1.79	87,89,91
AR	90,910	45	1.76	89,92,88
FL	81,770(?)	249	1.51	88,87,86
IA	77,684	50	1.39	89,90,88
NH	9,152	124	1.02	65,68,56
OK	66,637	46	0.97	92,90,87
ME	26,761	40	0.86	59,51,68
WA	56,000	77	0.84	—
UT	68,399	21	0.82	61,62,60[2]
ID	61,200	12	0.74	—

[1]Table in order of deer harvest per square mile for each state.
[2]For Utah, elk, pronghorn antelope, and bighorn sheep all had record takes in latest three years. Moose had the three second-best years in the past three years.

Source: Harvest statistics compiled from data supplied by states answering requests for information. Human population data from Wright 1994.

mile is calculated by dividing the number of deer harvested by the number of square miles of land for each state. The number may be a little deceptive and not be a perfect reflection of the true deer population. West Virginia subtracts the areas of the state where hunting is not possible. They also add in deer killed for reasons other than hunting. Therefore, West Virginia's official deer kill per square mile is higher than what we report.

Most western states have great variations in habitat, some of which may be

Table 4.4
Comparison of U.S. Deer Harvests by State

| State | Harvests and Years of Record | | Harvest Change Percent |
	First Four Years	Last Four Years	
AR	1,656 (38–41)	420,588 (89–92)	+25,298
AZ	38,409 (48–51)	76,769 (89–92)	+100
GA	256,117 (74,77)	1,142,559 (90–93)	+346
IA	14,978 (53–57)	437,811 (88–92)	+2,823
IL	44,918 (70–73)	350,773 (89–92)	+681
ID	35,851 (35–38)	297,600 (89–92)	+730
KY	22,612 (76–79)	327,724 (89–92)	+1,349
MD	83,895 (83–86)	190,331 (89–92)	+127
LA	35,830 (67)	214,900 (92)	+500
ME	28,102 (19–22)	108,935 (90–93)	+288
MI	54,110 (31–34)	17,045,567 (89–92)	+31,402
MT	290,856 (78–81)	660,000(89–92)	+124
NB	2,663 (45–51)	139,265 (90–93)	+5,130
NY	270,933 (55–58)	856,875 (90–93)	+216
OK	38,434 (86)	78,610 (92)	+105
PA	6,488 (15–18)	1,388,954 (88–91)	+21,308
TN	9342 (52,57,62,63)	503,660 (90–93)	+5,291
TX	1,262,051 (74–77)	1,849,966 (89–92)	+47
UT	33,050 (25–28)	236,741(90–93)	+616
VA	2,308 (23,24,27,28)	675,295 (89–92)	+29,159

Source: Harvest statistics compiled from data supplied by states answering requests for information.

totally unsuitable for deer. Where the habitats are suitable, the square-mile deer population may be among the highest in the nation. However, the average deer population for the average of all habitats within a state may be very low. Three of the four highest deer harvests per square mile occurred in such populous and highly developed states as Pennsylvania, Michigan, and New Jersey. Also shown in table 4.3 are years of the highest harvests. The first, second, and third record years for each state show that deer populations continued to increase in most states up to the last year of record.

Such sparsely populated and thickly forested states as New Hampshire and Maine have far lower harvests per square mile. Their record harvests were in the 1950s and 1960s. The old evergreen forests of much of these states are similar to New York's Adirondack forest. Such forests do not have abundant food for most wildlife.

Table 4.4 compares the magnitude of the first four harvests of record with the last four harvests of record for the states that answered our inquiries. The changes range from 100 percent increase to 29,159 percent increase, that is, from a doubling of the population to an increase of about 300 times. The exact increase is generally a function of the number of years between the earliest to latest—the longer the period, the greater the change.

The deer population of the Rocky Mountains and West Coast states has not greatly increased; in fact, in some states it has declined. Populations of other big game are somewhat variable as indicated by state harvest data. Generally, harvests of pronghorn antelope, elk, bison, javelina, and wild pigs (in the Southeast) are increasing. And turkey harvests are increasing everywhere.

Populations of mountain lions, wolves, and coyotes are expanding in most areas. Bears are also generally on the rise, but not so strongly. Moose, bighorn sheep, and mountain goat harvests have generally been decreasing since about 1965 but not to endangered levels. We suspect that poaching has caused the decrease. However, moose and bighorn sheep are at near record levels in Utah.

The big game populations in the West would probably be larger if forest fires were allowed to burn or if there was more lumbering.

Wildlife in the Midwest—A Special Case

Probably nowhere in the United States are the changes in the character of wildlife since 1492 as great as in the Midwest. The prairie was barren when the first white settlers arrived. Welsch (1992, 112), writing about Nebraska in the mid-1800s, says: "And there were few birds: no cardinals, no robins, no orioles, no owls, no thrushes, no siskins, no goldfinches, or wood ducks." Lewis and Clark did report turkeys and some deer, although their observations were largely limited to the wooded areas immediately along the Missouri and Yellowstone rivers on which they traveled. The major wildlife in the plains area of the Midwest consisted of great herds of bison, a few predatory or scavenging animals and birds, prairie chickens, and prairie dogs.

The Audubon Society's *Field Guide to North American Birds* (Bull and Farrand 1977) shows that *all* the birds reported to be absent by Welsch are now present throughout the Midwest. An example of the impact of the new trees in the Midwest is the probable reuniting of northern oriole populations. Apparently, after the Indians burned the trees, perhaps five thousand years ago, two oriole populations developed. The eastern population evolved into the Baltimore oriole and the western population into the Bullock's oriole. They were thought to be different species. But "When trees were planted on the Great Plains, the two forms extended their ranges and met" and "they interbred freely" (Bull and Farrand 1977, 547). Thus, they were actually the same species.

Along with birds, white-tailed deer and many other animals requiring trees for habitats reoccupied the Midwest and proliferated. Typically, deer harvests in Arkansas, Nebraska, Iowa, and Oklahoma are sharply up since records were first kept, from nearly 3000 percent for Iowa to over 25,000 percent for Arkansas. The deer population continues to increase. While certainly not natural, the present tree cover (and wildlife therein) is far more like it was before the Indians created major areas of prairie. Contrary to prevalent environmental thought, industrial man greatly improved nature as measured by the much larger diversity of wildlife in the Midwest.

Among birds, incidentally, wild turkey and geese harvests are strongly increasing in the Midwest, while duck harvests are decreasing. Overall, the current wildlife population in the Midwest is more diversified than any time in the past five thousand years, the time that the Indians started to maintain and expand the prairie by burning (Anderson 1990). Of course, certain plains species like bison are obviously depleted. Additionally, of course, woods do not favor some small game such as prairie chickens and pheasants that require open grasslands.

Other Wildlife

In some ways, the most significant increases in wildlife populations are those of gulls and such raptorial birds as hawks, vultures, and owls. Since these birds to varying degrees live off other wildlife, increases in their populations indicate an increase in the total volume of wildlife available to them as food. Most raptorial and scavenging bird populations are increasing.

Robbins et al. (1986) show that about 61 percent of America's birds are expanding their populations, 8 percent holding even, and 31 percent decreasing. Of the latter group many are migratory birds that spend time each year in South and Central America, where habitats are currently being destroyed. Many of the rest are field birds whose populations decrease as forests expand.

Populations of many other forms of life are not catalogued, but we assume that wildlife that need wooded areas for habitats have proliferated. Some of these may be very abundant and important in the food chain, yet are rarely seen by people. For example, according to Breisch (1994) the total weight of redback salamanders in New York is larger than that of any other species of bird or mammal, including the white-tailed deer. Data about actual numbers of "minor" living forms are not available.

WILDLIFE IN OTHER NATIONS

If wildlife have proliferated in reforested and afforested areas in the United States, it is logical to conclude that they have proliferated in reforested and afforested areas of other nations as well. The United Kingdom has both pluses and minuses. Although extensive reforestation, particularly of steep hillsides, has helped wildlife, removal of many hedgerows to consolidate fields for efficient farming has resulted in some loss of wildlife (Goudie 1990, 90). Overall, wildlife in the United Kingdom has probably increased in recent decades because the volume of forest gained is undoubtedly much larger than the volume of hedgerows lost. According to Goudie (p. 327), over the past fifty years no species of bird has been lost in Britain because of lack of protection, and several species have recolonized and are increasing.

Goudie (p. 106) also cites the expansion of the saiga antelope population in Russia from about one thousand in 1920 to over 2 million in the 1970s because of good game management.

Deforestation and general devegetation throughout the Third World are having a profound and continuing negative influence on wildlife. McNeely (1990, 46, 47) concludes that for forty-two sub-Saharan African nations, including the island of Madagascar, the wildlife habitat loss is 65 percent; for nineteen tropical Asian nations, the loss is 67 percent.[2] Deforestation of areas of Latin America must also be having a negative influence on much wildlife.

Humans have been influencing wildlife habitats for so long it may not always be clear what is natural. Probably all Asian forests have been cleared by humans at one time or another. This is also true of much of Central America and even some of the Amazon Basin largely because of devegetation by early Indians. Nonetheless, the loss of wildlife habitat in Third World nations is considerable because much cleared land remains cleared. The land is needed for agriculture or the forest is needed for fuel.

CONCLUSIONS

Populations of wildlife rise and fall for many natural as well as anthropogenic reasons. The natural reasons include viral, bacterial, fungal, and parasitic diseases; weather conditions; and availability of water. Habitat changes caused by forest fires can help many types of wildlife although sagebrush fires can be harmful to the pronghorn antelope that largely feed on sagebrush at some times of the year. Predatory animals can have a significant effect locally.

Humans influence wildlife populations by altering habitats and by legal and illegal hunting. Fighting forest and brush fires, reforestation and afforestation, agricultural practices, road kills, and general development all influence wildlife populations. Some human influences are favorable to wildlife and others are unfavorable. However, the overall impact through the past seventy years in the United States has been to greatly increase most woodland wildlife species, particularly in the eastern two-thirds of the nation. Generally in states where development is greatest, populations of such game as white-tailed deer and turkeys are the largest. Some woodland wildlife in the United States, such as white-tailed deer, turkeys, opossums, beavers, and Midwest birds, are probably more abundant today than they were in 1492. In addition, horticultural activities in suburban areas lead to a significant increase in the number of species of wildlife over the number found in more pristine areas. The common position of environmentalists that industrial man destroys nature is not borne out by the facts.

The concern expressed by many environmentalists that pesticides harm wildlife is also not based on reality. Actually, pesticides bear a major responsibility for the expansion of many wildlife populations. They are responsible for much of the decreased need for agricultural land (see chapter 2), and hence have made a major contribution to the expanded woodland wildlife habitats.

Such great increases if wildlife populations are rare in human history and appear to be an inevitable result of industrialization and the wealth it creates. Contrary to statements by Peters and Lovejoy (1990) legal hunting pressures are *not* keeping big game populations down in America, except as planned by game managers. Pollution and loss of habitat are *not* significant factors. Many wildlife populations are strongly rising in such industrialized and otherwise developed states as Michigan, New Jersey, New York, and Pennsylvania. The trend toward expansion of woodland wildlife should continue for a few decades.

As forests get old, as they are in New York's Adirondacks and much of New Hampshire, Vermont, and Maine, the populations of much woodland wildlife could decrease if wildlife habitats are not properly managed. For similar reasons, expanding old forests of the West could also cause a decline in wildlife. Proper wildlife management, primarily through lumbering to create clearings (or letting fires burn), could prevent the decline. Popular environmentalist thought that old forests are better for wildlife is not corroborated by the facts.

How wildlife populations in America fare in the future is largely a matter of politics. *If "activists" are successful in preventing logging of old forests throughout the nation, or if they successfully reduce agricultural efficiency, or if they raise energy prices sufficiently, most wildlife population gains will ultimately reverse.* (We analyze the reasons for activists' apparent counterproductivity in later chapters.)

While increases in wildlife populations in the highly developed United States and other industrial nations are probably unprecedented in the history of the world's civilizations, there is much evidence that primitive people have had an opposite effect and have been responsible for the destruction of many species. Currently, wildlife habitats in the Third World are in a downward spiral in virtually all nations. This downward spiral will continue as long as these nations remain poor. Reversal of the trend is possible only if these nations can increase industrialization and thus increase their wealth.

Looking at the world's wildlife, it is apparent that the "high-consumption" industrial nations are expanding wildlife populations. Conversely, the "low-consumption" Third World nations are depleting wildlife.

NOTES

1. A downtrend blip is now occurring for raccoons and some other species because of a rabies epidemic. Once over, these populations will again expand.

2. Much of the "habitat loss" is assumed to be forest habitat loss. With the loss of forests some species of insects, reptiles, amphibians, birds, and animals may become more abundant.

REFERENCES

Alabama Wildlife Federation. 1994. Alabama hunting survey estimates, 1963–93.

Anderson, R. C. 1990. The historic role of fire in the North American grassland. In *Fire in the North American Tallgrass Prairies,* edited by E. L. Collins and L. L. Wallace, 8–18. Norman: University of Oklahoma Press.

Andrle, R. F., and J. R. Carroll. 1988. *The Atlas of Breeding Birds in New York State.* Ithaca, N.Y.: Cornell University Press.

Anon. 1991. News release for aerial waterfowl survey. New York State Department of Environmental Conservation, March 13.

————. 1992a. Leave it to beavers. *Time,* August 24, 17.

————. 1992b. Hunting v. shooting. *The Economist,* December 12, 102.

————. 1993a. Cormorants and Lake Ontario fisheries. *Furbearer Management Newsletter,* New York State Department of Environmental Conservation, Winter, 1.

————. 1993b. Furbearer damage "downunder." *Furbearer Management Newsletter,* New York State Department of Environmental Conservation, Winter, 3.

————. 1993c. New York State black bear harvest—1992. New York State Department of Environmental Conservation.

————. 1993d. Are we running out of trees? *Reader's Digest,* November, 125.

————. 1995. Illegal hunting, kill the butterfly. *The Economist,* April 8, 28, 29.

Arizona Game and Fish Commission. 1993. Arizona game survey and harvest data summary.

————. 1988, 1993. Arizona game survey and harvest special data summary, historical 1919–87 data.

Arkansas Game and Fish Commission. 1973–92. Annual game harvest data (deer, turkeys, black bear). Arkansas Wildlife Management Division.

Avery, D. 1995. Saving the planet with pesticides. In *The True State of the Planet,* edited by R. Bailey. New York: Free Press.

Baden, J. A., ed. 1994. *Environmental Gore.* San Francisco: Pacific Research Institute for Public Policy.

Bailey, R., ed. 1995. *The True State of the Planet.* New York: Free Press.

Barrons, K. C. 1981. *Are Pesticides Really Necessary?* Chicago: Regnery Gateway.

Batcheller, G. 1994. The 1992–93 Beaver harvest: A major shortfall, *Furbearer Management Newsletter,* Winter.

B.C. Environment, Wildlife Branch. 1992. Estimate wildlife harvest in British Columbia, 1950–1991. Province of British Columbia, Ministry of Environment, Lands and Parks.

Bishop, P., et al. 1992. *Beaver Management in New York State: History and Specification of Future Program.* New York State Department of Environmental Conservation.

Breisch, A. 1994. Diversity, wild in New York, winter 1993–1994. New York State Department of Environmental Conservation.

Bull, J., and J. Farrand, Jr. 1977. *The Audubon Society Field Guide to North American Birds* (Eastern Region). New York: Alfred Knopf.

Bureau of Land Management. 1961–94. Public land statistics, U.S. Department of Interior.

Bureau of Wildlife. 1994. 1984 through 1993 deer take by county and town. New York State Department of Environmental Conservation.

————. 1993. Calculated legal deer take in New York State, statistics 1955–1992.

Carson, R. 1962. *Silent Spring.* New York: Houghton Mifflin.

Cartwright, M. E., and M. Pledger. 1990. Deer harvest, 1990. Arkansas Game and Fish Commission (1938–1992).

Conway, J. 1992. Eastern wildlife, bittersweet success. *National Geographic,* February, 66–89.

Easterbrook, G. 1995. *A Moment on the Earth.* New York: Penguin Books.

Fish and Game Department. 1994. Game harvest studies, 1992–1993, State of New Hampshire.

Fish and Wildlife Branch. 1993. New Brunswick big game harvest reports. Department of Natural Resources and Energy, Fredericton, N.B.

Flather, C. H., and T. W. Hoekstra. 1989. *An Analysis of the Wildlife and Fish Situation in the United States: 1989–2040.* U.S. Department of Agriculture, Forest Service, General Technical Report RM-178.

Florida. 1993. Estimated harvests by species, 1950–1993.

Game Division, Louisiana Department of Wildlife and Fisheries. 1967–90. Deer kill surveys.

Gore, A. 1992. *Earth in the Balance.* New York: Houghton Mifflin.

Gotie, R. F. 1995. Cars and wildlife don't mix. *Wild in New York,* 17.

Goudie, A. 1990. *The Human Impact on the Natural Environment.* Oxford: Basil Blackwell.

Halls, L. K., ed. 1984. *White-Tailed Deer, Ecology and Management.* Harrisburg, Pa.: Stackpole Books.

Hicks, A., and E. McGowan. 1992. Restoration of moose in northern New York State. Draft EIS, New York State Department of Environmental Conservation.

Idaho Department of Fish and Game. 1993. Idaho big game harvest, 1935–1992, Boise.

Illinois Department of Conservation. 1994. Illinois deer harvest summary (1970–1992).

Iowa Department of Natural Resources. 1993. Trends in Iowa wildlife populations and harvest, 1992 (deer 1953–1992).

Keller, J. 1982. From yellowthroat to woodpeckers. *The Conservationist,* July–August, 31–35.

Kentucky Wildlife Division. 1970–93. Statewide wildlife surveys, 1980–1993.

Lilienfeld, R. M., and W. L. Rathje. 1995. Six enviro-myths. *New York Times,* January 21, op-ed.

Line, L. 1993. Silence of the songbirds. *National Geographic,* June, 68–91.

Long, A., R. M. Hansen, and P. S. Martin. 1974. Extinction of the ground sloth. *Geological Society of America Bulletin* 85 (12): 1835–42.

Louisiana Department of Wildlife and Fisheries. 1980–93. Louisiana big and small game harvest surveys.

Maine Department of Inland Fisheries and Wildlife. 1994. Research and management report, 1992, 1993 and wildlife management statistics, 1919–1993. Augusta, Maine.

Marsh, G. P. 1874. *The Earth as Modified by Human Action.* New York: Scribner, Armstrong.

Martin, P. S., and R. G. Klein, eds. 1984. *Quaternary Extinctions: A Prehistoric Revolution.* Tucson: University of Arizona Press.

McCabe, R. E., and T. R. McCabe. 1984. Of slings and arrows: an historical perspective.

In *White-Tailed Deer, Ecology and Management,* edited by L. K. Halls. Harrisburg, Pa.: Stackpole Books.

McNeely, J. A., K. R. Miller, W. V. Reid, R. A. Mittermeier, and T. B. Werner. 1990. *Conserving the World Biological Diversity.* Washington, D.C.: World Bank.

Michigan Department of Natural Resources, Wildlife Division. n.d. History of deer populations in Michigan (with data from 1850s to 1989).

Michigan Wildlife Division. 1936–92. Legal game kills statistics, Michigan Department of Natural Resources.

Miranda, E. E. 1994. Tropical rain forests: Myths and facts. In *Environmental Gore,* edited by J. A. Baden, 153–69. San Francisco: Pacific Research Institute for Public Policy.

Mississippi Department of Wildlife, Fisheries and Parks. 1993. Mississippi mail survey of game harvest and hunter effort for 1972–1992, Jackson, Miss. (Also harvest data 1982–92.)

Missouri Department of Conservation. 1993. Yearbook of population trends for Missouri wildlife, 1944–1993. Jefferson City, Mo.

Nebraska Game and Parks Commission. 1994. Game harvest data, 1945–1993. Lincoln, Nebr.

Nelson, D. 1992a. State deer car-kill total rising. *Albany Times Union,* July 17.

——. 1992b. Wild about those dogs, hunters hardpressed to outfox coyote. *Albany Times Union,* March, 15.

——. 1994. Bad winter for state turkeys. *Albany Times Union,* April 19, 2–2.

New Jersey Department of Environmental Protection and Energy. 1994. Legal deer harvests, 1909–1993, and turkey and upland game harvests.

New York State Department of Environmental Conservation. 1973. Summary of New York's big game seasons (1928–1971).

——. 1982–91. New York State black bear harvests.

——. 1991. News release. March 13, regarding wintering Canada geese.

——. 1993. Deer take by country and town, 1983–1992.

Odom, R. R. 1993. Georgia wildlife harvest survey trends, Georgia Department of Natural Resources.

Ohio Division of Wildlife. 1966–93. Game survey results, Ohio Department of Natural Resources.

Oklahoma Department of Wildlife Conservation. 1993. Upland game harvest surveys, 1986–1992.

Pennsylvania Game Commission. Various dates. Big game kill, 1915 to 1992; small game special, 1983–1992.

Peters, R. L., and T. E. Lovejoy. 1990. Terrestrial fauna. In *The Earth as Transformed by Human Action,* edited by B. L. Turner, 353–69. Cambridge, Mass.: Cambridge University Press, with Clark University.

Peterson, J. 1992. About America's forests. *Evergreen* (Special Bonus Issue): 2–5.

Robbins, C. S., D. Bystrak, and P. H. Geissler. 1986. *The Breeding Bird Survey: Its First Fifteen Years, 1965–1979.* U.S. Department of Interior, Resource Publication 157.

Ryel, L. A., C. L. Bennett, Jr., M. L. Moss, and D. G. Parks. 1980. *A History of Deer Hunting in Michigan.* Michigan Department of Natural Resources, Wildlife Division Report No. 2868.

Severinghaus, C. W., and C. P. Brown. 1956. History of the white-tailed deer in New York. *New York Fish and Game Journal,* 129–67.

Skovlin, J. M. 1982. Habitat requirements and evaluations. In *Elk of North America,* Wildlife Management Institute, 369–413. Harrisburg, Pa.: Stackpole Books.

Steadman, D. W. 1995. Prehistoric extinctions of Pacific Island birds; Biodiversity meets zooarchaeology. *Science* 267: 1123–31.

Stickney, M. D. 1983. Addendum to the history of the white-tailed deer in New York, New York deer take, 1956–1982. New York State Department of Environmental Conservation.

Tennessee Wildlife Resources Agency. 1994. Big game harvest and range surveys (1952–1993).

———. 1993a. Small game harvest report, 1992–1993.

———. 1993b. Waterfowl report, 1992–1993.

Texas Parks and Wildlife Department. 1993. Big game harvest survey results 1983–84 through 1992–93; white-tailed deer survey, 1974–1992.

Thomsen, D. E. 1977. The great late Pleistocene extinctions: A slothful tale. *Science News* 112 (December): 196–98.

Virginia Department of Game and Inland Fisheries, Wildlife Division. 1992. Virginia deer harvest summary (1923–1992).

Welsch, R. 1992. A song for the pioneers. *Audubon,* November–December, 112–116.

West Virginia Division of Natural Resources, Wildlife Resources Section. 1994. 1993 big game bulletin (covers 1989–93).

Wright, J. W. 1994. *The Universal Almanac.* Kansas City: Andrews and McMeel.

Wyoming Game and Fish Department. 1993. Annual report 1993, Cheyenne, Wyo.

CHAPTER 5

Water and Water-Related Resources

In chapters 2, 3, and 4 we described the expansion of soil, forest, and wildlife resources in industrial nations. We showed that much criticism about the environmental effect of industry is not based on reality. Although problems can be found, the total dispersed effects of industrialization have been environmentally beneficial.

Similarly, handling of water resources by industrial societies has been continuously criticized. For example, construction of dams has long been criticized and some environmentalists take the extreme position of recommending that they all be removed. Their idea: return to a wild planet.

Gore doesn't take quite such a radical view. According to him (1992, 100), "Unfortunately, the dramatic change in our relationship to the earth since the industrial revolution, especially in this century, is now causing profound damage to the global water system." He attributes much of the potential damage to global warming and melting ice because of the greenhouse effect caused by an increase in carbon dioxide. He also names local diminishing rainfall, deforestation, contamination by industrial pollutants, depletion of groundwater, irrigation, and Third World water use as major problems. And Gore (p. 143) is alarmed at the 500 percent increase in fishing worldwide.

Characteristically, Gore sees environmental liabilities. Is there a balance? Are there any benefits in our handling of water and water resources in general?

Eckholm (1976, 115–17) gives us a first clue. He describes how in 2400 B.C. in Mesopotamia, average grain yield was 2,537 liters per hectare; by 2100 B.C., the yield was 1,470 liters per hectare; and by 1700 B.C., the yield dropped to 897 liters per hectare. He attributes the change to soil salination caused by irrigation. A second clue is that during the height of the cultures of Mesopotamia, the land supported about 11.4 people per square kilometer. It now supports 239—over 20 times more people (Simmons 1993). The total impact of modern technology has been to reduce problems and to make the Earth more productive than ever. Could the situation with water be similar to that of soil, agriculture, forests, and wildlife?

In this chapter, we look at the total impact of modern industrialization and technology on water resources. That there are localized problems is undeniable. There always are. But what are the dispersed effects of human activities on water? As in previous chapters, we look at the situation in industrial nations and in Third World nations. To speak of them as one would invite confusion because the situation in the two worlds is radically different.

WATER FOR HUMAN CONSUMPTION

Water is abundant on Earth—the blue planet. Most of the Earth (71%) is covered with oceans. On a worldwide basis, there is no shortage of water. However, ocean water with its 34.48 grams of salts per liter—mostly sodium chloride—is not fit for human consumption. In even moderate quantities, it is poisonous. Only about 2.5 percent of the earth's water is not salty, and most of that is in ice caps and glaciers.

Nature makes ocean water fit for human consumption by the process of evaporation. Air circulates moist air—some of it as clouds—over land masses, and water falls on the land as rain and snow. This precipitation contains virtually none of the salts found in oceans. Water that falls on soil largely ends up in streams; some sinks into the ground.

Water that remains in the ground becomes groundwater. The abundance and distribution of groundwater is highly variable, depending on rainfall and the nature of the rocks. Some rocks are sufficiently porous to hold large quantities of water. If rock pores are sufficiently interconnected, people can retrieve water in large quantities from springs or wells.

Water that runs off the land and from underground through springs mostly flows into streams and then back to the oceans. The movement of water from oceans into and over the land and back to the oceans is called the hydrologic cycle.

At first humans were no different from animals and obtained their water from streams, springs, lakes, and ponds. If they ventured too far from water or if rains suddenly failed, serious trouble resulted. Gradually, people found that they could interrupt the hydrologic cycle by damming waterways and holding water in ponds or reservoirs. This made people somewhat more independent of the vagaries of nature. To this day, it allows them to live in areas that might otherwise be too dry to support human life.

Humans also found that they could improve springs by collecting water flow in basins or ponds. It was then a short step to develop wells to tap groundwater.

The use of water by people does not change the basic hydrologic cycle in the sense that most of the water they "consume" is, in the long run, returned to the oceans. Human consumption is but a small interruption in the hydrologic cycle.

HISTORICAL PERSPECTIVE

All major civilizations of the world developed in the dynamic environment of the great warming trend after the last glacial period, which ended about ten thousand years ago. The development of water resources contributed to the domestication of plants and animals as well as the development of stable agriculture. Farmers transported food into cities that were at the centers of transportation infrastructures. With the development of cities, the religious, philosophical, artistic, political, and technical components of societies evolved.

Ancient Hydraulic Civilizations

Ancient China, India, Mesopotamia, and Egypt were hydraulic (or riverine) civilizations. They had strong, central governments that took responsibility for major projects that supplied and managed water, largely for agricultural purposes. Even in pre-Columbian America, about 75 percent of the Indians lived in hydraulic societies. Incas, Aztecs, Mayas, and Pueblos, for example, were all hydraulic peoples because they collected and distributed water to their croplands. Mayans on the Yucatan Peninsula used a grid of canals that acted both as drainage ditches for their fields and as transportation infrastructures for canoes to carry food to their cities.

Ancient Groundwater Supplies

Groundwater has always been important for human development, particularly in arid and semiarid lands. Wells were some of the earliest artificial sources of water supply. Historians refer to important wells in ancient Egypt, Greece, Assyria, India, Persia, and China. Humans went to great trouble to develop groundwater. The Chinese had wells over 1,500 feet deep. Egyptians excavated Joseph's well at Cairo 279 feet into solid rock. The upper shaft was 18 by 24 feet and 165 feet deep; the lower, 9 by 15 feet and 130 feet deep. They raised water in buckets on endless chains, operated by mules in a chamber at the bottom of the upper shaft. Ancient Jerusalem and Carthage stored rainwater in underground cisterns.

Public Water Supplies—Early Europe

Some of the best-engineered water supplies in Europe were developed quite early. Between 312 B.C. and A.D. 305 Romans constructed reservoirs. They distributed the water by 14 aqueducts, which had a total length of 359 miles, including 59 miles of stone arches to carry their water over depressions. The aqueducts of Rome varied from 3 to 8 feet deep and 2.5 to 5 feet wide. Roman construction is still in use in places in Europe.

Romans distributed water through ceramic and lead pipes to public baths, fountains, public buildings, and some private homes. Most people got their water from public fountains. Different aqueducts carried water of varying quality— the highest quality for drinking and the others for baths. The Romans used sedimentation basins to remove silt and improve quality. Rome distributed about 50 million gallons a day to a population of about one million.

After the decline of the Roman Empire, European water quality and distribution facilities deteriorated. Improvements came slowly.

Water Supplies—United States

U.S. cities developed high-quality, reliable municipal water supplies before most European cities. The first was Boston, which brought in spring water by gravity in 1652. The first mechanical operation was a wood pump at Bethlehem, Pennsylvania, in 1754. Americans used wood pipes initially; cast iron pipes first appeared in Philadelphia in 1804. In 1822 Philadelphia built the first large-scale metal pipe distribution system. New York and Boston followed suit later. The western United States continued to use wood pipes because of the high cost of iron.

Improvements in cast iron pipe construction and machinery to provide low-cost pumps allowed both direct-pumping systems for small towns and development of ground and artisan supplies in western America. By 1900 most towns with over two thousand residents had a public supply.

Since 1900 filter systems have improved water quality. In 1900 only 6.3 percent of the population had filtered water, but by 1940 it was over 40 percent. Contaminated water caused several epidemics of typhoid, dysentery, and cholera between 1890 and 1920. Starting in 1908, Americans began using chlorination in addition to filtration to guard against water-borne diseases.

CURRENT WATER MANAGEMENT IN THE UNITED STATES

Water management consists of capturing, diverting, and (if needed) purifying water for multiple human household and industrial uses. Water management also involves flood control, power generation, recreation, and transportation. Management for one purpose may conflict with management for other purposes. Obviously, water has not always been managed well. Still, First World nations have managed their water resources well enough to provide for most of the needs of their people.

Abundance

About 30 inches of water as rain and snow fall annually on the 48 contiguous states. This amounts to about 4,400 billion gallons a day. The U.S. Geological Survey has estimated that about 21.5 inches of the 30 inches evaporate from vegetation and soil and water surfaces. The other 8.5 inches represent the usable water supply. Of this, the nation withdraws and uses about 2 inches, of which 0.5 inch evaporates. The rest of the water used joins the unused flow to make a total of about 8 inches returning to the oceans. That is about 1,150 billion gallons a day (McGuinness, 1963, 10).

The 100th meridian west longitude divides the contiguous 48 states into two areas of about equal size but of different climatic conditions. A narrow band from Texas to northern Minnesota has an average annual rainfall of 20 inches. East of that, precipitation in the northern states averages 30 inches and the southern states 60 inches. To the west of that 20-inch belt the land is arid or semiarid, with average annual precipitation of 10 inches to 20 inches. The Northwest coastal area is an exception, with over 100 inches (Carr et al. 1990).

In the East, water projects are primarily for domestic water supply, power, and transportation; the West also uses water for irrigation and mining.

Storage

People store water in reservoirs so they are not at the mercy of variations in natural flow. The United States and Puerto Rico have 2,654 reservoirs and controlled natural lakes with capacities of 5,000 acre feet or more (1 acre foot equals 325,850 gallons). This is a combined normal storage (excluding any flood control storage) of 480 million acre feet (609 billion cubic meters). The 574 largest reservoirs account for 90 percent of the total. In addition, there are at least 50,000 reservoirs with capacities of 50 acre feet to 5,000 acre feet and about 2 million smaller farm ponds (U.S. Geological Survey 1984). The total pond and reservoir capacity approaches 550 million acre feet (about 698 billion cubic meters). About half the major reservoirs of the world are in North America (Goudie 1990, 155).

Incidentally, the capacity of the world's largest lakes (nature's reservoirs) is much larger than that of the world's largest reservoirs. The largest lakes hold thousands of times more fresh water than all the world's reservoirs. The Aswan High Dam in Egypt holds 169 billion cubic meters of water; the Kariba Reservoir in Zambia, 160 billion cubic meters. America's Lake Powell (mostly in Arizona) holds 33 billion cubic meters, while Lake Meade in Arizona and Nevada holds almost 37 billion cubic meters. For comparison, Lake Baikal in Russia holds 22 trillion cubic meters; Lake Superior in North America, over 12 trillion cubic meters. This is 17 times more water than that held in all of America's reservoirs. However, lakes, being natural, are not always ideally located for human use. Hence, we build reservoirs to compensate.

Storing water for future use may be an almost instinctive human characteristic, akin to planting gardens and crops in the spring. A traveler can get a feel for the water stored in small ponds in the contiguous forty-eight United States when flying over the Midwest at a time of the day when the sun reflects upward from water surfaces. Thousands of small ponds and reservoirs act as mirrors. Comparing ponds on old and new topographic maps shows that land owners have steadily increased the number of ponds. President Franklin Delano Roosevelt started a farm pond program through the Department of Agriculture. Its purpose was to increase America's water and fish resources. Although voluntary, it has been highly successful. America now has over 2 million farm ponds.

Major water storage projects can be enormously expensive and obviously are most common in industrial nations. First World nations have about three-quarters of the world's dams and about 70 percent of the world's twenty-five largest reservoirs. They also have 70 percent of the world's twenty-five largest dams. Most of the world's major reservoirs have been constructed in the past seven decades. America built 95 percent of its major reservoirs after 1920. The large reservoirs in Third World nations have all been constructed with money from the industrial world.

Distribution

Some of the world's largest engineering projects involve moving water from reservoir to areas of use. An early example of a public water supply project in the United States is the 1923 completion of the O'Shaughnessy Dam on the Tuolumne River in Yosemite Park.[1] The water crosses California by pipe to supply reservoirs in San Mateo County for use by the population of the San Francisco Peninsula. Cooper Lake in the Catskill Mountains supplies water for New York City via an underground aqueduct. A more recent example in the United States is the California Aqueduct, which takes water via canal from the Mt. Shasta area of northern California some 650 miles south to the Los Angeles area. The new Central Arizona Project carries water over 200 miles from the Colorado River to the Phoenix–Tucson area. The water was originally for agricultural use, but is now used for municipal supply as well (Anderson et al. 1992). Many environmentalists have objected to both the California aqueduct and the Central Arizona Project.

Major water diversion projects are concentrated in the industrial nations because they have the wealth required to distribute their water resources.

In 1985 about 18 percent of the nation's total population was self-supplied from private wells and surface waters (Carr et al. 1990). Over 95 percent of the serviced population is supplied by 106 major metropolitan utilities. Small public utilities, each servicing less than 1,000 persons, supply the other 5 percent of the population (U.S. Environmental Protection Agency 1982).

Public water systems used 36.3 billion gallons a day (bgd) in 1985, up 78 percent from 1960. That rise was about 1.5 times the rate of growth of the population served. About two-thirds of the withdrawal was for residential use. The rise in the number of households is considered responsible for the increase (Carr et al. 1990).

Industrial Use

Quantity of water per unit of production has decreased continuously since 1960 due to changes in technology, changes in production, and pollution abatement requirements. Industry now treats and recycles much more process water than formerly. Additionally, a major water use, steel production, dropped from 131.4 million tons in 1970 to 92.9 million tons in 1992.

In 1983, 3 percent of some 358,000 manufacturing firms used more than 95 percent of the water required in manufacturing. The five major sectors (paper and paper products, chemicals and allied products, steel, petroleum refining, food processing) had water intake of 27.5 bgd.

Thermoelectric power generation converts water into steam to turn turbines. Fossil fuel or nuclear energy provides the heat source. Increases in efficiency resulted in 11 percent less water required for cooling steam in 1985 (187 bgd) than in 1980, although there was an increase of 36 percent in power generated.

Agricultural Use

Agriculture uses about 97 percent of its water supply for irrigation and about 3 percent for livestock and aquaculture.

In 1984 the 17 western states used 91 percent of the irrigation water used in America. Irrigation used 137 bgd in 1985, an increase of 54 percent since 1950. Of that, crop and field evaporation consumed 73.8 bgd and leakage or evaporation from the conveyance system lost 23.6 bgd (Carr et al. 1990). About two-thirds of irrigation water is from surface supplies, the rest from groundwater. About 80 percent of the total consumption of water in the United States (water not available for reuse) is for irrigation.

Of the total western irrigated acreage, about 20 percent uses water sources developed by the Bureau of Reclamation; 80 percent is funded by nonfederal, primarily private investment. Bureau of Reclamation water is partially federally funded because the government until recently charged no interest.

Management of irrigation water includes maintaining both quantity and quality. Properly done, irrigation water helps maintain water flow during dry seasons, improves wildlife habitats, and may increase wetlands.

Energy

Water has long been a source of power. In early America, into the 1900s, any place where water dropped enough to drive a water wheel became a potential source of power. Many American cities are located at the fall line around the eastern and southern Appalachians, where water runs off the rocks of the mountain cores onto the sediments of the coastal plains. In the eastern United States, the relics of old mills and manufacturing sites are common at any location where water suddenly changes elevation.

With the introduction in the late 1800s of water-driven electrical generators, the waterwheel rapidly became less important. Some waterwheel sites became sources of electrical power, but most were abandoned. Large hydroelectric projects that could supply inexpensive electricity to wide areas are more efficient. For example, electric companies developed the power potential of Niagara Falls in New York from 1890 until the 1950s.

Hydroelectric power in America increased about 186 percent from 1950 through 1991. It is about 4 percent of the total energy consumed (not counting wood) for home heating. Hydroelectric power is renewable, inexpensive, and clean. However, few undeveloped, efficient sites remain. Additionally, many people emphasizing local problems and largely ignoring the dispersed benefits have blocked much development of hydropower. We consider hydropower a resource multiplied, a resource that did not exist before industrialization, a resource that lessens the pressure on wood and other fuels as energy resources.

Transportation

Throughout the 1800s North Americans (and Europeans as well) developed their inland water resources for transportation purposes, largely through systems of canals, locks, and dams. The 760-mile St. Lawrence River seaway is a more recent development that allows oceangoing vessels to enter through the heart of the continent through the Great Lakes. The Tombigbee project (362 miles) linking the Mobile River to the Tennessee River is also a recent addition. Barges and ships move from the Gulf of Mexico throughout America's agricultural heartland. America has 12,278 miles of major canals. (New York State's Barge Canal and Erie Canal system are not included in America's total because of the limitations of barge size.)

With the construction of railroads and highways, competition reduced the value of canal transportation. Still, high-bulk, low-value commodities such as grain, stone, coal, and liquid fuels are moved far less expensively via water than by other carriers. Thus, limestone and dolomite move down the Mississippi from the Ohio River–St. Louis–Cape Girardeau areas to the New Orleans market. Hard granite rock moves from the St. Paul–Minneapolis area to the Gulf Coast, where it is used in a skid-resistant surface material for asphalt-concrete highways. Water transportation is inexpensive. For example, the haul cost of stone from the upper Midwest to the Gulf Coast is from $5.00 to $10.00 per ton.

The development of water resources for transportation resulted in the creation of a major resource. This resource has contributed significantly to the efficiency of the industrial system and to America's wealth. (Offsetting the economic benefit is the cost of controlling the zebra mussel.)

Fish Resources

The importation and stocking of non-native fish date to early China and the Greco-Roman empires (2000 B.C. in China). However, the industrial nations have greatly expanded this practice. The benefits gained may vary from the added pleasure of new and different species to having fish where there had been none. Larkin (1978) points out that British Columbia is now considered a fisherman's paradise. However, nearly all game fish in the interior of the province were introduced to the lakes and streams. The stocking of streams and the introduction of new species creates a new resource or, at the very least, enhances an old one.

The total freshwater fish resource in America has greatly increased. Since President Franklin D. Roosevelt's farm pond program first started constructing ponds and stocking them with fish in the 1930s, the program has greatly expanded our nation's fish and water resources.

And fishing is good. For example, the New York State Department of Environmental Conservation keeps annually updated historic records for largest fish for forty-four species. The earliest record fish on the January 1995 list is a northern pike caught in 1940. Ninety-one percent of the record fish were caught from 1983 through 1994. The best years for the number of record fish were 1990 and 1992, with six record fish each; 1991 and 1994 followed with five each; 1989 was next with four. Included in the records of the past twelve years are all five species of bass, all five species of salmon, and all five species of trout. Comparing 1981's twenty-two official freshwater fish records, 86 percent were broken by the 1995 records. Fishing has never been better!

The increase of fish populations, however, has not been uniform. Although most sports species have increased and aquaculture is expanding, some species are declining and are considered endangered. A recent article in the *New York Times* summarizes the endangered species of freshwater fish in America. For each state the number of native species along with the number of endangered species are shown. But the numbers are misleading. Totaling the number of endangered species does not produce the total endangered species in America. Some species may be locally endangered for any of many reasons, but they may thrive in other areas. For example, the round whitefish is not faring well in New York's Adirondacks but is thriving throughout north-central and northwestern Canada and Alaska.[2] The spoonhead sculpin may be extirpated in Lakes Ontario and Erie but is common in other Great Lakes and in much of central Canada. Some species, like the deepwater sculpin and some of the darters, may be endangered in several states and hence may be counted several times.

The reasons for species being "endangered," "threatened," or of "special concern" are highly variable. Some are endangered because of natural causes; that is, at any given time in geologic history, some species are thriving, some are not. Usually, the latter ones either evolve or become extinct. The causes of the endangered status include predation, disease, overfishing, turbidity, siltation, high acidity or alkalinity, competition, chemical contaminants, and loss of habitats.

The practice of farming fish has greatly increased in America since 1980. Fish aquaculture is practiced primarily in the Pacific Northwest, lower Mississippi, and south Atlantic-Gulf regions. Modern fish farming involves sophisticated food, temperature, disease, and production controls. In addition, fish aquaculturists develop new species. From 1980 through 1990 America's output volume of farmed fish quadrupled, so it now supplies from 10 percent to 15 percent of America's seafood needs (Hanfman 1993). During the same interval America's fish consumption doubled. Thus, the rate of production of fish aquaculture is twice the rate of increase in fish consumption. The U.S. Department of Agriculture anticipates a continued rapid expansion of fish aquaculture in America.

Currently, America cultivates thirty species of fish and shellfish. This includes special new varieties, such as the hybrid striped bass, which is a cross between a striped bass and a white bass. Catfish, trout, and crawfish are the major domestic fish produced in aquaculture. In the 1975–91 period catfish production increased by 2400 percent. America now produces catfish from about 151,860 acres of ponds and crawfish from 140,000 acres (Hanfman 1993, 3).

Additionally, Norway produces much of America's imported salmon. Some Norwegian fish farmers have started production also in eastern Canada. The efficiency of production has driven the price of salmon downward by about 25 percent. Characteristically, the innovative fish aquaculture has decreased pressure on the natural salmon resource as well as other fisheries.

Quality of farmed fish is far more tightly controlled than that of natural fish and efficiency of production keeps prices low. Aquaculture is another example of multiplication of resources.

Other Wildlife Resources

The large increase in the surface area of water in America has benefited other wildlife as well as fish. Migrating waterfowl stop at farm ponds and reservoirs during their travels. Ponds in arid areas of America's West are sources of water for both birds and animals. Farm ponds often attract herds of antelope in the West, and Canada geese may be found on many of America's ponds, lakes, and reservoirs. Some of the increase in wildlife in the United States can be attributed to expanded water resources.

Recreation

Ponds and reservoirs are centers for recreation throughout the United States. Fishing, boating, water skiing, swimming, and scenic vistas have enormously expanded in recent decades. The large reservoirs of America's West, Lakes Meade and Powell, for example, are spectacular recreational facilities. Often overlooked, however, are the millions of ponds and smaller reservoirs that are used for recreation. The combination of new forests, often surrounding ponds and reservoirs, means that extensive travel is no longer needed to find excellent water-based recreational facilities in scenic settings. In 1991, 35.6 million U.S.

residents 16 years old and older enjoyed freshwater fishing areas (U.S. Department of Interior 1993).

Recreational resources are increasingly important to Americans. For example, between 1941 (the first year of record) and 1987 visits to state parks increased approximately 45 percent to about 280 million per year. Visits to national parks increased about 7900 percent from 1924 to 1987; visits to national forests, 3400 percent (Clawson and Harrington 1991). (Population increased 114 percent during this period.) The ability to take advantage of recreational facilities depends on income, availability of transportation (largely automobiles), quality of roads, and the vacationer's time. As people have more wealth, they use recreational facilities. (For further discussion, see chapter 9.)

Starting in 1935 the Civilian Conservation Corps (CCC) built many small dams to form attractive, artificial recreational lakes. They also built thousands of miles of access roads.

As of 1981, there were almost 11 million acres of state parks and 90.8 million acres of wilderness areas. As of 1988 America had 258,683,000 acres of national parks. The number of visits to state parks shows the particular importance of local recreational facilities. The proliferation of ponds and reservoirs throughout the United States contributes significantly to local recreation. Added to camping, hunting, and hiking in the new woods, America has done well in providing recreational facilities for its population.

The future should see a continued expansion of water-based recreational facilities. However, if environmentalists are successful in eliminating the internal combustion engine (Gore 1992, 326), the whole recreational picture could change. Getting to recreational areas would become very difficult.

Problems with Water in America

We have largely stressed the asset side of water as an environmental resource. Of course, there are problem areas, as for any human activity.

Gore summarizes some:

- *Drought conditions in California.* Development and the correlative demand for water is now large enough that in times of drought reservoirs do not contain enough water.

- *The greenhouse effect.* Gore considers the greenhouse effect a serious water problem that can cause flooding because of melting South Pole and Greenland ice. However, whether we are in a significant warming or cooling cycle is controversial.

- *Deforestation.* Gore believes deforestation is a problem for water supplies. For the industrial nations, this is not true. Deforestation in Third World nations is a problem. How the problem can be solved will be discussed in later chapters.

- *Industrial pollution.* Although Gore names industrial pollution as a major problem, such contamination is steadily decreasing. In America, it is no longer significant. Easterbrook (1995, 629) says: ''Degradation of pristine rivers by new water pollution has essentially ended in the United States.'' He points out that only ''1.6 percent of U.S. river miles'' contain ''harmful'' levels of synthetic chemicals. Europe is behind America in cleaning up industrial pollution, but it is catching up.

- *Groundwater.* Gore also talks about the problem of excessive groundwater withdrawal. For example, in some areas of the southwestern United States water is ''mined,'' that is, pumped from underground and not replaced. The water table has dropped from 50 feet to 450 feet in areas of Arizona, New Mexico, and California, resulting in land subsidence, fissures, and depleted steam flow (Anderson et al. 1992). The Ogalalla aquifer in the western high plains is being depleted. Gore also describes the depletion of groundwater resources in some areas of the Third World. He is correct. These are problems. Whether depleting groundwater resources can be recharged artificially is a technical problem that can be locally solvable. These local problems need to be faced and solved in a rational manner.

Problems also occur where surface streams are the only source of water, as in some areas of the Midwest. When drought reduces stream flow, communities are forced to ration or even haul water. California cities have had the same problems at times.

Farmers pump fresh water from delta and flood plain areas of the lower Sacramento–San Joaquin river system, allowing saltwater intrusion into the groundwater. Florida and Long Island have a similar problem in some areas.

Salinity occurs naturally. At Hoover Dam about half the salinity is attributable to natural sources and the remainder from water use. Of the total water used, about three-fourths comes from irrigation. The salinity of the Colorado River increases from 50 parts per million (ppm) at the headwaters to about 800 ppm at Imperial Dam. Hydrologists predict salinity at the dam will increase to about 1,000 ppm by the year 2010. Agricultural yields for some crops and soil types decrease and production costs increase when salinity reaches 700 ppm to 850 ppm.

These problems certainly exist and cause local decreases in per acre agricultural production. However, in the context that production per acre is enormously increasing in America, and in industrial nations in general, the concerns may be overblown.[3]

WATER FOR THIRD WORLD NATIONS

Quality

Over two-thirds of the world's drinking water supply may be hazardous to human health. (See chapter 6 for effects of poor water quality on health.) The most serious contaminants are human body wastes, *not* industrial chemicals. Sewage treatment plants are rare in Third World countries, and most human wastes from cities and towns end up in streams. Wells and springs are often unprotected from contamination by surface wash, which flushes human and animal feces into them.

We discuss water quality in the next chapter under sanitation. It is sufficient to say here that many characteristics of water that are tightly controlled in First World nations are considered too costly by Third World nations.

Quantity

Worldwide, even with great anticipated increases in demand by the year 2000, the world's total use will still be only half the stable renewable supply (United Nations 1990, 80). The problem is "underdevelopment of water resources relative to needs and potential, and the uneven distribution of water resources."

According to the Population Fund (1991, 35), "as many as 2 billion people live in areas with chronic [water] shortages." Linden (1990) reports that some eight thousand villages in India have no water supply. Similarly, many people in Africa must walk long distances every day for water.

People excessively stress water supplies when the amount available per year is less than 500 cubic meters per person. Africa, Burundi, Kenya, Malawi, Rwanda, and Tunisia should all see such stress by the year 2025 (Population Fund 1991, 40). However, First World nations have helped Third World nations construct large reservoirs. They include the Kariba in Zambia, Lake Nasser in Egypt, and the Akosomba in Ghana, with capacities of 160 billion m^3, 169 billion m^3, and 148 billion m^3, respectively. To date, however, these nations have not attained the full potential benefits of these supplies for irrigation, fish culture, and public drinking water supplies. Distribution and development are expensive.

Reservoirs in developing nations often have very short lives because population pressure on the land and forests does not allow control of drainage areas feeding the reservoirs. High erosion rates on stripped land have caused rapid sedimentation, filling many Third World reservoirs and thus greatly reducing storage capacities. Eckholm (1976) describes many cases in which reservoir capacity has diminished rapidly after completion of a dam. For example, the Anchicaya Dam in Colombia was completed in 1955 but by 1957 nearly a quarter of the reservoir capacity had been lost to sedimentation. Sedimentary filling by the silt-laden Indus River reduced the capacity of the Tarbela reservoir in Pakistan to one-seventh of its capacity. The reservoir behind the Ambuklao Dam in the Philippines had a predicted life of sixty-two years; instead, it will last only thirty-two years. And public health programs are set back in cities such as Bangkok, Nairobi, Lagos, and Abidjan because deforestation of upland catchment areas causes high erosion of sediments, which fill reservoirs and reduce availability of potable water. There are many such examples.

Fish

Fish offer a source of protein. People of many Third World nations have insufficient protein, and kwashiorkor (a disease caused by protein deficiency) is common in many areas. In Senegal, protein is absent from most diets nine months of the year, yet off the coast of Senegal is one of the most prolific fisheries in the world, fished by South Africa, Japan, and Russia. Senegal does not have the required fishing boats and refrigeration to take advantage of the resources.

Many small nations recognize the potential of fish agriculture, but the means of establishing the industry are elusive. Control of diseases, feed, and suitable water containment are all expensive. Additionally, lack of refrigeration makes distribution of fish almost impossible. Developing the new resource requires wealth that is not available.

CONCLUSIONS

Throughout the ages humans have learned much about the conservation and use of water resources. Humans have made mistakes. However, a result of water policies in First World nations has been to multiply water resources. First World people are no longer so dependent on vagaries of rainfall or water that naturally flows by them. First World nations, by catching and storing water, are much less dependent on the whims of nature. They control most of their water environment. Control is most apparent in the ability for virtually all First World people to turn on a faucet, take as much water as they like, and drink it without fear.

In multiplying water resources, First World nations have multiplied their potential freshwater fish resources and the habitats for much wildlife. They have also multiplied their recreational resources. By making the world better for themselves, they also improve the world for other life on Earth.

Most Third World nations are not able to properly develop their water resources. Hence, much of their water is dangerous to drink, is not collected in viable reservoirs, and is not distributed to points of need.

NOTES

1. The fight between John Muir, "Sierra Poet" and founder of the Sierra Club, and Gifford Pinchot, U.S. Division of Forestry and Pinchot School of Forestry, Yale University, about the O'Shaughnessy Dam was an early and classic fight between preservationists (Muir) and "wise use" proponents (Pinchot).

2. Data are courtesy of Endangered Fisheries Unit, Bureau of Fisheries, New York State Department of Environmental Conservation.

3. The concern about decreased agricultural production that has been expressed by environmentalists is curious. The same people are likely to want farmers to stop using

chemicals, internal combustion engines and bioengineering, all of which can reduce per acre production.

REFERENCES

Anderson, T. W., G. W. Freethey, and P. Tucci. 1992. Geohydrology and water resources of alluvial basins, in South Central Arizona and parts of adjacent states. U.S. Geological Survey, Professional Paper 1406-B.

Carr, J. E., E. B. Chase, R. W. Paulson, and D. W. Moody, comps. 1990. National water summary 1987—hydrologic events and water supply and uses. U.S. Geological Survey, Water Supply Paper 2350. Denver: United States Geological Survey Federal Center

Clawson, M., and W. Harrington. 1991. The growing role of outdoor recreation. In Frederick, K. D, and R. A. Sedjo, *America's Renewable Resources.* Washington, D.C.: Resources for the Future, p. 249–282

David, S. D. 1988. National water summary, 1986—hydrologic events and groundwater quality. U.S. Geological Survey, Water Supply Paper 2325.

Easterbrook, G. 1995 *A Moment on the Earth.* New York: Penguin Books.

Eckholm, E. P. 1976. *Losing Ground.* New York: W. W. Norton.

Frederick, K. D., and R. A. Sedjo. 1991. *America's Renewable Resources.* Washington, D.C.: Resources for the Future.

Gore, A. 1992. *Earth in the Balance.* New York: Houghton Mifflin.

Goudie, A. 1990. *The Human Impact on the Natural Environment.* Oxford: Basil Blackwell.

Hanfman, D. T. 1993. The status and potential of aquaculture in the United States: An overview and bibliography. Beltsville, Md.: National Agriculture Library.

Larkin, P. A. 1978. Where next in wildlife management? *American Forests,* March, 30–33.

Linden, Eugene. 1990. The last drops. *Time,* August 20, 58–61.

Matthews, T. 1989. Rescue plan for Africa. *World Monitor,* May.

McGuinness, C. L. 1963. The role of ground water in the national water situation. U.S. Geological Survey, Water Supply Paper 1800.

Population Fund. 1991. *Population, Resources and the Environment, Critical Challenges.* New York: United Nations.

Simmons, I. G. 1993. *Environmental History.* Oxford: Blackwell.

Stevens, W. K. 1995. Earth Day at 25: How has nature fared? *New York Times,* April 17, C1, C5.

United Nations. 1990. *Global Outlook 2000.* United Nations Publications, United States.

U.S. Corps of Engineers. 1988. Inland waterway review, Fort Belvoir. Virginia Institute for Water Resources.

U.S. Department of the Interior. 1993. *1992 National Survey of Fishing, Hunting and Wildlife-Associated Recreation.* Washington, D.C.: U.S. Government Printing Office.

U.S. Environmental Protection Agency. 1982. Survey of operating and financial characteristics of community water systems. Springfield, Va.: National Technical Information Service.

U.S. Geological Survey. 1984. National water summary 1983—hydrologic events and issues. U.S. Geological Survey, Water Supply Paper 2250.

CHAPTER 6

Sanitation and Disease—
The Human Environment

In the previous chapters, we have shown how First World nations have effectively multiplied their soil, forest, wildlife, water, and fish resources. In this chapter, we show that First World nations have a similar record for human health. They have extended the years of human productivity, thus multiplying the human resource.

Health problems are in two broad categories: those of First World nations and those of Third World nations. Many measures taken to improve the health of people in developed nations are not applicable to developing nations. Largely, people in developing nations must go through the same process that people in developed nations went through to improve their health. The health of people in developed nations is often related to individual lifestyle preferences. Excessive smoking, drinking, or eating and lack of exercise are major health problems for people of wealthy nations. First World people *create* many of their health problems. In the Third World, the environment *imposes* health problems on people. They have relatively little control over their health.

What factors have brought First World countries to their present position? What should they do to continue enjoying the benefits? How can Third World nations achieve the same benefits?

The answers are, of course, in medical technology, including diet and sanitation. Medical availability is also important. Wealth is the essential common denominator.

Human life expectancy throughout the world has increased significantly over the past seven or eight decades. Improved medical knowledge has been the primary cause. The changes coincide with the industrialization process and with the resulting general knowledge explosion. People in First World nations have the longest life expectancy. Longevities well into the seventies are the rule. However, the transfer of medical knowledge has resulted in a higher percent of improvement occurring in Third World nations. Though improvement has been

Table 6.1
Comparison of Some Disease-Caused Deaths, United States and World

Cause of Death	United States, 1900[1]	Percent Mortality 1991[2]	World, Percent Mortality 1990[3]
Tuberculosis	18.0	‹0.1	8.0
Pneumonia and influenza	18.7	4.4	15.9
Diarrhea	13.2	‹0.1	39.8
Malaria	—	—	4.0
Cancer	5.9	29.9	—
Cardiovascular	32.0	60.1	—
Typhoid fever	2.9	‹0.1	0.07
Dengue fever	—	—	31.8
Intestinal parasites	—	—	0.5

[1]Adapted from Gotchy 1994.
[2]Wright 1994.
[3]World Health Organization 1993.
Notes: Whooping cough, measles, scarlet fever, diphtheria, and croup were significant causes of death in America as late as about 1900 but now are not important.

From 1900 to 1990 deaths per 100,000 people from accidents in America dropped 49% (after Gotchy 1994).

Cancer and cardiovascular diseases are diseases of the wealthy and of "old age." They increase as people no longer die from preventable diseases.

significant, it is still far less than it should be (for statistical details, see chapter 8).

In this chapter, we analyze factors that influence human health and longevity and relate them to technology and wealth. The components are sanitation, nutrition, and medical availability, all tied together by the wealth factor.

DISEASES—THE UNSEEN ENVIRONMENTAL ENEMIES

Table 6.1 compares the causes of death in America for the year 1900 with the causes of death in America in 1991 and for the world in 1990. The causes of death in America in the late 1800s are similar to the current causes of death over most of the world today. Causes of death from disease in modern America are primarily those associated with old age—cancer and cardiovascular diseases. America and other First World nations have neutralized the common diseases found in most of the rest of the world. People of First World nations tend to die as a result of their lifestyle choices. Cancer, heart disease, pulmonary disease, diabetes, AIDS, liver disease, and prenatal-related conditions are often the result of individual sexual, eating, smoking, or exercise preferences. People of First World countries create much of their own health environment.

The leading causes of death for most other people of the world are quite different. Environmental conditions over which they may have little control impose diseases on them.

Before discussing methods of disease prevention throughout the world, we will briefly review the nature of common diseases. Table 6.2 is a summary of the extent of major communicable disease worldwide. The World Bank publishes information about the extent of diseases every ten years. The data are compiled by the World Health Organization (WHO). By far, the largest number of people who die of environmental diseases are in Third World nations. Many diseases are found only in tropical nations. Some common causes of death worldwide (pneumonia, diarrhea, or tuberculosis) are present in First World nations, but now are rarely fatal.

Zoonotic Diseases

Initially, AIDS (Acquired Immune Deficiency Syndrome) was a zoonotic disease, that is, transmitted from animals to humans. Other zoonotic diseases have been observed but are rare and will not be discussed. AIDS causes significant mortality in First World nations. However, data presented at the Ninth International Conference on AIDS and STD (Sexually Transmitted Diseases) in Africa showed the far greater severity of the AIDS epidemic in Third World nations. The conference was held in Kampala, Uganda, December 10–13, 1995, with over 3500 delegates from 113 countries. Dr. Peter Piot, Executive Director of UNAIDS, a UN agency scheduled for operation January 1, 1996, said that between 14 and 15 million people worldwide are now infected with the AIDS virus (8.5 million adults with HIV in sub-Saharan Africa). He also reported that many are unaware of it and so infection continues. Nine out of ten infected are in developing countries. The virus is spreading along preexisting fault lines, propelled by poverty and lack of education. Another report indicated that 50 percent of those infected in that part of the world are between 15 and 24 years of age (Anon. 1995a).

The consequences are many, including lowered life expectancy, reduced productivity, and severely strained public health budgets. Funds to control other diseases such as malaria and tuberculosis, which remain unabated, have been reallocated to AIDS. Many household heads have been lost, along with trained personnel in business, agriculture, manufacturing, education, and government. Food crises have occurred locally, and many children have left school because of reduced school budgets or loss of parents.

WHO presently estimates that by the year 2000, 10 to 15 million children worldwide under 18 years of age will have lost one or both parents to AIDS, with approximately 90 percent of those children in Africa. In Uganda, a 1991

Table 6.2

Major Communicable[1] Environmental Diseases, and Worldwide Extent, 1990

Disease	Estimated Population At Risk		Population Infected		Deaths per Year and Some Other Impacts
Enteric Diseases					
Primarily diarrhea	Worldwide		3	billion	10–20 million children 160,000 adults
Shigellosis (Bacillary dysentery)	Worldwide		6	billion	60% children under 10
Intestinal Parasites	Worldwide				205,000
Roundworm			1	billion	20,000
Hookworm			900	million	60,000
Tapeworm			50	million	50,000
Amoebas			500	million	75,000
Respiratory Diseases Influenza, pneumonia	Worldwide				1/4 to 1/3 of childhood mortality
Tuberculosis			1.7 billion 20 million active cases; 8 million new cases annually		3 million
Mosquito-Borne Diseases	5	Continents			
Malaria	2.1	billion	150	million[2]	1 to 2 million
Dengue fever	—		30-60	million	5–50% mortality
Filariasis (lymphatic)	900 76	million Countries	250	million	Disfiguring
Schistosomiasis	600-700	million	200-300	million	Major health problem
Typhoid fever	Worldwide		1	million	25,000
Trachoma (eye infection)	Tropical		400–500	million	6–9 million with loss of eyesight

[1]Communicable is person to person or from nature to people.

[2]World Health Organization (WHO 1990) estimates 267 million cases. Malaria appears to be increasing according to some WHO data.

Note: Virtually all of the above deaths and debilitation are preventable since they occur as a result of malnutriton, lack of clean water, lack of sanitary facilities for disposal of human waste, and insect disease vectors that could be controlled by pesticides, etc.

The annual total death from the above causes for the world is about 39 million or about 928 per 100,000 for the Third World nations where almost all of the deaths occur.

Source: Adapted from Listori 1990.

survey found that 1.2 million children under 18, 11.6 percent of the nation's population, were orphaned (Anon. 1995b).

Enteric Diseases

Enteric diseases, especially diarrhea, are perhaps the most important cause of morbidity and mortality. A range of chemical and biological agents cause enteric problems.

Diarrhea in newborns and children claims 10 million to 20 million lives yearly. High body temperatures cause rapid dehydration, a major cause of death. Mortality can exceed 50 per 1,000 per year in preschool children or as high as 40 per 100 in premature or low-birthweight infants. Transmission usually occurs because of ingestion of pathogens in or on food, water, toys, pets, clothing, and unclean hands of mothers and children. Protein-calorie malnutrition is commonly associated with acute diarrhea attacks. Typically, 275 attacks per 100 children per year may occur (Listori 1990).

The house fly is a major problem because it can transport pathogenic bacteria either in its alimentary tract or on the external surfaces of its body. Although long known, knowledge about the dangers from house flies has not been sufficiently incorporated into preventive health programs in Third World nations.

Uncontaminated drinking water, improved housing, food protection, proper disposal of feces, use of insecticides and window screens, and education about personal hygiene can prevent most enteric diseases in Third World countries.

Respiratory Diseases

Colds, Pneumonia, Influenza. Airborne particles carry the common cold virus. A cold can predispose the body to such secondary infections as pneumonia or influenza, particularly among the aged, the malnourished children, and the chronically ill. Pneumonia and influenza are major causes of mortality. According to WHO, these infections cause approximately one-fourth to one-third of childhood deaths. Particulates in the air caused by smoke from heating and cooking with charcoal, wood, kerosene, or dung in crowded areas such as houses, slums, and squatter settlements of Third World countries favor the spread of these diseases. Education about personal hygiene has helped, but the lack of good ventilation in homes of the poor is not easily solved.

Tuberculosis. Tuberculosis is quite common. Most healthy people overcome it without ill effect because of natural resistance. Decline of the disease in Europe started long before the discovery of the tuberculosis bacillus because of improved public health and sanitation. This disease is a drag on the economies of Third World nations, where 80 percent of tuberculosis occurs in the 15–59 age bracket, the most productive years. About 3 million people die annually from tuberculosis.

Transmission can be through unpasteurized milk from infected cattle or from exposure to droplets carrying the bacilli from infected persons (sneezing, coughing, or spitting). Intervention requires pasteurization, screening and immunization, reduced overcrowding, improved nutrition, knowledge of personal hygiene, and better ventilation.

Intestinal Parasite Diseases

Various intestinal parasites, particularly intestinal worms, interfere with digestion, absorb nutrients, cause anemia and diarrhea, and result in malnutrition, dehydration, vitamin deficiency, and even death. Secondary effects include heart disease, damage to the reproductive system, and infant and maternal mortality. Proper disposal of feces, protection of water supplies, prevention of contamination in living quarters, particularly children's play areas, and attention to personal hygiene and food handling are preventive measures.

Shigellosis (Dysentery)

Interpersonal contacts, flies, and food poisoning spread shigellosis. The mortality rate can exceed 20 to 25 percent. Failing to wash hands and fingernails after defecation is the major cause of transmission. Reduction depends on availability of clean water, sanitary disposal of feces, personal hygiene, fly control, and proper cooking and storage of food.

Mosquito-Borne Diseases

Malaria, filariasis, yellow fever, and dengue are mosquito-borne diseases infecting some 450 million people and causing over 2 million deaths a year. Three mosquito genera are responsible—*Aedes, Anopheles,* and *Culex*—and each has its own breeding habits. Their flight range is up to three miles for the malaria-carrying mosquito (*Anopheles*) and up to one hundred miles for *Aedes;* the average is about three-fourths of a mile. Drainage to remove the mosquito habitat and proper disposal of solid waste are critical controls.

Malaria. Humans get four types of malaria. *Anopheles* mosquitoes transmit all of them, they are of the genus *Plasmodium: P. falciparum, P. vivax, P. ovale,* and *P. malariae. P. falciparum* is the most dangerous, resulting in life-threatening complications such as anemia and cerebral malaria. The fatality rate of malaria exceeds 10 percent. It is the number one cause of death in Africa.

The WHO (1993) emphasized, "Malaria is acknowledged to be by far the most important tropical parasitic disease, causing great suffering and loss of life." The report estimates the loss of life in Africa "is no less than 500,000 to 1.2 million deaths annually, mainly among African children below the age of 5 years. Worldwide, it is estimated there are about 120 million clinical cases of malaria" (p. 15). Total cases appear to be rising, with estimates as high as 267 million (WHO 1990). Its debilitating effect is considerable. For Africa the estimated annual cost, direct and indirect, for 1987 was U.S. $800 million. Despite that cost and demonstrated need, development of controls has been slow. Poverty is one obstacle. In addition, as conditions for loans, First World nations have banned some pesticides that prevent control of mosquitoes.

In America, because of a ban on some pesticides and an increase in wetlands, mosquito populations have increased and malaria and encephalitis have also increased. Both declined in the United States until the mid-1970s, but both are on the rise since. Malaria was once limited to a small part of southern Illinois. Now it occurs in the southeastern states and as far north as Philadelphia.

In 1975 an epidemic of encephalitis in the Midwest resulted in over four thousand confirmed human cases with ninety-five confirmed deaths. There is no vaccine. Another mosquito-vectored virus related to the midwestern encephalitis and found in large areas of the Midwest causes mild flu-like symptoms at onset. Some cases result in serious brain damage delayed up to three years after onset. Control of these diseases requires control over mosquito breeding areas. However, the federal government often construes such programs as violating the Endangered Species Act or the Wetlands Act (Hazeltine 1991).

Filariasis. Filariasis is an infection by filarial worms spread by insects. Lymphatic filariasis is an infection causing inflammation and blockage of the lymphatic system. It is carried by *Culex* mosquitoes, which bite at night. They breed in pit latrines, open sewer drains, and waste water, predominantly in urban areas. Filariasis infects some 250 million people. In Africa, the vector is *Anopheles,* which breeds in clean water. River blindness, elephantiasis, and guinea worm disease are examples of filariasis.

Yellow fever. Yellow fever is an acute infectious disease caused by a virus that enters the body through the bite of an infected mosquito (*Aedes egypti*). It causes chills, fever, aches, jaundice, vomiting, kidney damage, uremia, and often death. Protection is through vaccination. The fatality rate is 20 percent to 30 percent.

Dengue fever. Dengue fever is a sudden-onset, acute fever, with intense headaches, muscle pains, and rash. It usually lasts five days. The insect vector is the mosquito *Aedes egypti* (*Aedes albopictus* in the Philippines). It is a vicious daytime biter that breeds in or near human habitation and will remain in houses throughout its life span. It is spreading rapidly on five continents. Untreated, dengue fever fatality rates reach 50 percent; treated, 5 percent.

Other Diseases

Cholera. Cholera is spread by organisms in the intestinal discharges of people who have cholera or are carriers (they carry the infective organism without disease symptoms). Infection is spread through water and food (by house flies, by use of contaminated water for washing food, or by hands of carriers). Seven epidemics occurred in the United States from 1835 to 1884. Today's cholera epidemics occur predominately in lower socioeconomic groups because of malnutrition or poor hygiene.

Peru had a cholera epidemic in 1991–1992 with a reported 625,259 cases and 4,396 deaths (Communicable Disease Center 1995). The epidemic occurred when Peruvian authorities stopped chlorination of drinking water in response to the EPA's concern that chlorination could cause cancer. After the epidemic started, Peru resumed chlorination. However, by that time many carriers had traveled into adjoining countries and spread the disease. From January 23, 1991, through September 1, 1994, 1,041,422 cases of cholera developed with 9,642 deaths in 20 countries in Latin America (Communicable Disease Center 1995).

Schistosomiasis. Schistosomiasis is an infection caused by a worm parasite in the veins around the intestines, bladder, and liver. A snail that lives in slow-moving water and usually under lily pads transmits the parasite. People discharge the eggs of the worm in both urine and feces. The eggs hatch in fresh water and enter the snail, where they develop into free swimming worms able to penetrate the skin of humans and animals. Where humans stand in irrigation canals to get water and discharge their body waste into the canals, there can be continuous reinfection. The disease causes low mortality; effects range from skin rash to liver disease and urinary and intestinal complications. Women and children are particularly at risk because of higher exposure.

Interruption of the life cycle of the worm is essential. Improved irrigation, proper disposal of human excreta, covered storage, and use of pipes or covered flumes for transmission of water eliminate the sources of the infection.

Sleeping Sickness (Trypanosomiasis). The tse-tse fly is the insect vector and is found primarily in rural areas. Two main types of disease result in different effects. The riverine type (Gambiense) spreads through a human-fly-human cycle in central western Africa. The savanna type (Rhodosiense) prefers cattle and wild animals in eastern Africa. The savanna type causes more human deaths. It also interferes with the development of the livestock industry. In some areas, the lack of cattle leads to kwashiorkor, a debilitating disease caused by insufficient protein.

Clearing brush along streams near villages and the use of insecticides help control the fly habitat.

Trachoma. Trachoma is a treatable eye infection; untreated, it can cause blindness. It spreads by contact with eye discharges or articles soiled by patients. Flies also carry the disease. Improved personal hygiene and increased availability of clean water are effective and crucial interventions. Currently, some 6 million to 9 million have lost their eyesight and 8 million are at risk. Some 400 million to 500 million people have the disease.

Tetanus. Tetanus is an infection causing painful contractions of neck and trunk muscles. It is introduced into the body via puncture wounds, burns, and scratches. In Third World countries, it may infect the stump of the umbilical cord when a poultice of animal dung is used. Animal feces may enter cuts and bruises of farmers and animal meat-packing house employees. Again, availability of clean water for cleaning wounds is a most important preventive measure. Education of midwives is essential. If treatment is inadequate, the fatality range can be from 30 percent to 90 percent.

Typhoid and Paratyphoid Fevers. Human feces spread typhoid and paratyphoid infections. The fever is not accompanied by diarrhea. The mortality rate is about 10 percent; when patients use antibiotics, the rate drops to about one percent. Improved water supply is the single most important factor in controlling typhoid. A reduction of as much as 80 percent can occur within five years of installation of water filtration facilities. Humans are the main source of the disease. Transmission is by ingesting food and water contaminated by human feces. Individuals who have no evidence of fever may be carriers and able to infect food and water.

Pandemic Diseases of History. A pandemic is a global disease spread over an extended period. Plagues are particularly severe examples. Plagues are as old as human civilizations and have profoundly influenced history. The worst plagues (bubonic, largely) were the plague of Justinian (A.D. 540–590); the Black Death (1346–1361); and the so-called Great Plague of London (1665–1666). They all apparently resulted from the bite of fleas carried by the black rat. The Black Death probably killed about 24 million people—about 25 percent of the European population at the time.

Typhus (transmitted by the body louse), typhoid fever, cholera, and syphilis have all been major pandemic diseases at various times in history. But the great pandemics of history could not now become a problem in First World nations because of modern sanitation. Clean water, proper disposal of trash and bodily wastes, and control of rodents and insect vectors all make recurrence of the historic pandemics unlikely in First World nations.

Conditions in Third World nations, however, are another matter.

SANITATION

Sanitation is the means of improving the environment to reduce human disease. The factors most influencing human health are water supply, excreta and waste disposal, insect and rodent control, food storage, food markets, personal hygiene, and the living environment. The living environment includes ventilation, amount of crowding, heating, lighting, screening, plumbing, and play area conditions. Maintaining human health requires simultaneous attention to all these factors.

Sanitation—First World

We discuss first sanitation procedures used by First World nations. We distinguish between First and Third World procedures, because what is practical in one world may simply be useless, silly, or impossible in the other. Further, many diseases are different and require different controls.

Potable Water. Most First World nations now have abundant clean water available for their people. Most of it flows from taps and comes from central municipal supplies. In rural areas, water usually comes from individual wells.

Until about 1910 typhoid fever, dysentery, and cholera outbreaks in America were common. Now they are very rare, thanks to clean water. Waterworks facilities treat most water. Much of the treatment attacks characteristics that do not affect human health (e.g., hardness, odor, flavor, or excess mineral matter). From a health standpoint, filtering and chlorination are most critical. Harmful microbes rarely reach the consumer. The result is that throughout the First World people can drink tap water without danger of acquiring water-carried diseases.

Sewage Collection and Treatment—America. "Modern sewerage (in the United States) has followed closely upon urban development and that, in turn, for the most part, has been consequent upon the industrial evolution, the establishment of the mechanical age and its progress. In terms of both population numbers and rate of growth, urban development in the United States practically dates from the middle of the last century" (Hyde 1938, 1). Hyde recognized the essential role of industrial growth to provide the wealth necessary for construction of sewage treatment systems.

In 1855 Chicago started the first comprehensive sewerage[1] project in the United States. In 1860, when the population of the United States was 31,400,000, about one million people had access to some kind of sewerage connections. Then, about 7 million resided in towns of more than 2,500. That meant that 17 percent of the urban population resided in sewered communities. By 1935, 69,500,000 persons—91 percent of the total urban population of 75,500,000—lived in sewered communities. The total U.S. population was 132 million.

At first, disposal was by dilution in a receiving body of water. The more advanced chemical precipitation and sand filtration procedures were first used in Great Britain and on the Continent. By 1900, 60 municipal treatment plants in the United States serving a population of about one million persons—4 percent of the population—lived in sewered communities. By 1935 approximately 3,700 municipal plants served a total population of over 28 million, or 41 percent of the sewered population.

Black and Phelps in 1910 developed procedures for estimating the self-purification capacity of receiving waters. If properly used, this self-purification capacity is a natural resource of economic significance in effective water management (Hyde 1938, 1–3). However, public objections to even treated sewage in streams have largely eliminated this natural economic benefit. Raw sewage was mostly eliminated from America's waterways by the 1980s.

For rural homes and small institutions, the septic tank, properly designed and with an adequate drainage field, has proved most serviceable. In 1934 among the 3,500 municipal plants in the United States, 41 percent (1,450) used septic tanks. Some 800 municipalities used trickling filters, a process that was able to withstand sudden increases of loads by using an improved method of distributing the waste water to the filter. This process also removed organics more efficiently.

Irrigation for disposal of sewage and treated effluents was used not only in the arid and semiarid West but in several eastern cities as well. The first application of this technology was at the state asylum in Augusta, Maine, in 1872 (Hyde 1938, 7).

As late as the mid-1900s raw municipal sewage entered many rivers in the United States. Currently, America treats over 90 percent of all sewage. By the year 2000 all sewage should be treated. Treating sewage is very expensive. Treating 100 percent of it in municipal areas is very difficult, especially in times of heavy runoff from storms. In many areas sewerage carries both sewage and storm water runoff. (Essentially, industrial wastes do not now enter the nation's waters.)

Because of the differences in requirements among the states and among the regions of the federal government, sewage treatment cost per capita is variable. Many small communities have found maintenance and operating cost to achieve complete or advanced waste treatment prohibitive. The practical effect of treatment on a receiving stream could be nil. However, adherence to uniform requirements has replaced engineering design with inflexible bureaucratic regulation.

Garbage Disposal. The disposal of garbage in First World countries is usually through collection trucks that take the material to environmentally controlled sites (landfills) or incinerators. Usually waste food products are picked up from garbage cans or other tightly covered containers. At disposal sites, garbage is regularly covered with soil. These procedures, whether landfills or incineration, reduce the possibility of rat infestations. Thus, the likelihood of rat-carried diseases from central garbage disposal in First World nations is remote. However, an infestation in large cities is a potentially serious health problem. Areas of poor sanitation practices, including improper disposal of garbage, attract rats (Washington, D.C. is an example).

Indoor Air. Often overlooked as a major contributor to good human health in First World nations is the purity of indoor air. We take it for granted that our air will not be a source of disease. Indoor air relatively free of smoke, other particulates, or harmful bacteria or viruses is the rule in most First World homes.

Crowding. Most people in First World nations live in relatively spacious surroundings. Isolation of sick people is usually easy and, therefore, transmission of infections is generally retarded. People crowded into small living quarters share their diseases. The British, in detailed epidemiological studies (Lawther 1978), conclude that lower socioeconomic status "is very important in development of chronic disease—constitutional weakness resulting from malnutrition, bad housing, damp housing, overcrowding where there is cross-infection in the household, inadequate treatment of the infection."

Hygiene. People of First World nations take two more items for granted: soap and abundant, clean water. These two items enable First World people to bathe frequently. Simply washing the hands is a major factor in disease control.

Sanitation—Third World

Clean water, sewage collection and treatment, ample living space, adequate indoor ventilation, window screens, and soap all cost money. For nations that have annual per capita GNPs of less than $200, First World solutions to sanitation problems are not always feasible. Still, Third World people can and have benefited from First World medical knowledge. Thus, education is the first requisite to solving Third World sanitation problems.

Education. Between the intervals 1960–1965 and 1980–1985, child mortality rates (deaths per 1,000 children) have dropped 27.4 percent in Africa; 34.6 percent in Asia; and 36.6 percent in South America (Population Fund 1991, 54). Most societies significantly increased average human longevity in the 1970–90 interval. For Third World nations, the increase was about 17 percent. Over the intervals 1950–1955 to 1980–1988, life expectancy for Africans increased 32.5 percent; Asians, 40.5 percent; and South Americans, 22.4 percent (United Nations 1991, 54).[2] Education has been a major factor. For Third World nations, education pertained largely to control of major environmental diseases through personal hygiene. Education about the causes of diseases, immunization, and pre- and postnatal care can be very helpful for people of developing nations.

Education may be frustrating. Knowing that control of mosquitoes, flies, rodents, or bodily wastes can reduce many diseases may be of little value for people who cannot afford remediation. Knowledge about personal hygiene may be of little value to people who have neither soap nor clean water. And knowing about the importance of boiling water before human consumption may not be useful for people who are short of fuel. Still, education is necessary and should be ultimately beneficial.

Sewage and Sewage Disposal. Third World nations have considerable difficulty handling human bodily wastes in both rural and metropolitan areas because of the cost of collection and treatment. In rural areas, disposal of waste is often near the home, along a trail, or in fly-infested latrines. Also, people may use the wastes as fertilizer on crops. Both flies and some crops transmit disease. Septic systems are not feasible for most rural people because there is no connected water supply.

Sewage disposal for metropolitan areas also has financial hurdles. Sewers discharge to streams; pit latrines are not all fly-protected; water supply is unreliable and often out of operation for days. Ground or street curb drains are often used as toilets and flushed only when it rains.

Without facilities for collection and treatment of sewage, cholera, typhoid, and dysentery will continue to take a high human toll until money is available to build and maintain such systems.

An interim solution in many Third World countries is a pit latrine (or "drop hole'') for individual homes. Commonly, however, pit latrines and septic tank disposal fields contaminate water wells when the septic wastes are too close to the wells. In Uganda, by regulation, pit latrines must be thirty feet deep. Wastes in such deep pits, however, contaminate groundwater in large areas. Construction guides furnished by the U.S. Agency for International Development (USAID) detail design of the pit and recommend covering the pit area to allow use in rainy weather. However, they do not describe how to locate the pit so as not to contaminate groundwater. The result is that too often the latrine and well are adjacent, under the same roof, and both below groundwater level.

Drinking Water. Improper handling of human wastes leads, of course, to contaminated drinking water, a serious problem throughout the world. The contamination is generally by human feces, although animal feces can also be a problem. In 1984 safe drinking water was available to only 19 percent of the people in Sri Lanka; 18 percent in Paraguay; 16 percent in Uganda; 14 percent in Sierra Leone; 13 percent in Mozambique; 11 percent in Nepal; 10 percent in Afghanistan; 6 percent in Mali; and 4 percent in Ethiopia (United Nations 1991, 36).

Water-borne pathogens contribute to typhoid, cholera, amoebic infections, bacillary dysentery, and diarrhea. These pathogens cause 88 percent of all disease in Third World nations and 90 percent of the 13 million child deaths annually (United Nations 1991, 36). Contributing to the problem is the declining size of catchment basins in many areas due to deforestation. This leads to excessive erosion. Eroded materials rapidly fill reservoirs, reducing available water and creating yet another setback to public health.

Disease Vector Control. Blood-sucking or disease-carrying insects walking on food transmit disease. These include flies, mosquitoes, and fleas. They spread diseases by mechanically transferring the causative agent. Insect-borne diseases prevail where insect hosts are indigenous and where conditions for their breeding are suitable. Controls are meant to prevent the insect host from biting humans or animals. Specifically, destroying habitats of the insects (draining swamps or emptying containers of water, poisoning breeding areas with insecticides, poisoning habitat areas with pesticides such as DDT), using insect repellant, and screening sleeping areas all help control insect vectors. However, many Third World nations cannot afford the common, successful methods used in the First World.

Rats and some other rodents carry and transmit diseases to humans. The rat, for example, serves as a host for the rat flea (which carries bubonic plague). The rat is also the animal reservoir for typhus fever (transmitted by the body louse). It also transmits diseases by carrying the causative organisms from waste material (e.g., human excreta) to people's food. Rats can carry intestinal parasites, particularly tapeworms, as well as the agent for infectious jaundice. The bite of a rat may cause rat bite fever.

Another reason for rodent control is the amount of food they consume from storage. Reported losses from rodents and spoilage in India exceed 25 percent.

It is virtually impossible to eliminate rats if they have access to a food supply. Control of rats involves poison and eliminating access to household food and garbage.

Living Environment. The less affluent in the Third World live in mud-brick, straw-roofed, dirt-floor homes, and usually do not have potable water. Women and children may walk miles, often twice a day, to get water. A First World citizen would usually get sick from the water so laboriously obtained. There is no plumbing. Ventilation is simple air exchange through an open door. Heating is nonexistent. The first cold snap causes many deaths because malnutrition is common and resistance is low. Flies that carry excreta from humans and animals abound in children's play areas outside the house. The outskirts of the yard are bounded by excreta on the ground or in poorly designed "drop holes," exposed to flies that can carry waste to nearby homes. No refrigeration leads to spoilage of food; no screening promotes contamination of food. Any artificial lighting is with kerosene lanterns, which give off smoke and fumes. Cooking is with wood, charcoal, or dried dung either inside or outside the building. If inside, the smoke level can be high. Smoke particulates contribute to high rates of respiratory disease, especially in children. Even wealthier rural citizens, those who have property and an automobile or truck, have a limited diet and may not have access to potable water or window screening.

Markets. Open markets supply goods in Third World nations. These include vegetables that may have been grown in fields fertilized with human excreta. Butchers carve meat as ordered, from fly-covered carcasses that have no cover or refrigeration. Fish receive similar treatment. Spread of disease in these open markets is common.

Garbage Disposal. Third World nations dispose of garbage using methods that are thousands of years old. Without garbage trucks available, they must leave garbage close to their homes. Dogs, chickens, and pigs clean up much food debris. This is fortunate because the job would otherwise be done mostly by rats. Rat-caused epidemics would then be more of a problem.

Health Care

Survival of the sick often depends on availability of health care. In developing countries, most hospital facilities are in urban areas. Gradually, clinics are being constructed in rural areas and immunization is reaching more children. Still, Third World nations will not have enough doctors until their per capita income rises enough so they can afford to pay for them.

Third World nations often lack sufficient refrigeration to store drugs. With the expiration of patents on chlorofluorocarbons (CFCs) such as Freon, there was the expectation that Third World countries would be able to cheaply produce their own chlorofluorocarbons and, perhaps, even refrigerators. However, fear of ozone depletion by people in industrial nations is resulting in a phasing out of CFCs. This is a step backward for Third World health. (Whether the CFC-ozone "problem" is significant is covered in chapter 11.)

NUTRITION

Generally, nutrition is not considered an environmental factor. Yet abundant good food has contributed greatly to the improved health of First World people. Conversely, poor nutrition greatly reduces the ability of Third World people to withstand the onslaught of disease. In addition, poor nutrition itself can cause problems.

Nutrition—First World

People of the First World now have more stamina, and are bigger, faster, and stronger than any previous generation. It is startling to see suits of armor used by medieval fighting men. They are too small even for boys in their early teens of today's First World nations, much less for average adult males. Today's average man would have difficulty getting into the bunks used by sailors of old sailing ships. The record books for swimming and track and field attest to a steady increase in the strength, speed, and stamina of modern men and women. Better techniques, training, and equipment are factors. But the increase in the size of football and basketball players is obvious to anyone looking at a contemporary team roster compared with a similar roster from thirty years ago.

Beal (1980, 35) describes how the physical fitness level of American draftees for World War II was far superior to those of World War I. She attributes lower incidence of physical impairments and general all around good health to "good nutrition and better environmental conditions from infancy on through the period of rapid growth."

Nutrition has several components. We need sources of energy (such as sugars, fats, and carbohydrates). We need sources of proteins (vegetable and animal), high-bulk foods (vegetables, whole grains) to keep the intestinal tract healthy, and vitamins and minerals. Sources of major minerals (calcium, magnesium, and phosphorous) and minor trace elements (iodine, copper, zinc, selenium, and cobalt) and vitamins are also important.

The average First World person eating a balanced diet selected from all the major food groups generally gets all the components needed for health. Additionally, many people take supplements to ensure the intake of sufficient vitamins and minerals.

A major health plus is the availability of fresh fruits, vegetables, and meats throughout the winter months. This does two things: it assures a healthy diet containing all of the required megaconstituents. It also greatly improves the probability that needed trace elements required for human health are sufficient. A diet consisting of only local foods will usually be short of one or more trace elements.

Nutrition—Third World

The Third World has serious nutritional problems. Some 500 million people in sub-Saharan Africa are undernourished, although the majority of undernourished persons are in Asia. More than 150 million children in Third World nations are undernourished (United Nations 1991, 54). While moderate malnutrition is survivable, it makes people more susceptible to disease.

Like many predictions, especially those that may have a political purpose, famines anticipated by some authorities did not occur. Starvation has occurred locally, but political conflicts are far more to blame than agricultural failure. Still, the Population Fund (1991, 34) says: "there has been an environment-population debacle building up for decades in the agricultural sector, covert and largely disregarded until the last few years." If the dire predictions are true, malnutrition should increase.

Third World people will continue to have nutritional problems until they achieve Second World status (see chapter 8). Even where there is sufficient food, the diet may not be balanced. For example, shortage of protein produce kwashiorkor in some areas; and a shortage of vitamin A is a problem for many children. Vitamin A deficiency has caused some 10 million cases of xerophthalmia worldwide, with about five hundred thousand resulting in blindness. A few cents' worth of vitamin A could prevent this problem (National Research Council 1993, 128–29).

CLEAN WATER

Throughout the world keeping rivers, lakes, and oceans clean has historically been a low environmental priority. The following reasons are apparent:

- Streams are nature's sewers. They carry inorganic sediments; the chemical wastes of weathering; and such organic matter as wood, leaves, animal feces, rotted animal carcasses, and fish feces. Humans in most countries add raw sewage and industrial wastes. The water of most rivers in Third World nations is not safe for human consumption. River water in First World nations, although now largely clear of raw sewage, is still not suitable for direct human consumption. The eroded sediments and other debris off the land create huge deltas. The Mississippi Delta consists of sedimentary debris over forty thousand feet deep, and the delta of the Colorado River contains all the debris eroded from the Grand Canyon complex. A delta is nature's garbage dump.

- People in most nations add their own debris to the existing load.

- Cleaning streams is very expensive. Human sewage contaminates most waterways. The process of sewage treatment is expensive, and Third World and even Second World nations usually cannot afford it. For example, even in America, treating sewage from many major cities was not economically possible until the 1960s and 1970s. To some extent, cleaning sewage from rivers is a luxury.

- Normally, oxidation in moving water cleanses it of the microbes that cause human sickness. However, if people live closely spaced along rivers, there may not be sufficient distance between outfall and intake for oxidation to occur. Lakes also cleanse themselves of organisms that are harmful to human health. Contaminated water can enter a lake and clean water can leave the other end. Similarly, the oceans cleanse themselves of harmful organic material. Organisms or other contaminants that are harmful to humans in both cases are likely to be food for other organisms.

- The debris of human activity—the junk that too often ends in waterways—is generally not harmful to human health. However, most people are aesthetically offended by the presence of the castoffs of civilization in their streams.

DISCUSSION

For Third World nations, simple, inexpensive environmental controls will greatly improve their health and longevity. Monies spent in developed countries for the ultimate in environmental control could accomplish far more in human terms in undeveloped countries.

The World Bank (Listori, 1990, vii), speaking of First World health says: "no single intervention has been wholly responsible for such health improvement"; "interpersonal contacts are an extremely important mechanism of transmission" of disease. In western Europe during the nineteenth and twentieth centuries, major respiratory and diarrhea diseases often had already begun to decline ahead of medical breakthroughs. In similar manner, reduced mortality in North America started long before improvement in water supply and waste disposal.

Improved health results from general economic development and improvement in living standards, including education and income. That education in sanitation is essential is obvious. But clearly the poor and disadvantaged, the people in most need of improved quality of life, must experience economic growth before enhanced environment occurs. We illustrated this earlier in the brief summary of diseases that debilitate or cause the death of millions yearly. Many diseases could be controlled with the application of fundamental sanitation measures. Some of these measures are community in nature (e.g., potable water supply) but many require personal expenditure (e.g., facilities for excreta disposal, screening to limit disease transmission by flies and mosquitoes). Personal expenditure requires income. Developing sources of income that increase the wealth of a nation is important. But also limited funding imposes the necessity for limiting expenditures to programs that are essential rather than "desirable."

NOTES

1. *Sewerage* is the pipes, pumps, and related equipment used for sewage treatment; *sewage* is the water-carried waste material.

2. Significant though these changes are, Third World people would live far longer if First World nations would allow greater use of pesticides and would not block industrialization (see chapter 13).

REFERENCES

Anon. 1995a. Questions addressed to Dr. Peter Piot, UNAIDS Executive Director, Kampala, Uganda. *The New Vision,* December 11, 1.

———. 1995b. The repercussions of the pandemic on the African economy, Kampala, Uganda. *The Sunday Vision,* December 11, 1.

Beal, V. A. 1980. *Nutrition and Life Span.* New York: John Wiley and Sons.

Communicable Disease Center. 1995. *Morbidity and Mortality Weekly Report.* U.S. Public Health Service, Atlanta, Ga.

Dunham, G. C. 1938. Military preventive medicine, U.S. Army.

Gotchy, R. L. 1994. Nuclear risks: Perceptions vs. reality. *Technology: Journal of the Franklin Institute* (331A): 41–51.

Hazeltine, W. 1991. Testimony, Water Resources Subcommittee, U.S. House of Representatives, hearing on wetland protection, October 31.

Hyde, C. G. 1938. Review of progress in sewage treatment during the past fifty years. In *Modern Sewage Disposal,* edited by L. Pearse. New York: The Federation of Sewage Works Associations.

Lawther, P. J. 1978. Private communication, November 10.

Listori, J. A. 1990. *Environmental Health Components for Water Supply, Sanitation and Urban Projects.* World Bank Technical Paper No. 121.

National Research Council. 1993. Effects of health programs on child mortality in sub-Saharan Africa. Washington, D.C.

United Nations. 1991. *Population, Resources and Environment.* New York: Fund for Population Activities.

Whitney, E. N. 1981. *Nutrition.* St. Paul: West.

World Commission on Environment and Development. 1987. *Our Common Future.* Oxford: Oxford University Press.

World Health Organization. 1990. *Tropical Diseases.* Geneva: United Nations.

———. 1993. *Tropical Disease Research Progress, 1991–92.* Geneva: United Nations.

——. 1994. *Weekly Epidemiological Record.* Geneva: United Nations.

Wright, J. W. 1994. *The Universal Almanac.* Kansas City: Andrews and McMeel.

PART II

Wealth and Resources

Conclusions

- The public sees industry as the major source of America's environmental problems and regulation of industry as the answer.
- Conversely, the Third World sees increased industry as the answer to their environmental problems.
- The Third World is correct. People of wealthy nations are not knowledgeable about how they solved their own major environmental problems. Nor are they knowledgeable about how to continue the improvement.
- The amount of improvement of the human and natural environments is directly proportional to the amount of wealth created.
- For First and Second World nations, deindustrialization, that is, going back to the land, would reverse all human and natural environmental gains.
- Urbanization of the human population is wrenching for the newly urbanized who usually live in slums. However, because so many people have left the land (are no longer farmers), the land can return to nature.
- Industrialization is the surest, noncoercive way to reduce the human population.
- Environmental conditions can be separated into three major categories related to wealth:

Third World. Those nations in which the annual per capita gross national product (APCGNP) is less than $1,000 are in the human survival phase. People are preoccupied with matters of human health. Birthrates are high; lives are short. Most people live directly off the land, and most GNP is from agriculture. Per capita, the people use the least materials. However, natural resources are being consumed at a very high rate because deterioration of the Third World's natural environment is ubiquitous.

Second World. APCGNP is from $1,000 to $3,000. This is a transition phase in which increasing industrialization, largely in metropolitan areas, and the higher resultant incomes, encourage people to move from the land to the cities. Birthrates drop. As people leave marginal agricultural lands, the land "begins to rest." Natural resources, including wildlife, forests, and soil, begin a rejuvenation process.

First World. APCGNP is above $3,000. First World nations use the most materials. However, they are characterized by multiplication of natural resources, including soil, water, forest, and wildlife. They also have low infant mortalities and birthrates and low population growth. Agricultural productivity increases at a far higher rate than the population. Farm incomes are at parity with other industrial incomes. Therefore, the flow of people from the land to towns and cities is slow.

- The concept of sustainability, that is, balancing population with resource use, is a second best goal. The resource multiplication that characterizes First World nations is far more appropriate.

CHAPTER 7

The Environment, Rich and Poor

To an extraordinary extent, few people in America appear to be aware of the major environmental gains that we have described in the previous chapters. Environmentally, Americans are not well educated. In this chapter we describe the differences in environmental perspectives of the rich and the poor. Because of their perspectives, the educated wealthy have difficulty helping the poor. They may also not know how to further improve their own environments. The impediments to improvement of the poor nations have proven to be great. Even after over $300 billion in aid over almost five decades, no Third World nation receiving such aid has evolved to First World status (Bandow and Vasquez 1994). In fact, many aid recipients have actually regressed in terms of both human and natural environments. Understanding the nature of the different perspectives and how education can create blindness are steps toward improving the whole world's environment.

COMPARISON OF ENVIRONMENTAL PROBLEMS

An April 29, 1990 poll sponsored by the *Wall Street Journal* and the National Broadcasting Company found that 66 percent of Americans believe the environment is getting worse.

Following are three lists of environmental problems. Table 7.1 summarizes the environmental concerns of the American public. Table 7.2 is the EPA's list of most significant environmental problems and a comparison with public ranking of concerns (Roberts 1990). Table 7.3 is a list of environmental concerns of Africans personally communicated by a U.S.-trained Ethiopian geologist, Mahdi Mohammad Shumburo. The Shumburo list first appeared in an unpublished paper by Dunn and Kinney (1992) written for distribution at the 1992 UN Environment and Development meeting in Rio de Janiero. It was quoted later by Shaw (1994). Shumburo was director of the Ethiopia Institute of Geo-

Table 7.1
Public Ratings of U.S. Environmental Issues

1.   Active hazardous waste sites (67%)
2.   Abandoned hazardous waste sites (65%)
3.   Water pollution from industrial wastes (63%)
4.   Occupational exposure to toxic chemicals (63%)
5.   Oil spills (60%)
6.   Destruction of the ozone layer (60%)
7.   Nuclear power plant accidents (60%)
8.   Industrial accidents releasing pollutants (58%)
9.   Radiation from radioactive wastes (58%)
10.   Air pollution from factories (56%)
11.   Leaking underground storage tanks (55%)
12.   Coastal water contamination (54%)
13.   Solid waste and litter (53%)
14.   Pesticide risks to farm workers (52%)
15.   Water pollution from agricultural runoff (51%)
16.   Water pollution from sewage plants (50%)
17.   Air pollution from vehicles (50%)
18.   Pesticide residues in foods (49%)
19.   Greenhouse effect (48%)
20.   Drinking water contamination (46%)
21.   Destruction of wetlands (42%)
22.   Acid rain (40%)
23.   Water pollution from city runoff (35%)
24.   Nonhazardous waste sites (31%)
25.   Biotechnology (30%)
26.   Indoor air pollution (22%)
27.   Radiation from x-rays (21%)
28.   Radon in homes (17%)
29.   Radiation from microwave ovens (13%)

Note: % = Percentage of population that considers the problem serious.
Source: Roberts (1990).

Table 7.2
EPA Ratings of U.S. Environmental Issues

	Ecological Risks	Public's Rating (7.1)
1.	Global climate change	19
2.	Stratospheric ozone depletion	6
3.	Habitat alteration	—
4.	Species extinction and biodiversity loss	—
	Health Risks	
5.	Criteria air pollutants (e.g., smog)	17
6.	Toxic air pollutants (e.g., benzene)	10
7.	Radon	28
8.	Indoor air pollution	26
9.	Drinking water contamination	20
10.	Occupational exposure to chemicals	4
11.	Application of pesticides	18
12.	Stratospheric ozone depletion	6

Note: Risks that EPA's experts feel should concern us most.
Source: Adapted from Roberts 1990.

logical Surveys, and for eight years was first director general of United Nations' Eastern and Southern African Mineral Resources Development Center in Zaire. He was also a geologic consultant with Dunn Corporation.

The EPA's and the American public's lists are similar in character although they differ considerably in their ranking of individual risks. The first three concerns of the American public, all pertaining to industrial wastes, do not appear on the EPA's list. Several other items are not on the EPA's list. Habitat alteration and species extinction (and biodiversity loss) are on the EPA's list but not on the public's list.

With the exception of concern about indoor radon, the problems on both lists are caused by industry. Habitat alteration, species extinction, and biodiversity loss on the EPA's list may not be related to problems in America. We have shown in chapters 3 and 4 that wildlife habitats and diversity of species of plants and wildlife are greatly improving in America. Thus, the EPA's concern would seem to be more related to loss of tropical rainforests and to budding commercial agriculture in Third World nations. The EPA's listing of stratospheric ozone depletion as an ecological risk, as well as a human health risk, resulted from the reported burning by UV-B of the eyes of sheep in Patagonia and New Zealand (the problem turned out to be pink eye infection rather than UV-B).

Twenty-eight of the twenty-nine concerns of the American public are health-related. This suggests that the public feels that human health should be the major concern of regulatory agencies. And, in fact, most EPA regulations have improved health as their stated purpose.

Table 7.3
Shumburo's Environmental Concerns

1.   Disease (sleeping sickness, malaria, cholera, typhoid fever, dysentery, bilharzia, AIDS, tuberculosis, trachoma, etc.)

2.   Soil erosion (caused by deforestation, devegetation, over-tilling, over-grazing, high energy costs)

3.   Soil nutrient loss (lack of fertilizer caused by poverty and energy-related high fertilizer costs)

4.   Lack of sewage treatment and contamination of water by human bodily wastes

5.   Insufficient drinking water treatment facilities

6.   Lack of refrigeration and other means of food preservation, poor food distribution

7.   Climatic and rainfall changes (resulting in part from deforestation and desertification)

8.   Depletion of water resources

9.   Loss of wildlife habitats (concern is primarily because wildlife attracts tourist dollars)

10.   Human-caused floods (resulting from deforestation and devegetation in general)

Source: Mahdi Mohammad Shumburo, personal communication.

The concern about nature in the EPA's list (items 3 and 4) puts the agency more in line philosophically with those environmentalists who have greater concern for nature than for people (see chapters 11 and 13).

The list of tables 7.1 and 7.2 have a nearly 100 percent lack of correlation with the Shumburo list. The U.S. public's list is actually a media list in the sense that the public must be told about most problems (that is, most citizens do not really see or feel the problems on a daily basis). Conversely, the African problems are obvious to even the most casual observer.

On comparing the lists, we reach the following conclusions:

1. Africa's environmental problems are Third World megaproblems—noncontroversial, pervasive, and highly visible. They are caused by low or decreasing food production, poor indoor air and sanitation, disease, severe social problems, low average human productivity, low average income, and generally poor quality of life. Third World African nations are economically inefficient. Their environmental problems will not be solved until this changes. Shumburo's problems are mostly related to life and death and the availability of the next meal or next drink of water.

2. America's problems, although often speculative or controversial, are routinely described as "catastrophic" or "devastating." There appear to be no words remaining in our vocabulary to describe problems of the Shumburo type, which may be from a hundred to a million times more severe in human terms (see chapter 12).

3. America could solve all environmental problems of the public's and the EPA's lists and virtually all the urgent environmental problems of Third World nations would still be present. In fact, they would undoubtedly be worse because *America could have helped the poor,* but chose to spend its wealth elsewhere.

4. The United States could solve all problems on its public's list and the earth would be no greener.

5. Solving several problems on the Ethiopian's list *would* make the world greener.

6. Solving problems on the American public's list could lead to reversal of many environmental gains of the past decades. Nonproductive use of national wealth has an environmental cost (see chapter 8, 10, and 13).

7. Environmental problems of Third World countries will influence more bird populations in America than anything else on the American list, because many of America's birds winter in poor countries where wildlife habitats are deteriorating.

8. The American public's list of environmental problems conclusively shows that America sees industry as the major environmental culprit. In contrast, no industry-caused problems are on the African's list. In fact, Shumburo sees industrialization as the *only way out* of the downward environmental spiral. (We conclude that Shumburo is correct.)

9. The American public's environmental problems are usually measured in parts per million, billion, or trillion. The health effects are often difficult or impossible to measure and are often based on opinion rather than factual proof (see chapter 12). The public must be told of their existence. Conversely, the Shumburo problems are obvious and noncontroversial.

10. The American public's environmental problem list will constantly change, depending on what the public sees in the media. However, the Shumburo problems will not change for any poor nation until that nation can industrialize.

11. The cumulative impact of all environmental positives and negatives on the health of Americans is overwhelmingly positive because Americans continue to live longer.

12. The cumulative health impact of all environmental factors in most poor nations is overwhelmingly negative because the people have short life spans and high infant mortalities (see chapter 8).

13. The cumulative impact on the natural environment of all activities in First World nations over the past seventy years has been beneficial in terms of forests, wildlife habitats, quantity of water, water cleanliness, soil erosion, and soil productivity.

14. Industrial nations multiply their natural resources.

15. The cumulative impact of all human activities in Third World nations causes destruction of all components of the natural environment.

16. Third World nations consume their natural resources.

17. Third World nations are likely to believe that First World nations' environmental problems are trivial.

18. Africa's list might have been America's list in the nineteenth century.

19. Americans largely look to *regulation* of industry to solve their environmental problems. The developing nations look to *development* of industry to solve theirs.

20. Solving or minimizing of the Shumburo-type environmental problems in the United States largely occurred *before* the environmental revolution and was a *normal result* of the industrialization process. Government regulations had virtually nothing to do with this success.

21. The American public's list is largely a summary of rich man's problems; the African list, a summary of poor man's problems.

22. In the Ethiopian's opinion, the best thing that could happen to the African environment is somehow to acquire America's list of "catastrophic" problems in exchange for theirs.

With such a huge difference in perspectives, the people of poor nations are very skeptical of the ability of the rich to really understand them, much less help them—and rightly so.

On comparing these lists we must ask: To what extent are America's—and other industrialized democracies—environmental concerns trivial? For example, were Americans to solve all problems on their list, how many lives would actually be saved? Specifically, would the longevity of the average person be increased at all? Is the wealth America spends on environmental problems money well spent, or could the same amount spent elsewhere be more beneficial to the natural and human environments? To what extent can "solving" America's problems actually be a source of environmental problems? And how many of America's problems are real problems? Finally, do Americans have any knowledge about the environmental trade-offs involved in solving their environmental problems? We answer these questions in later chapters.

THE EDUCATION PARADOX

The people of the wealthy nations are "highly" educated. Through television, newspapers, magazines, books, computerized data sources, and electronic mail, they have ready access to virtually all data ever collected by humankind. Computer technology makes data retrieval ever more efficient. Yet the people of industrial nations are woefully ignorant about the human and natural environments in which they live. Further, some people of industrial nations idealize the life of the primitive societies (see chapter 1).

Most people of the Third World nations are not well educated and have little access to data about the world. Yet their view of the industrial nations is that the industrial environment for both humans and nature is superior to their own. They are correct. They show their opinion with their feet, because so many are clamoring to get into industrial nations by any means possible.

Thus the education paradox. The less educated people of the world are more knowledgeable about the environmental realities of the industrial nations than are the "well-educated" people who live in those nations. (How education can lead to ignorance is described in part III.)

Finally, because it is so obvious to the poor that the wealthy do not know what they have or how they got it, they are skeptical of advice from the wealthy. And, again they are correct. Much of the failure to move Third World nations to Second or First World status is the result of blindness on the part of wealthy nations. In spite of America's expenditure of some $300 billion (see Bandow and Vasquez 1994), there are few, if any, cases in which any significant improvement in living standards has occurred. Clearly, education in wealthy societies may be an environmental hazard. (We expand on these subjects in chapters 10 through 15.)

SUMMARY

The environmental problems envisaged by the U.S. public are subtle, usually not readily visible, and often controversial. We call them "media problems." The environmental problems of the Third World are mostly visible everywhere, obviously life-threatening, and not controversial. The United States once had environmental problems similar to those of Third World nations but has been able to overcome them as an indirect result of industrialization and the wealth produced.

The American public, despite its unlimited access to information, is less knowledgeable about the industrially caused gains for the human and natural environments than people in Third World nations. Third World nations correctly see industrialization as the answer to their environmental ills.

REFERENCES

Bandow, D., and I. Vasquez., eds. 1994. *Perpetuating Poverty.* Washington, D.C.: Cato Institute.

Dunn, J. R., and J. E. Kinney. 1992. UNCED, environmentalists vs. humanity. Unpublished report to U.N. meeting in Rio de Janiero, May.

Roberts, L. 1990. Counting on science at EPA. *Science* 249: 616.

Shaw, J. S. 1994. Things are better than we think and could be better yet. *The Freeman,* June, 276–78.

Shumburo, M. M. 1992. Personal communication.

CHAPTER 8

Wealth and the Environment Quantified

In this chapter we show that improvements in the human and natural environments occur in a logical sequence related to a nation's annual per capita gross national product (APCGNP). The most significant improvements occur without government regulations. By quantitatively relating environmental changes to wealth, First World nations can better understand the origin of their own environmental gains as well as how to reverse deteriorating environmental conditions in Third World nations.

We relate the quality of various environmental components, human and natural, to wealth. We define wealth in terms of APCGNP, because these data are most readily available. Other measures of wealth, such as gross domestic product (GDP) or per capita income, would show the same correlations because the numbers are very similar. The GNP is an imperfect measurement, because it includes income from the service sector. Such income is really income redistribution. Industry creates new wealth. Perhaps fortuitously, the GNP usually reflects the amount and diversity of industrialization.

We can relate several aspects of the human environment to wealth. The most significant statistic for the human environment is longevity. The better the human environment, the longer people live. Other quantifiable parameters of the human environment that we can correlate with wealth are sanitation, water purity, and infant and general mortality rates.

The amounts of forests, wildlife, stored water, and soil erosion are measures of the quality of the natural environment. The major indicator of reversal of environmental degradation is reforestation or, more broadly, revegetation, and this can be quantified. Although quantitative information about wildlife for many nations is not available or is difficult to relate to wealth, qualitative relationships may be obvious.

THE HUMAN ENVIRONMENT AND WEALTH

Such agencies as the World Health Organization (WHO), the World Bank, and the Food and Agricultural Organization (FAO) have collected much quantitative information about the human environment. This can be related graphically to the wealth of various nations. Most of the data in the following pages are from Wright (1993, 1994).

Longevity

The most cursory look at APCGNP and longevity of the world's people shows wealthy people live longer. We can conclude, therefore, that the rich create a better physical environment for themselves. Even within a nation, people with high incomes live longer than people with low incomes. Figure 8.1 is a plot of APCGNP versus longevity of people of the world's nations.

The figure plots ranges for nations with APCGNP from $100 to over $20,000. The income divisions relate to the number of nations in each category, and therefore, the intervals are irregular. The APCGNP means are from $100 to $16,000.

Without exception, people of the twenty wealthiest nations live longer than people of the twenty poorest. Populations of almost all nations increased their longevity in the twenty years from 1970 to 1990. The health of the world's people is improving. Guyana is an exception. Russia is also a major exception because significant drops in longevity have been reported (Specter 1995). Russian men now have a life expectancy of less than sixty years. This reversal throws Russia back to Third World status as far as health is concerned.

As noted in chapter 5, increased longevity over the 1970–1990 interval in Third World nations is about 17 percent[1]; for First World nations, about 11 percent. Increased longevity in the United States since 1900 has been about 55 percent. The rate of improvement for Third World nations is greater than for the First World. Part of this improvement is because wealthy nations have transferred medical knowledge and technology to poorer nations. Also, small increases in wealth among Third World nations cause much greater beneficial environmental changes than do comparable wealth increases in First World nations.

The point at which a nation has the proper mix of enough food, disease control, and medical care for its people to reach an average life expectancy of 65 years is about $1,600 APCGNP; $3,000 for a life expectancy of 70 years. Of the 143 nations for which information is available, the populations of 54 have reached the 70 year average longevity mark. This includes all major industrial nations.

Figure 8.1
Human Life Expectancy and Per Capita GNP for the World's Nations

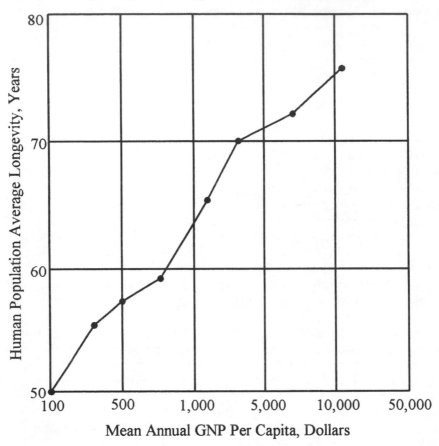

Source: Adpated from Wright 1994.

Drinking Water

Human bodily wastes contaminate much of the world's drinking water and are the major cause of such diseases as cholera, dysentery, and typhoid (see chapter 6). Figure 8.2 plots APCGNP against percent of nations' populations for which safe drinking water is available. Twenty-four nations have safe water supplies for 100 percent of their populations. Included are all the major industrial democracies, and all but 2 of the 24 nations have APCGNPs of over $4,800. The two exceptions are North Korea ($1,390) and Mongolia ($1,000). The Mongolian exception may be partly because the population of 2,200,000 occupies a large area. Therefore, they contaminate very little water with sewage. North Korea is anomalous for unknown reasons.

Figure 8.2
Availability of Clean Water and Annual Per Capita GNP

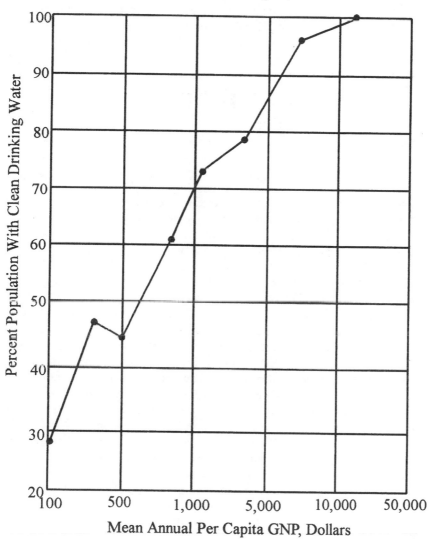

Source: Adapted from Wright 1994.

Forty-seven nations have safe water for 90 percent of their people. They have an average APCGNP of almost $6,000.

For the 33 poor nations with safe drinking water for less than half their populations, the average APCGNP is $440. Availability of clean water improves most rapidly with APCGNP changes between $200 and $1,750 per capita per year.

Sanitation

Figure 8.3 plots APCGNP against the percent of a nation's population with good sanitation available. The 25 nations in which 100 percent of their populations have effective sanitation include all major industrial nations. At the 90 percent level, 43 nations have good sanitation, and these have an average APCGNP of $7,000. The 36 nations in which less than 50 percent of the population have access to sanitation have an APCGNP of less than $800.

Between $1,750 and $3,000 APCGNP, the curve reverses from 76 percent to 69 percent availability. (The significance of this reversal is discussed under the heading "Second World, Urbanization Phase.")

Control of Diseases

Tables on world health do not indicate the economic point at which major diseases come under control. However, longevity increases rapidly to $1,750 (figure 8.1). Most of this rise is probably the result of controlling major diseases and the living environment. Drinking water quality, sewage treatment, and the infant mortality ideal levels all occur at a higher income. Somewhere between $600 and $1,200 APCGNP, the major debilitating diseases start coming under control.

Some indication of the ability to control diseases and other ailments can be found in the 92 nations for which per capita annual expenditures for health are available. The highest expenditure is in West Germany at $1,195, followed closely by France at $1,194. The United States is at $536. Perhaps surprisingly, Sweden is at $80 and Denmark is at $70. The people of all these nations have average life expectancies of 75 years or more. For First World nations, longevity is more related to general wealth and living conditions than to measured per capita expenditures on health.

The 36 nations that spend $10 or less per capita on health include the poorest on earth. Only the following 7 nations of this group have APCGNPs of $1,000 or more: Paraguay ($1,000), Camaroon ($1,040), Guatemala ($1,180), Colombia ($1,300), Syria ($1,600), Mexico ($2,680), and Turkey ($3,100).

Birthrates

Human proliferation can be a major environmental problem for Third World nations. They may be unable to produce and distribute sufficient food. Additionally, populous Third World nations excessively stress their forest, wildlife, and soil resources, because larger populations need more land for agriculture. The average birthrate per 1,000 people for 1990 for the world was 26. According to Whitmore et al. (1990), the population growth rate for North America and Europe has been below replacement level since the mid- to late 1970s. The eastern European nations that were formerly part of the Soviet bloc are currently

Figure 8.3
Availability of Good Sanitary Conditions and Per Capita GNP

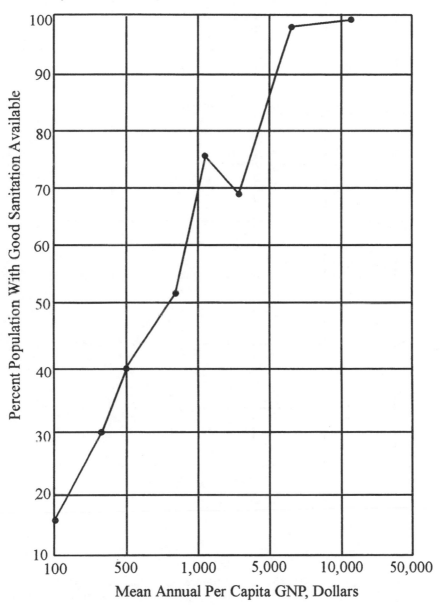

Source: Adapted from Wright 1994.

Figure 8.4
Birthrate and Per Capita GNP for the World's Nations

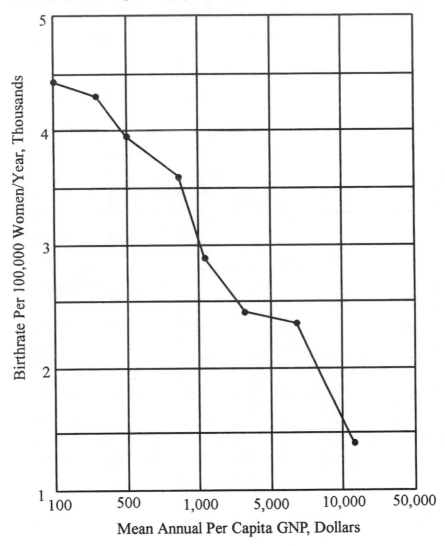

Source: Adapted from Wright 1994.

approaching this level. The average birthrate for Africa is 43 per 1,000; for Latin America and Asia, 27; and for Melanesia, 32. The highest for any nation is Malawi, which has 55 births per 1,000. Its APCGNP is $175.

Figure 8.4 plots mean APCGNP against average birthrates per 100,000 women per year of the world's nations, for the years 1990–95 (data from Wright

1994).[2] The mean income levels are the same as in the previous figures. It appears an APCGNP of over $3,000 correlates with birthrates at about the replacement level. Decline in birthrates is most rapid when the APCGNP is between $100 and about $3,000. The first major break in the slope of the curve occurs at $1,750.

Fertility rate is the number of children per woman and is another way of looking at birthrates. The 28 nations with the lowest fertility rates (less than 1.9 children per woman) include all major industrialized nations plus Cuba. Replacement level is slightly over 2.0 for industrial nations. For Third World nations it is considerably higher, varying from nation to nation depending on infant mortality and average longevity. The nations with fertility rates of 6.5 or more include the world's poorest nations plus Saudi Arabia.

The statement by Easterbrook (1990, 26), "and today there is one proven nonviolent means to bring down population growth: industrialization," is largely true. However, education and technology have resulted in Third World countries' use of contraceptives increasing from 31 million women in 1960–1965 to 381 million women in 1985–1990. Fertility rates for these nations dropped from 6.1 to 3.9 during that interval (World Health Organization 1991).

Infant Mortality

In Figure 8.5, the APCGNP per capita per year for nations is plotted against infant mortality per 100,000 births using the same income divisions as used previously.[3] Infant mortalities drop rapidly between a mean of $100 APCGNP and $1,750 APCGNP. At $1,750 infant mortality is 3,900 per 100,000 births. Infant mortality then *increases* to 4,200 per 100,000 births at $3,000 APCGNP. This coincides with a reversal in sanitation conditions that also occurs between $1,750 and $3,000. (We discuss this reversal later in this chapter under the heading "Second World, Urbanization Phase.")

The 21 nations with infant mortalities of 1,000 or less per 100,000 births include all the major industrial nations. Of these, Israel at $10,500 has the lowest APCGNP. The highest infant mortality is in Sierra Leone, which has 14,300 deaths per 100,000 births; the lowest is in Finland, which has 500 deaths per 100,000 births.

The 33 nations with infant mortalities between 1,000 to 2,000 per 100,000 births include some nations with APCGNPs of around $2,000: Chile, $2,130; Costa Rica, $1,810; Cuba, $2,000; Malaysia, $2,460; and Mauritania, $2,000. An infant mortality rate of less than 2,000 per 100,000 births appears to become possible at an APCGNP of about $2,000 per year but may not become general until about $11,000.

Infant Mortality versus Birthrates

Figure 8.6 plots infant mortalities against birthrates. We suggest that although infant mortality correlates with wealth, higher birthrates may be related more to

Figure 8.5
Infant Mortality and Annual Per Capita GNP for the World's Nations

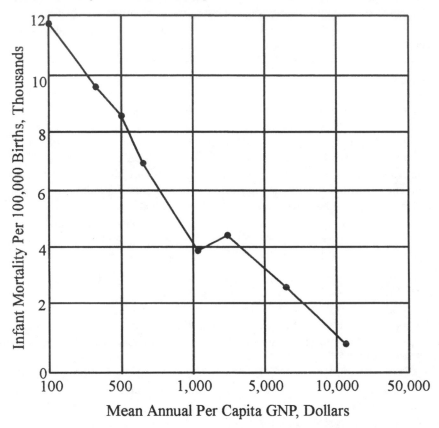

Source: Adapted from Wright 1994.

infant mortality than to wealth. This would account for Gabon, which has an APCGNP of $3,090, with a high birthrate of 4,300 per 100,000 women, and a high infant mortality of 9,400 per 100,000 births; Libya, with a birthrate of 4,300 and infant mortality of 6,800; and Saudi Arabia, with a birthrate of 4,200 and a high infant mortality rate of 5,800. These nations have average APCGNPs in the $4,000 to $10,000 range and should, to be consistent with other wealthy nations, have much lower birthrates.

It is a basic human characteristic that when infant mortality rates are high, birthrates are high. This is consistent with Easterbrook's (1994, 63) quote from Chivian, who said, "The technical literature is unanimous that when you improve basic health, especially child and reproductive health, birthrates go down." However, this is apparently not the only factor at work because the increased use of contraceptives has resulted in a significant lowering of birth-

Figure 8.6
Infant Mortality and Birthrates for the World's Nations

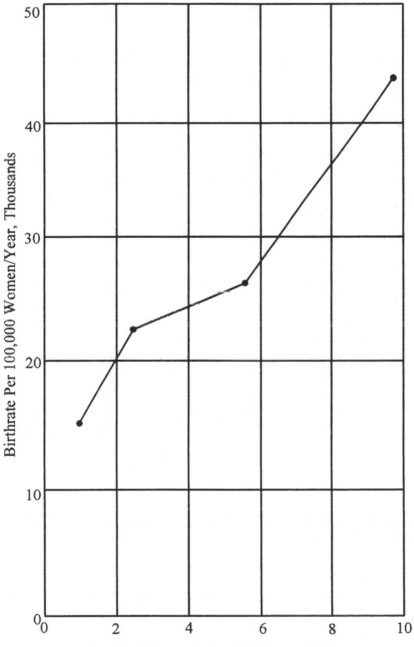

Infant Mortality Per 100,000 Births, Thousands

Source: Adapted from Wright 1994.

Figure 8.7
Percentage of Educated Population and Annual Per Capita GNP

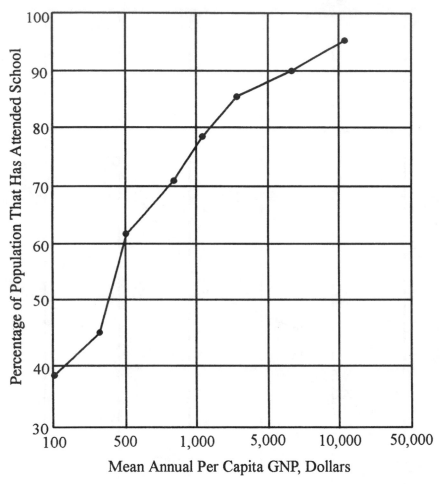

Source: Adapted from Wright 1994.

rates. Clearly, availability of contraceptives can be a major factor in some developing nations.

Education

The amount of education is an environmental factor. Figure 8.7 plots the percent of nations' populations that attend schools against APCGNP using the same financial groupings of nations as in previous graphs. As can be seen, the number of people educated increases rapidly with increases in APCGNP up to about $1,750. It increases more slowly to $3,000 and then very slowly after that. The curve is similar to most of the other curves presented in this chapter.

Education is important for the wealth-creating process and, therefore, is an important environmental factor.[3] Additionally, education about sanitation and personal hygiene can have a great influence on infant mortality and death rates even without appreciable increase in wealth. This suggests that technology transfers can allow Third World nations to evolve to First World status more rapidly than the current First World nations evolved. (In chapters 13 and 15 we discuss political factors that may influence this evolution.)

THE NATURAL ENVIRONMENT AND WEALTH

Chapters 2 and 3 demonstrated that improvements in the natural environment correlate with agricultural populations leaving the land to live in urban areas where new industries proliferate or old industries expand. In addition, high agricultural productivity per acre and efficient food handling go hand in hand with urbanization and restoration of nature.

Urbanization

Coinciding with an increase in wealth is an increase in percent of nations' populations living in urban areas. Berry (1990) summarizes the data. We have plotted percent urbanization in Figure 8.8 against APCGNP in dollars. The poorer nations are the most rural. In these nations, APCGNP rises only slightly as populations move toward cities. At $800 to $3,000, APCGNP rises faster, and 44 percent to 62 percent of the population reside in towns and cities. Between $3,000 and $7,000 APCGNP the rate of increase in the percent of people living in cities slows.

Reforestation

The thirty-four nations that are reforesting (growing more wood than is being cut) include all major industrial nations (see chapter 3). Currently, all nations with an APCGNP over $3,000 are expanding their forests.

Figure 8.9 is a plot of wood cut and used for construction (data from World Resources Institute 1990). As the figure shows, poor nations use most of the wood they cut as fuel. It appears that forests can expand when the APCGNP is between $3,000 and $4,000. The wood cut and *not* used for firewood is then about 50 percent. After this point, the rate of use of wood for fuel declines slowly with increase in APCGNP.

India and China, which have APCGNPs of $300 and $370, respectively, may also be expanding their forests, although the information about India is contradictory. A major reason may be the so-called green revolution of recent years in which these nations suddenly became independent of outside food sources. Their improved per acre agricultural productivity caused a decrease in pressure on the land, allowing them to reforest some areas. Whether they are able in the

Figure 8.8
Percentage of Population in Cities and Annual Per Capita GNP

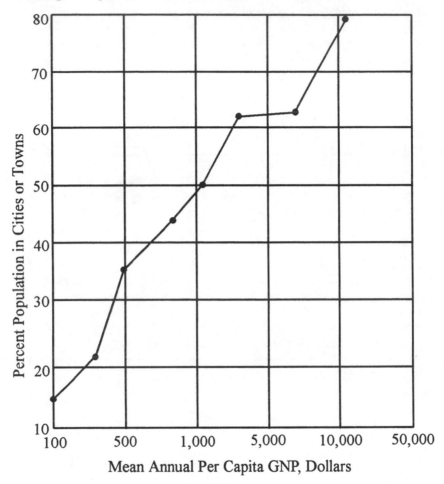

Source: Adapted from Berry 1990; Wright 1994.

future to balance population, agricultural productivity, and affordable nonwood energy is not certain.

Agriculture and Land Use

As shown in chapters 2 and 3, high agricultural efficiency is mandatory for forest expansion. In the United States, improved agricultural efficiency coincided with the shift of people from the land to urban areas. Forest acreage started to expand in 1920 when the farm population was 30.1 percent. Wood-cut balanced with wood-grown by 1940 when the farm population was 23.2 percent. Cur-

Table 8.9
Percentage of Wood Cut and Used for Construction and Per Capita GNP

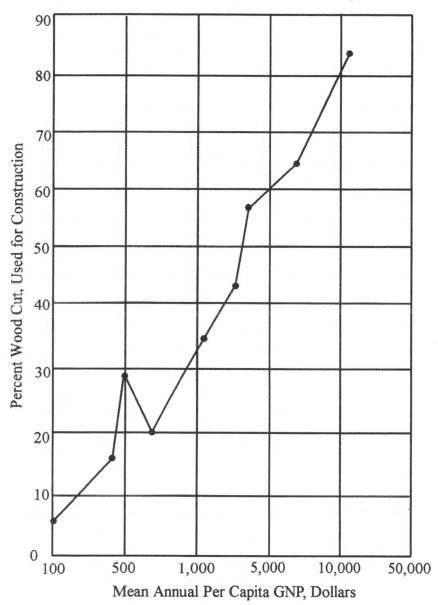

Source: Adapted from World Resources Institute 1990.

Figure 8.10
Annual Per Capita GNP vs. Percentage of GDP from Nonagricultural Sources

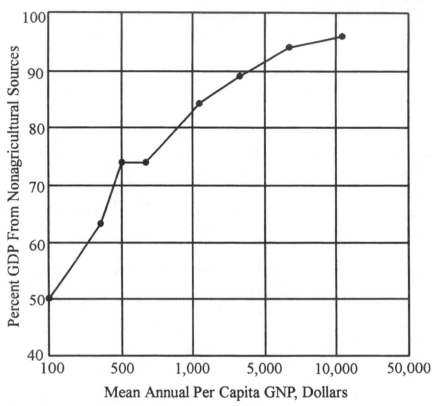

Mean Annual Per Capita GNP, Dollars

Source: Adapted from Wright 1994.

rently, with the farm population at 1.9 percent, forests are expanding at over 4 million acres per year, the highest rate ever. The shift of population from rural to urban areas also coincides with an expansion of nonagricultural GNP. The development of high-paying, nonagricultural industries motivated farmers to leave marginal agricultural lands for jobs in urban industrial areas. Thus, plotting APCGNP against percent GDP from nonagricultural sources is a reflection of the ability of a nation to sustain reforestation (data from Wright 1993, 1994). The major break in the curve of figure 8.10 is at $1,000 APCGNP. At this point 50 percent of nations' people live in cities (figure 8.8). Afforestation and refor-estation become possible after $1,000 APCGNP because a significant population has left the land.

If nations expand their agricultural industry relative to nonagricultural indus-try, their economies tend to regress. Table 8.1 summarizes the twenty-one nations that increased (or had the same) percent of GDP for their agricultural

Table 8.1
Real Growth and GDP from Agriculture

Nation	Real Growth 1980–1991	Percent GDP from Agriculture 1970	1990
Algeria	−0.8	10	13
Argentina	−1.5	13	15
Bolivia	−2.0	17	24
Central African Rep.	−1.5	35	42
Ghana	−0.3	47	53
Guinea - Bissau	+1.3	47	51
Guyana	−3.2	19	38
Iran	−1.1	19	21
Ivory Coast	−3.4	40	46
Madagascar	−2.4	30	33
Nicaragua	−4.6	25	35
Saudia Arabia	−4.2	6	7
Sierra Leone	−1.3	28	43
Somalia	−5.5	59	65
Suriname	−4.5	7	11
Syria	−2.1	20	28
Tanzania	−1.1	41	59
Uganda	+3.3	54	66
Venezuela	−1.5	6	6
Zaire	−1.6	16	30
Zambia	−2.9	11	17

Source: Adapted from Wright 1993, 1994.

sector between 1970 and 1990. The table also summarizes the real growth as a percent from 1980 to 1991. Although the year intervals do not match, the trend is clear. Most nations expanding their agricultural economies relative to their total economies are *reversing* their ability to create wealth. The only real exception is Uganda, whose real growth increased 3.3 percent and whose GDP from its agricultural sector increased from 54 percent in 1970 to 66 percent in 1990. However, Uganda also increased its food exports to neighboring nations. Thus it expanded its agricultural sector while increasing its GDP. Venezuela seems like an exception because it had negative real growth from 1980 to 1991, but the percent GDP from its agricultural sector remained constant at 6 percent. The drop in real growth, however, was more related to a drop in oil prices than to any real expansion of the agricultural sector. Sucre (1995, Λ 11) blames much of the problem on the International Monetary Fund (IMF) and the World Bank and the strings attached to making financial resources available to soften payments on loans. As a consequence, there is "a massive transfer of resources from the private sector to the pocket of the wasteful government." The results have been disastrous and typical for nations "blessed" with IMF loans (see chapters 13 and 15).

"Deindustrialization," in the sense that income from agriculture increases relative to other industrial income, *can be expected to reverse the quality of both human and natural environments.* We visualize nations undergoing such change as "traveling backward" down all curves in this chapter. *The idea that deindustrialization or "agriculturalization" of industrial nations will somehow help the environment is not valid.*

Wildlife

Changes in wildlife populations relate to per capita GNP in a general way, but specific information is not available. We described some changes in wealthy nations and in poor nations in chapter 4, and showed some remarkable gains in the United States. Great losses have occurred in sub-Saharan Africa (65% loss of habitat) and in tropical Asian nations (67% loss of habitat). Wildlife populations increase when people leave the land for the cities and when forests start to expand. This generally occurs between $1,000 and $4,000 APCGNP.

Erosion and Soil Regeneration

Ability to control soil erosion caused by human activities is far greater in wealthy nations than in poor ones. High per acre agricultural production allows the wealthy to till only the best and flattest land. Revegetation of steep, highly erodible slopes is a natural outgrowth of the industrialization process. As people leave rural lands and move to cities, erosion rates decrease; soil regenerates in large areas so more soil is created than lost. These changes occur at around $3,000 GNP per capita per year.

MISCELLANEOUS WEALTH—ENVIRONMENTAL CORRELATIONS

For hilly and mountainous areas, the average angle of tilled slopes is largely a function of wealth; the lower the angle, the wealthier the nation. However, we know of no systematic measurement of angles of tilled slopes. Steep, stripped slopes in such nations as Haiti, the Philippines, and Nepal are not to be found in industrialized nations. However, they were common in America and Europe in the 1800s (Marsh 1864, 1874).

The number of domestic goats, including those that have reverted to a wild state, is largely a function of wealth; wealthiest nations have fewer goats. Goats are among the most destructive animals on earth because their sharp, cloven hooves damage soil and because they eat almost any vegetative cover. A high goat population probably correlates with high erosion rates, but statistics are not readily available.

DISCUSSION AND CONCLUSIONS

To summarize the environmental changes that occur as nations became richer, we see three phases.

Third World, Human Survival–Resource Consumption Phase

Nations in this phase generally have APCGNPs of less than $1,000. The environmental problems that most occupy the attention of their populations concern water, food and human health, or, simply, survival. The problems are summarized in the Shumburo list in chapter 7. High birth, infant mortality, and death rates caused by smoke-laden indoor air, uncontrolled insect vectors, and unsafe water characterize the human environment. Their people are also poorly educated. However, small increases in national wealth permit large improvements in the human environment of these countries.

With human environmental conditions so obviously in need of improvement, people give little attention to improving nature. Over half the populations are rural, living directly off the land. Inefficient use of human resources is ubiquitous. People who must spend hours a day obtaining fuel or water and people who are chronically sick cannot be economically efficient. Producing the wealth needed to improve their human and natural environments is very difficult. In addition, wasteful agricultural practices and inefficient food transportation and handling cause a huge waste of agricultural produce. Inefficient use of land and energy resources is endemic. Thus, Third World nations consume their forest, wildlife, land, soil, and water resources.

Second World, Urbanization Phase

Phase II starts at $1,000 APCGNP and continues to about $3,000 APCGNP. The urban population starts at about 50 percent and expands to about 60 percent, and the wealth from nonagricultural sources rises from about 80 percent to about 90 percent. The force driving the urbanization process is economic, as reflected in the annual per capita GDP for agriculture relative to other industries. For Uganda, the APCGNP for the agricultural sector is $203 and for other industries is $1,583; for Zaire, $85 and $1,353; for Thailand, $264 and $5,224 (data from Wright 1994). The economic force driving people from the land is enormous. By comparison, agricultural incomes for the United States are about the same as for other industries.

Newcomers to urban areas cannot afford good housing, and consequently live in slums. This causes a decline of average national sanitation conditions and an increase in infant mortality rates. Industrial slums may be inevitable. However, most of the people who live in the slums have voluntarily moved there to be close to industrial areas where they believe they will have opportunities to improve their lot. Presumably, people living in industrial slums of the developing world are "on their way up." Bad though conditions are, in their opinion opportunities are better there than where they formerly lived.

The percentage of people who attend school starts at 80 percent, and the number rises to about 90 percent.

Because people leave the land, marginal agricultural lands start to revegetate with natural grasses, forbs, and trees. Nature starts restoration in wide areas—an early dispersed benefit of the industrialization process.

First World, Resource Multiplication Phase

At $3,000 APCGNP, over 90 percent of a nation's income is from nonagricultural sources and human longevity is over seventy years. Natural ground cover, including forests, continues to expand. New forests become more secure as less wood is used for fuel. As natural vegetation expands, soil erosion lessens and the wildlife that require trees and other natural ground cover for habitat increases. Agricultural efficiency improves at a far higher rate than population growth. Populations continue to shift to urban areas until the APCGNP for agriculture equals that of other industries.

Sanitation and clean water are available for most people. Industrial waste can be cleaned from waterways. Then, late in the wealth-creating process, nations are increasingly able to treat waste so raw sewage rarely enters rivers. As the wealth of nations increases, the human environment continues to improve, birthrates drop, and education levels increase.

Technology continuously shows the way to use new materials so that the total resource base expands.

NOTES

1. Although the 17 percent increase in life expectancy is impressive, it should be much better. We show in later chapters that First World policies about Third World pesticide use and development has actually caused millions of premature deaths. The 17 percent increase should be more like 25 percent.

2. Birthrate per 100,000 is used here to be consistent with data in chapter 10.

3. We conclude later that the wrong kind of education can reverse many environmental benefits.

REFERENCES

Berry, B.J.L. 1990. Urbanization. In *The Earth as Transformed by Human Activity,* edited by B. L. Turner III et al. Cambridge: Cambridge University Press.

Easterbrook, G. 1990. Everything you know about the environment is wrong. *New Republic,* April 30, 14–27.

———. 1994. Forget PCB's, radon, Alar (the world's greatest dangers are dung, smoke and dirty water). *New York Times Magazine,* September 11, 60–63.

Marsh, G. P. 1864. *Man and Nature; or Physical Geography as Modified by Human Action.* New York: Scribners.

———. 1874. *The Earth as Modified by Human Action.* New York: Scribner, Armstrong.

Specter, M. 1995. Russian health care in a dismally poor state. *(Albany) Times Union,* February 19, A-24.

Sucre, A. 1995. Mexicans beware! What IMF austerity did for Venezuelans. *Wall Street Journal,* February 24, A11.

Turner, B. L., III, et al., eds. 1990. *The Earth as Transformed by Human Activity.* Cambridge: Cambridge University Press.

Whitmore, T. M., B. L. Turner, D. L. Johnson, R. W. Kates, and T. R. Gottschang. 1990. Long term population change. In *The Earth as Transformed by Human Activity,* edited by B. L. Turner III et al. Cambridge: Cambridge University Press.

World Health Organization. 1991. *Reproductive Health, A Key to a Brighter Future.* Geneva: United Nations.

World Resources Institute. 1990. *World Resources.* New York: Basic Books.

Wright, J. W. 1993. *The Universal Almanac.* Kansas City: Andrews and McMeel.

———. 1994. *The Universal Almanac.* Kansas City: Andrews and McMeel.

CHAPTER 9

Sustainable Development versus
Resource Multiplication

Most environmental leaders have been reluctant to admit that there are benefits from industrialization. When such benefits have been shown, however, the usual answer has been, "Yes, but those benefits are not sustainable." The idea of sustainability became prominent with the 1972 publication of Meadows et al.'s *Limits to Growth*. They conclude that since all nonrenewable resources are finite, the world will soon run out of all such resources. The United Nation talks of "excessive demands and unsustainable lifestyles among the richer segments, which place immense stress on the environment"; "sustainable development is the dominant economic, environmental, and social issue of the 21st Century" (United Nations, 1992, 31). Leguey-Feilleux (1995, A) says: "our present economic model of prosperity is not ecologically sustainable." Nonsustainability is clearly an environmental "given," and not arguable. But are the lifestyles of the "richer segments" really unsustainable?

The concept of sustainability implies several things. First, resource-rich nations should be more prosperous than resource-poor nations. Yet Africa and South America have many resource-rich nations that are not doing well financially. According to Thatcher (1995, 4), "If resources were the key to wealth, the richest country in the world would be Russia." Conversely, countries like Belgium, Holland, and Japan should be the poorest. Natural resources, renewable or nonrenewable, are not as critical as other factors. Second, sustainability implies that we should save nonrenewable resources for future generations. However, the very definition of a mineral resource is highly time- and technology-sensitive. The American Indian's idea of valuable nonrenewable resources was radically different from that of the white pioneers. And their idea was different from that of modern technological societies. Third, sustainability implies that resources are static. Yet, as we have shown, the amount of natural resources available to technological societies is enormous, much greater than for any previous societies. *Technology creates resources.*

In this chapter we show that the industrial nations have already evolved be-yond sustainable development and that sustainable development is a second-best goal. The real goal should be to multiply or otherwise improve resources. As shown in chapters 2 through 6, the major industrial nations have long been improving or expanding resources. They can do even better.

PROBLEMS WITH THE SUSTAINABLE DEVELOPMENT CONCEPT

"Sustainability is the simple, common-sense notion of providing for society's needs today without compromising future generations' ability to do the same" (Porter 1994, 66). According to this concept, humans to the greatest extent possible should fill their material needs by such renewable resources as sun, wind, water, trees, and agricultural products. The population should balance use and availability of these resources. We should recycle nonrenewable resources or leave them in the ground for future generations as appropriate. Yet renewable resources alone cannot sustain a modern industrial society. Implied in the sus-tainable development idea is that the population will, somehow, get along with less, be more in harmony with nature, and be more agricultural (see Maxey 1990, 3; and Fumento 1993, 353). Yet virtually every nation becoming more agricultural is regressing economically and degrading its renewable resources (see chapter 7). Is "sustainable development" as it has taken form really viable? We see the following problems with the sustainability idea in the area of mineral and energy resources:

1. Mineral Reserves. Reserves measured by oil and mining companies are usually limited to twenty years or so because the cost in present dollars of proving reserves beyond that period is generally prohibitive. Consequently, reserve fig-ures are *always* finite and measured reserves are *always* depletable in a short time. This has been the case ever since minerals were first used. Measured reserves are economic numbers used in mine planning and financing and are proportional to demand, *not* supply.

2. The Earth as a Mineral Resource. The earth itself is a mineral resource. Even after human use, a resource is still part of the earth system. A cubic mile of average continental earth crust contains a significant quantity of the annual mineral needs of the whole world. Table 9.1 summarizes the average content of three common, useful metals, titania for white pigment and titanium metal, the fertilizer oxide (potash), and silica (SiO_2) for glass, in an average cubic mile of continental earth crust. The content varies from 90 percent of approx-imate annual demand for iron to 7,500 percent for silica. There are 57,800,000 cubic miles to a depth of one mile. The probability of ever mining the average cubic mile of earth's crust for any of its elemental substances is remote. How-ever, the point is that the substances are abundant and available if people need them.

3. Changes in Mineral Use. The idea of sustainability implies a static technology.

Table 9.1
Availability of Chemical Materials per Cubic Mile of Continental Crust Relative to World Demand

	Short Tons per Cubic Mile	Percent Annual World Demand (1992)
Aluminum	1,010,563,000	5,550
Iron	633,932,000	90
Magnesium	259,788,000	4,600
Titania (TiO_2)	130,515,000	1,900
Silica (SiO_2)	7,463,000,000	7,500
Potash (K_2O)	314,000,000	1,290

Yet the minerals used by modern industrial societies are largely the result of rapidly changing industry and technology. The American Indian knew virtually nothing about how to use titanium, talc, silver, iron, phosphate, potash, limestone, cadmium, zinc, lead, kaolin, bentonite, or any of the myriad mineral substances used by a modern technical society. Industrial societies, in a sense, create their own resources by learning how to extract and use them. For example, we extract copper from lower and lower grades of ore as the technology of extraction improves. Yet the price in constant dollars per pound of copper has not increased significantly. Primitive societies are primitive largely because they have not learned how to use the materials on which they walk.

4. Ocean Floor Nodules, the Untouched Metal Resource. Advocates of sustainable development ignore a major resource. Metal oxide nodules pave much of the floor of the oceans of the world. These nodules consist largely of oxides of iron and manganese with varying amounts of more exotic metals such as copper, cobalt, nickel, molybdenum, lead, and zinc. These nodules have three virtues: (1) the known reserves were worth $900 trillion in 1976 dollars (Krug 1995, 7); (2) they are growing faster than they could ever be mined; and (3) they are recoverable by dredging (Mero 1972). In 1970 the United Nations put a moratorium on deep-sea mining, effectively blocking development. Who shares the wealth? Who owns the nodules? Blocking the use of such an important resource is curious for an organization that is highly vocal about the need for sustainability (see chapter 14). In later chapters we show that making predictions of problems come true is a preoccupation of the political Left.

5. Substitution of Materials. Advocates for sustainability usually ignore the fact

that materials used by industry are constantly changing as technology and market conditions change. Substitution of one mineral resource or technology for another has occurred throughout the millennia and continues at an accelerating rate. Archeologists have named the major ages of early human history after the ability of civilizations to use minerals—Stone, Copper, Bronze, and Iron ages. These ages are really ages of substitution. Humans learned to replace stone tools with copper, copper with bronze, and bronze with iron.

Such substitutions continue. For example, silica fibers now replace copper in some telephone lines, and satellites replace long-range transmission lines for some uses. The much more common calcium carbonate now replaces clay in high-quality papers (which contain up to 30% clay mineral or calcium carbonate). We construct airplanes, automobiles, and boats, to an increasing extent, of silica and/or carbon fibers and plastics. Even bridges can now be made of such things and are lighter, cheaper, longer-lasting, and easier to maintain. Incidentally, the total annual volume of plastics in industrial nations now exceeds the volume of steel, up from a fraction of a percent in 1990 (Rogich 1991). The use of plastic composite materials is just beginning. The new materials, silica and carbon (in many forms), are largely from nondepletable resources. They are either from the Earth itself, can be grown, or can be extracted from the atmosphere.

6. Efficiency. Sustainability advocates ignore the fact that industrial societies move from low efficiency to high efficiency in terms of energy. They also use evermore common and economical materials. For example, industry has replaced the early material-and-power-hungry computers with small, energy-efficient equipment that uses silicon as its primary working component. Silicon is the most common metal on Earth; about 3.5 billion tons occur in the average cubic mile of continental crust. Additionally, the power consumed by computers steadily decreases with the energy from light powering most small calculators. Because of such changes, the GNP of the United States grew 58 percent between 1972 and 1990 while the total energy consumption grew by 14 percent (Malone 1993). Japan uses 50 percent less energy per unit of GNP than it did fifteen years ago and the United States uses 30 percent less.

7. The Bureaucracy Problem. Implied, but rarely stated, is the need to administer sustainability of mineral and energy resources. This requires a bureaucracy that is flexible, intelligent, wise, efficient, and, above all, omnipotent. It would foresee all changes in technology and the use of materials to administer the sustainability process. The power of this bureaucracy over the future of the human and natural environments would be awesome. Few people can imagine such an entity. There is little question that one result of such an all-powerful bureaucracy would be to freeze all technology and innovation. Imagine what might have happened if a ''Sustainable Development Bureaucracy'' controlled resource use starting in 1850, 1900, 1920, or even 1940? We would not have the abundant natural resources (forests, wildlife, etc.) discussed in the first chapters of this book.

Humans have an essentially inexhaustible supply of mineral materials provided they have technology and energy. Technology is limitless, but energy would appear to set limits. Fossil fuels have limits; coal may last but another thousand years, for example. The limits on forms of energy based on fusion or radioactivity are less certain, but ultimately may prove to be limitless.[1] Meanwhile energy is abundant and only governments and OPEC keep prices high.

The so-called environmentally friendly wind or sun as major sources of energy cannot provide the energy required to drive an industrial society. Further, a landscape covered with solar collectors or windmills is not attractive to most people and both may render large areas of land unsuitable for most other purposes.

Nor is biomass a reasonable alternative energy source. Burning wood for fuel has deforested large areas of the Middle East, Africa, South and Central America, Southeastern Asia, and Oceania. It is not possible for the present world population to use only biomass as its major energy source without rapidly destroying the world's forests, soil, and woodland wildlife. Ultimately, this would lead to a worldwide ecological disaster and to unparalleled human misery. Sustainable development that advocates the greater use of "biomass" (wood, crop residues, and manure) is promoting an environmental calamity.

TO TURN BACK THE CLOCK?

Based on the belief that environmental changes caused by human activity are *always* deleterious, environmentalists have suggested remedies. They assume that industrial nations are the worst offenders and that their use of resources is unsustainable. Remedies range from stopping or reversing industrial growth ("reduce and eliminate unsustainable patterns of production and consumption," from Principle 8, United Nations 1992) to totally eliminating the human population.

Turning back the clock is as impossible as is eliminating the influence of humans. Human activities have modified almost every area on earth. We cannot erase such modifications nor should we.[2] For example, we cannot deintroduce introduced plants or wildlife. We cannot easily remove man-made ponds, lakes, and reservoirs. Further, a world without modern pesticides, herbicides, lime, and mineral fertilizers would be a world stripped of forests and depleted of wildlife because humans would need much more land for food production. The new forests and expanded wildlife populations are products of the industrialization process, indirect creations of the system. *Turning back the clock would be environmentally destructive on a massive scale.* Yet many environmental leaders say that they want to turn back the clock (see chapter 1).

The alternative is to admit openly that we cannot reverse most human development without endangering both the environment and the human race. That said, we can look at the world as a place for humans to live in and enjoy. We should, without guilt, improve the world as a place for humans. In so doing, we will also make the world better for much wildlife. Larkin (1978, 33) said, "The future of the fish-and-wildlife movement does not lie in protectionism alone but rather in the vigorous pursuit of opportunities to improve on nature.'' He might have added, ''and to improve the future of the human race.'' (Protectionism, incidentally, is an attempt to maintain the status quo. It is akin to sustainability. Both protectionism and sustainability are second-best goals.)

BEYOND SUSTAINABILITY

Sustainability implies the production of resources at a constant (and sustainable) rate in equilibrium with a constant population. For thousands of years much of the impact of humans has been environmentally destructive, that is, nonsustainable. However, in the past seventy years, industrial societies have reversed many negative human impacts on the environment, thus showing the way beyond sustainability. Some land has produced agricultural products for thousands of years. For most such land, the yield of crops is *higher* now than at any previous time; that is, that land is not producing sustainably, but its production has improved *beyond* sustainability. Similarly, by expanding forests and wildlife populations and by expanding water resources, industrial societies are multiplying natural resources. Again, they have evolved beyond sustainability.

The future holds even more promise, because via genetic engineering humanity can accelerate changes in plant and animal life to better fill human needs For example, a new hybrid willow suitable for fuel can grow up to fifteen feet a year (Johnson 1993). Additionally, it may be impossible to predict the sorts of foods that will be available even in a decade. The resultant changes should make agriculture more efficient, consistent with predictions of the USDA (1989, 146).

The resource picture, particularly in industrialized nations, is not bleak. Although the industrial nations have done well as measured by forest, land, wildlife, water resources, and the human condition, *they can and should do better.* They should continue to expand resources beyond mere sustainability.

Multiplication of Resources through Mining

Mining can multiply resources. Stone quarries or sand and gravel operations when completed often leave lakes. Most lakes in the Chicago area are in excavations resulting from mining operations. Such lakes and ponds are common throughout the United States. The act of mining has: (1) created another resource, a lake; (2) enhanced the groundwater resource by replacing rock or sand and gravel with water; (3) increased the nation's wealth both by the original mining and by improving land value around the lake; (4) improved the habitat for some water birds; (5) increased the fish resource because most such lakes are stocked; and (6) expanded scenic and recreational resources. Not too many decades ago this sort of conservation was inadvertent, but mine operators now plan for such future uses.

Table 9.2
Gross Wealth Created per Acre, Agriculture and Stone Mining

Product	Gross Wealth per Acre per Year in Dollars	Years to Get Equivalent of Crushed Stone Value
Silage Corn	3,306	274
Wheat	1,344	674
Common Hay	141	6,428
Crushed Stone 50-foot depth	$906,408/acre[1]	—

Note: Crushed stone taken as 11.86 cubic feet per ton; assumed value $5.00/ton, production losses not considered; agricultural gross value per acre calculated from New York Agricultural Statistics Service 1992 (New York State Department of Agriculture and Markets).

[1]Generally three or more acres would be mined per year.

Mining improves the environment and multiplies resources in other ways:

- Strip mining of coal has disturbed about one million acres (Johnson and Paone 1982). The coal has driven much of the nation's economy. Environmentally, the use of coal for energy bears much responsibility for America's 140 million acres of new forest. The small "point problem"[3] of coal mining has helped create a dispersed benefit that is 140 times larger. In addition, mine operators have reclaimed most strip coal mine areas and put the land to other uses.

- The mineral and petroleum industries are among the best ways to create national wealth. The creation of wealth is essential for both the natural and human environments (see chapters 8 and 13). However, the whole mining industry has disturbed less than 0.3 percent of the United States since 1776 and about one-third has been reclaimed (Petty et al. 1980).

- The value of minerals per acre is highly variable, with the lowly common crushed stone toward the bottom end of the spectrum. Table 9.2 shows how the per acre wealth from farming compares with the per acre wealth from mining rock for crushed stone.

- Higher-value mineral products would, of course, create larger per acre gross wealth. Additionally, once the mineral is depleted, most mined land still has value for other uses. By far, the largest volume of mineral produced is crushed stone and sand and gravel, and most such excavations, by plan, have valuable later uses, multiplying resources even more.

- Mineral industries are at the very base of industrial society. Availability of minerals is essential to the production of wealth.

- Mined potash, nitrate, and phosphate are needed for production of mineral fertilizers. The very small area disturbed (a few thousand acres) has a positive influence on some billion acres of agricultural land in the United States and throughout the world—again, a very favorable ratio. Keep in mind that after mining, most mined land is put to other productive uses. (People often notice where reclamation has not occurred. However, mines were once on Manhattan Island and Maryland was once a mining state. Most people would be hard put to find a single sign of mining in either area. Most of the myriads of excavations have disappeared.)

- Strong domestic mineral and energy industries reduce the need to drain national wealth to buy mineral materials produced in foreign nations. The wealth needed to buy foreign mineral materials is enormous and contributes billions of dollars annually to America's hemorrhaging wealth. As America becomes poorer, the environmental gains from wealth will be in jeopardy. Yet the development of virtually any new mineral or energy source in the United States is fought on "environmental" grounds.[4]

- A strong mineral industry contributes to a nation's independence. A nation dependent on imports from "friendly" nations is militarily weakened if there is a war.

- Extensive use of mined materials instead of wood for home construction in America, Europe, the Middle East, and North Africa has helped decrease pressure on forests and contributed to reforestation (see chapter 2). Were the United States to encourage greater use of mineral materials for home construction, a further reduction of pressures on America's forests would result. The small area used for mining could result in the dispersed benefit of larger forests.

- Mineral materials, such as stone, concrete, and steel, are the major components of tall buildings. People living and working in cities need less land area, allowing more land for other uses such as forests and recreation. Also, per capita energy consumption in cities is low. Wyoming residents consume four times as much energy per capita as highly urbanized residents of New York State, the lowest in the nation (modified from Famighetti 1994, 152). From several perspectives, urbanization is good conservation.

The nation can do even better. For example, many crushed stone operations are underground mines. Underground operations have the potential of leaving space that is valuable for other uses. Underground space is inexpensive to cool and to heat, thus requiring little energy and insulation. It also requires little maintenance. Thus the use of one resource has created another resource: efficient space. Were tax breaks or zoning regulations adapted to encourage such operations, there could be many more. The whole nation would benefit.

Substitution

As previously described, the substitution of products characterizes the industrialization process. Substitution of plastic for metal, glass for copper, titanium pigment for white lead, and calcium carbonate for clay in paper are but a few examples. Such substitutions are done for economic, health, or technological reasons. Substitution is one more assurance that depletion of resources will never be a serious problem.

Industrial Efficiency

Industries are becoming increasingly efficient, largely through application of new technologies. For example, new computerized fuel injector systems in automobiles have improved gasoline mileage from about 12 miles per gallon to about 22; we once needed 115 pounds of aluminum to make 1,000 cans; now it takes only 30 pounds (Asmus 1993).

Use of the waste products of manufacturing occurs throughout industry and is a method of improving economic efficiency. For example.

1. Cattle in Florida feed on the peels that remain from the manufacture of orange juice. In a sense, buying fresh oranges is environmentally wasteful if we discard the peels. In addition, making one's own orange juice is economically wasteful. *Consumer Reports* (February 1995) says that a serving of fresh-squeezed orange juice is about four times the cost of manufactured juice (Anon. 1995). A half gallon of orange juice at $2.50 to $3.00 is both an economic and conservation bargain. Enough oranges to make a half gallon of juice cost about $5.00. Adding the cost of a half hour juicing the oranges adds another $2.50. Then most people discard the peels. The industrial process leading to a half gallon of orange juice creates multiple values.

2. Manufacturing steel in Detroit produces a waste product consisting of slag and pieces of steel. The steel company sells this mix to another company that breaks it up and magnetically extracts the metal. The reclaimed metal along with some slag is sold back to the steel company. The steel company uses the slag as a "starter" and the metal becomes part of a later metal charge for steel manufacture. The remaining slag is crushed and graded for size and used for highway pavements. The companies waste nothing.

3. The production of high-quality gravel in the Shorter area of Alabama resulted in millions of tons of waste sand after the gravel was exhausted. Now the owners of the waste sand ship it via railroad to the Atlanta area where it fills a need for sand in a sand-short area. Meanwhile, they spread the fine particles of sand and clay that have no use in construction on fields for use as soil for farming. They have stocked the excavated lakes with fish and waterfowl and other wildlife also use the water.

Efficiency in industry is pervasive and constantly improving. Improved efficiency is inevitable in an open modern industrial society. (Government may be the only component of society that appears to be decreasingly efficient.)

Multiplication, Modification, and Distribution of Living Resources

People have modified almost all useful trees, shrubs, flowers, vegetables, or domestic animals to improve their value (see chapter 2). With modern bioengineering technology, such changes should accelerate. Higher crop yields and other beneficial changes should continue as the USDA (1989) predicts, further multiplying resources.

Introduction of non-native trees has greatly improved the landscape throughout the industrial world. This also multiplies vegetative biodiversity. Shrubs and trees are not only used for decorative purposes, but people plant them for wildlife habitat enhancement (trees provide cover, habitation, or food). The wildlife population is, thus, greatly increased because people plant millions of such shrubs annually throughout the United States (see also chapter 4).

Fish

As shown in chapter 5, water impoundments have greatly increased the freshwater fish population in industrial nations. The greatly expanded water resource is stocked with fish. This was an original purpose of President Franklin Delano Roosevelt's farm pond program. In addition, some created ponds or lakes are used for fish farming.

Birds

Industrial nations have redistributed species of birds throughout the world and over their own nations. Wildlife agencies from the East through the Rocky Mountain States have reintroduced turkeys. The pheasant is from China and other nations. Of course, not all introductions have been favorable. The English sparrow and the starling are examples of birds that have no particular virtues but compete with native species for food and nesting sites. However, introductions have generally been favorable.

Animals

Introduction of wildlife is common throughout the industrial world. Sometimes introduced animals replenish extirpated species. Sometimes they improve a strain of wildlife. The stocking of turkeys, white-tailed deer, and piebald deer (a largely white variation of the white-tailed deer) as well as the reintroduction of moose in areas of the eastern United States and wolves in the western states are examples.

Of course, some introductions of animals have produced problems. The introduction of wolves is not a pure blessing, considering their predation on domestic sheep. The introduction of the non-native nutria in Louisiana (by mistake), the mongoose into the Hawaiian Islands, and the furry opossum into New Zealand has created problems. These animals have few natural enemies to balance their populations. Trapping controlled the populations of nutria, furry opossums, and beavers. However, the drop in the market for furs because of animal rights activists has caused their populations to get out of hand. The proliferation of these animals is at the expense of habitats for other wildlife.

Introduction of Crops

Few species of food crops are native to the region in which they are grown. Gore (1992, 134–35) has an excellent map showing how people have distributed food plants over the world. Much of this redistribution occurred before industrialization, but with newly bioengineered crops in the offing, the distribution of new food crops will probably accelerate. Even without the sophistication of most modern bioengineering, new strains of rice contributed greatly to the so-called green revolution in food production in China, India, and other areas of southeastern Asia.

Increasing Recreational Resources

Because of expanding forests and decreasing need for land for agriculture, the United States has seen a great expansion of recreational resources and the public's use of them. For example, there are now 34.4 million acres of wilderness area in Alaska and 56.5 million in the lower 48 states.[5] Between 1941 and 1989 the area of state parks increased from 4,260,000 acres to 10,983,000 acres (Clawson and Harrington 1991). During that same interval, visits to national parks rose 410 percent; to national forests, 1400 percent; and to state parks, 900 percent. This compares with a population increase of about 114 percent. The ability of an increasingly large number of people to enjoy recreational facilities is probably a function of increased wealth, better roads, better vehicles, and better recreational facilities.

RESOURCE SUSTAINABILITY, THIRD WORLD

The opposite of sustainability occurs in most Third World nations, *where forest, wildlife, and soil resources are consumed.* Efficient use of resources and human energy is the heart of resource multiplication. Third World populations do not produce efficiently.

Evans (1980, 396) pointed out that if we counted the calories lost in the wood burned in slash-and-burn agriculture, the ratio of calories grown in the crops to calories lost by burning trees is 1:20. Sustainability requires caloric efficiency. This sort of inefficiency does not occur in industrial nations.

It is only through development, urbanization, and the creation of wealth that the Third World can evolve to the condition of resource multiplication found in the First World. Will First World concepts of sustainability help the Third World achieve these things? Not according to Anderson and Leal (1991, 171): "Shed of its beguiling simplicity, sustainable development is a guise for political control reminiscent of the governments being rejected in eastern Europe. Not only has that form of political control despoiled the environment and deprived people of higher living standards, it has oppressed individuals.'' (We expand on the nature of the counterproductivity of much environmental activity in later chapters.)

SUMMARY

Industrial nations are expanding their forests, increasing many wildlife populations, improving soil productivity, enhancing water resources, and increasing biodiversity. In short, they have already evolved past mere sustainability to resource multiplication. Paradoxically, Third World nations, while using the least total resources, are depleting natural resources. Third World nations are threatening far more species of plant and animal life than industrial nations.

Industrial nations multiply their resources in other ways. The use of one resource can create others or one industry can live off the waste from another industry. Industrial nations are not running out of resources. *Industrial technology creates resources by learning how to use them.* Gramm (1978, 25) puts it clearly: "Civilizations don't die by exhausting their resources. They die by consuming the institutions that made their vitality possible." The critical institutions of mining, agriculture, bioengineering, science, and chemical manufacture are all under attack by the environmental community. According to Wolfe (1984, 15), ''To demand that production of minerals or fuels be halted or locked up in preserves is a demand for impoverishment of civilization.'' Impoverishment of civilization may be the exact purpose of the philosophical arm of the environmental movement (see chapters 10, 11, and 12).

We know of no reasonable alternatives to continuing the technologic changes that have been so successful in improving the environments of industrialized nations. Further, the only successful model for resource multiplication is industrialization and its associated technologies. To revert to former technologic conditions would inevitably destroy the huge dispersed environmental gains and reverse the multiplication of resources that characterizes the industrial nations.

Were the idea of sustainability as generally understood by the environmental community implemented by society, the result would be an environmental disaster. In particular, the present world population cannot rely on wood or other biomass as its major source of energy without destroying all the world's forests and the wildlife therein. Going back to the land would also be environmentally disastrous. It is the opposite, getting *off* the land, that leads to a better environment.

In addition, the implementation of the sustainability idea implies a massive bureaucracy that would be intelligent, wise, efficient, and omnipotent—clearly, the ultimate oxymoron.

NOTES

1. Most environmental leaders of the Left are against inexpensive, limitless energy (see chapter 10).

2. McNeeley et al. (1990, 51) suggest that human-caused changes are essential to many ecological systems that are considered to be natural by many people.

3. A "point problem" is akin to an excavation for a new home. We tolerate the unattractive excavation for the benefit of a new house.

4. We show that high energy prices are largely responsible for the deforestation of Third World nations.

5. Such large wilderness areas are a sort of ultimate luxury of America's industrial society. To block the development of mineral resources in such large areas may, in the long run, prove to be environmentally counterproductive.

REFERENCES

Anderson, T. L., and D. R. Leal. 1991. *Free Market Environmentalism.* Boulder: West-view.

Anon. 1995. Orange juice: How far from fresh? *Consumer Reports*, February, 77.

Asmus, B. 1993. Private sector solutions to public sector problems. *Imprimis* 22 (10).

Clawson, M., and W. Harrington. 1991. The growing role of outdoor recreation. In *America's Renewable Resources,* edited by K. D. Frederick and R. A. Sedjo, 249–82. Washington, D.C.: Resources for the Future.

Evans, L. T. 1980. The natural history of crop yields. *American Scientist* 68: 388–97.

Famighetti, R., ed. 1994. *The World Almanac and Book of Facts.* Mahwah, N. J.: Funk and Wagnalls.

Frederick, K. D., and Sedjo, R. A., eds. 1991. *America's Renewable Resources.* Washington, D.C.: Resources for the Future.

Fumento, M. 1993. *Science under Siege.* New York: William Morrow.

Gore, A. 1992. *Earth in the Balance.* New York: Houghton Mifflin.

Gramm, W. P. 1978. Debunking doomsday. *Reason,* August, 24–25.

Horn, D. R., ed. 1972. *Ferromanganese Deposits on the Ocean Floor.* Washington, D.C.: Office for the International Decade of Ocean Exploration, National Science Foundation.

Johnson, R. 1993. Electric utilities study an old, new source of fuel: Firewood. *Wall Street Journal,* December 2, A1, A5.

Johnson, W., and J. Paone. 1982. Land utilization and reclamation in the mining industry, 1930–1980. Washington, D.C.: Bureau of Mines information circular, IC 8862.

Krug, E. C. 1995. The wealth of Davy Jone's Locker. *Environment Betrayed,* December–January, 7.

Larkin, P. A. 1978. Where next in wildlife management? *American Forests,* March 30–33.

Leguey-Feilluex, J. R. 1995. European perspectives on the ecological crisis. *ITEST Bulletin* (winter): 3–5.

Malone, T. F. 1993. Ferment and change, science, technology and society. *Environmental Science and Technology* 27(6): 1026.

Manes, C. 1990. *Green Rage.* Boston: Little, Brown.

Maxey, M. 1990. *Managing Environmental Risks: What Difference Does Ethics Make?*

Center for the Study of American Business, Formal Publication No. 90, Washington University, May.

McNeely, J. A., et al. 1990. *Conserving the World's Biological Diversity.* Washington, D.C.: World Bank.

Meadows, D. H., D. L. Meadows, J. Randers, and W. W. Behrens, II. 1972. *The Limits to Growth.* New York: Universe Books.

Mero, J. L. 1972. Potential economic value of ocean-floor manganese nodule deposits. In *Ferromanganese Deposits on the Ocean Floor,* edited by D. R. Horn. Washington, D.C.: Office for the International Decade of Ocean Exploration, National Science Foundation.

New York Agricultural Statistics Service. 1992. *New York Agricultural Statistics 1991–1992.* New York: New York State Department of Agriculture and Markets.

Petty, P. C., et al., 1980. *Metals, Minerals, Mining.* Denver, Colo.: American Institute of Professional Geologists.

Porter, J. 1994. Saving mining is good business. *Engineering and Mining Journal,* October, 66–69.

Rogich, D. G. 1991. The future of materials: Plastic component is growing. *Minerals Today,* June, 30–32.

Thatcher, M. 1995. The moral foundations of society. *Imprimis* 24 (3): 1–8.

United Nations. 1992. *Earth Summit Agenda 21, The United Nations Programme of Action from Rio.* United Nations Department of Public Information.

U.S. Department of Agriculture. 1989. *The Second RCA Appraisal (Soil, Water, and Related Resources on Nonfederal Land in the United States).*

Wolfe, J. A. 1984. *Mineral Resources, A World Review.* New York: Chapman and Hall.

PART III

Politics and the Environment

Conclusions

- Far from leading to environmental enlightenment, America's extensive access to information has created an education paradox: the more we are taught about the environment, the less we understand (see chapter 7). Decades of consistent bias in education and the major media have created a misinformed public. This bias starts from the political Left.

- Obfuscation by the political Left is not random. It always exaggerates environmental problems. It minimizes, ignores, or denies most environmental gains. Paradoxically, the Left even minimizes improvements for which it is responsible.

- For decades, the leaders of the environmental movement have conducted a war against industry and the democracy in which it thrives. Indirectly, the war has also been against the enormous environmental gains resulting from industry (see chapters 2 through 6).

- Although attacked, industry is hardly a participant in the debate. And industry gives far more financial support to its enemies than its friends.

- The real environmental conflict has negative forces inspired by the political Left on one side. They see obfuscation as furthering their ends. The other side consists of positive forces that see facts as basic to defining and solving environmental problems.

- The major negative forces are within a culture that receives philosophical, financial, or political rewards from having a hysterical and misinformed public. They consistently stress the liability side of the environmental ledger. We call this group the Liability Culture. Included are most academic leftists, many schoolteachers, most environmental societies and clubs, most of the major news media, the environment and development component of the United

Nations, part of industry, some wealthy elite, politically correct "scientists," most government regulatory agencies, and the legislatures that enable the regulators to operate. It also includes many of the deceived "environmentally concerned" to whom this book is dedicated.

- The other side is the Asset Culture. It has produced most major environmental assets that are reviewed in the first chapters of this book. The Asset Culture has little awareness of its environmental virtues. It consists largely of "doers," people who work to manufacture products or render services. Included are most producers of wealth. The doers are so busy doing (manufacturing, growing, mining, or just working) that they may not even be aware that a cultural war is in progress, much less participate.

- The frontline philosophical arm of the Asset Culture consists primarily of market-oriented authors of many books and articles, some major media and minor media, mainstream scientists, and an increasing number of legislators.

- Some of America's government participates on the Liability side of the war through creating and implementing environmental and other regulations. In particular, regulation of industrial chemicals is done with virtually no attention to relative risks, economic realities, or environmental implications. This has led to a warping of priorities in which we squander enormous wealth. Regulatory expenditures bear little relationship to human health. Wealth expended tends to be inversely proportional to the number of lives saved.

- The regulatory parts of government are consistent with major media and environmental organizations, because they also exaggerate environmental risks while minimizing gains, even those for which they are responsible. A problem for environmental regulators and for environmentalists in general is that if they admit their own considerable successes, the public could conclude, "Who needs them anymore"?

- The Liability side of the environmental war is philosophically controlled by intellectual nihilists, the Neo-Luddites. They are mostly disillusioned leftist academic and intellectual idealists who seek the destruction of industrialization and Western civilization. They also seek reduction of the world's human population by any means possible. Leftist politicians, with the help of cooperating major media, have been able to attain power in part by hiding their leftist leanings behind a benign environmental face. However, the actual results of their legislation and regulations are far more compatible with the environmentalist statements of chapter 1 than with their benign environmental face.

- The Liability Culture is largely financed by hundreds of millions of dollars per year from wealthy foundations. The Environmental Grantmakers Association coordinates much of this activity.

- The Liability Culture has the best-financed legislative lobbying arm in America.

- The federal government is not monolithic. Nonregulatory bureaucracies such as the Department of Energy, the Department of Agriculture, the Department of Interior, and the National Academy of Science have often opposed the regulatory bureaucracies.

- If the Liability Culture wins the environmental war, it will continue to promote policies that have already needlessly shortened hundreds of millions of lives of Third World people. Its policies have also contributed to the loss of the Third World's forests, wildlife, and soil. Ultimately, continuing its policies will also be destructive of the human and natural environments of First World nations.

- With the possible exception of an intercontinental atomic war or the earth being struck by a huge extraterrestrial object, the nihilistic leaders of the Liability Culture are potentially the world's most destructive environmental force.

- The Liability Culture in America is now on the defensive because of the conservative political victories in the 1994 midterm congressional election. To improve the environments of the world, political moderates cannot compromise with the Liability Culture, particularly with the nihilistic arm. Compromise with a wholly negative, destructive force can only lead to incremental destruction.

- America's conservative talk radio shows led by Rush Limbaugh are major factors in the changes. For the first time conservatives have successfully challenged the predominately liberal (socialist) media. They have broken the liberal monopoly on dissemination of information.

- The future of both humanity and nature rides with the new political alignment. America's conservative, free market, and libertarian forces can win only if they and the public are both informed and vigilant.

CHAPTER 10

Causes of Public Confusion

Information Americans usually receive in school or obtain from standard media sources paints a bleak picture of the world around them. Because of this, the public accepts most environmental regulations along with the resultant costs.

In this chapter we analyze the mechanisms that have caused public confusion. As discussed in chapter 1, the major information sources have largely shown the public only the liability side of the environmental ledger. Many of the liabilities are fictional; virtually all are exaggerated. Environmental laws and regulations are meant to protect us from these liabilities.

Neither legislators nor regulators have established cutoff points that define when a given regulation should be terminated. For example, when is air or water clean enough? They do not define success. Hence, regulators are *encouraged* to perpetually find additional increments of chemicals to remove. Without a definition of success, environmental regulations are endless—endless, that is, if regulatory agencies can continuously cry wolf and, somehow, sound credible. Fortunately for regulators, the major communications media, the academic Left, and most private environmental organizations have found their interests to be compatible with those of the regulators. This group has created a misinformed public.

MECHANISMS FOR DECEPTION

Many authors have described examples of environmental deception. We review a few that are most related to the subjects covered in this book.

Anecdotal Reporting—The Bad News Syndrome

One of the most common methods of misleading the public is the use of anecdotal evidence. Using such evidence can discredit practically anything. All the deceiver has to do is to find failures or downside examples and publicize them. Simultaneously, the deceiver ignores any benefits. For example, a medical procedure may save a million lives a year and it may cause three deaths. If we hear only about the deaths, we might pass a law preventing the use of the procedure. Eliminating the procedure saved three lives, on one hand, but at a cost of 999,997 other lives. Environmentally, we have made such errors repeatedly. For example, anyone reading Gore (1992) would find it difficult to believe that any environmental benefits have achieved in America or in other developed nations because of industrialization. He stresses anecdotal negatives, while ignoring positives. This is intentional. For example, Gore says that the media should not discuss good environmental news (Anon. 1992). He says that the media should not give equal weight to both sides of scientific controversies (Gore 1992, 30, 39). In other words, Gore recommends that *the nonscientific media should decide the validity of scientific findings.* Such press accounts will "undermine the effort to build a solid base of support for the difficult actions we must soon take" (*Chicago Tribune* June 25, 1992; Gore 1992, 39). That Gore follows this dictum and that the major media have been following it for decades is obvious. Good news is hidden or its importance derided. This is a form of censorship.

The mechanism is clear. Gore says nothing about the 140 million acres of America's new forests and the contained wildlife, nothing about the vastly reduced soil erosion in America, nothing about the expansion of renewable resources in industrial nations. Instead, he says, "We are creating a world that is hostile to wilderness" (1992, 26). Anecdotally, Gore deplores the loss of a hundred acres of old forest in Virginia outside Washington, D.C., displacing the deer population (p. 25). His description would be more related to the real world if he had described the expanding forests of Virginia. He could have described the consecutive record deer harvests of 1990, 1991, and 1992, and how the number of deer harvested in Virginia has risen 29,159 percent from the first four years of record to the last four years. He could have shown similar data for adjacent Maryland or even for his home state of Tennessee. Instead, he leads readers of his book to believe that development destroys forests and wildlife. He implies we must stop or sharply curtail development. Chapters 2, 3, and 4 have shown that the dispersed benefits of development are exactly the opposite of the implications of Gore's words.

Similarly, G. H. Matschke, an authority on white-tailed deer populations, writing in the encyclopedic *White-Tailed Deer, Ecology and Management* (Halls 1984) says that Pennsylvania lost 2,059 square miles of forest deer habitat between 1961 and 1975. However, forests were expanding and during that interval the white-tailed deer harvest in Pennsylvania increased 147 percent, more than doubling. By 1991 it had increased 592 percent.

He also similarly describes the loss of white-tailed deer habitats in New Jersey, Louisiana, and Texas. Yet all three states have rapidly expanding deer populations. Clearly, any local loss of habitat has been more than offset by major improvements elsewhere. In each case, Matchke selected anecdotal problems while ignoring beneficial overall gains.

As another example, in 1979 the National Agricultural Lands Study[1] published a pamphlet entitled "Where Have the Farmlands Gone?" The pamphlet concludes that development is destroying America's farmlands. Using the anecdotal approach, the pamphlet shows that development often occurred on former farmlands. But:

- It fails to say that government is paying many farmers *not* to produce because we have agricultural surpluses.

- The USDA's own projections anticipate that by the year 2030 America should need up to 160 million acres less of the cropland now in use because of improved agricultural efficiency (USDA 1989).

- It implies that most loss of farmland is the result of development. However, the total developed land (cities, towns, homes, highways) in all America is only 46.5 million acres. Moreover, the USDA's own statistics show an overwhelming majority of that "lost" farmland and pastureland reverted to forest, a major conservation gain. Actually, the developed 46.5 million acres also contributed to 140 million acres of new forest because people left farmland to go to developed areas.

Tolman (1994) describes a similar situation with wetlands. Carol Browner, EPA administrator, claimed before Congress that 300,000 acres of wetland are lost every year. This number is wrong. A massive five-year government study released the week of July 11, 1994, shows that the actual amount is 66,000 acres per year. Even this is misleading. In a sense, the 66,000 is an anecdotal number. The government's own wetlands programs aimed to restore 157,000 acres of wetlands in 1994 alone. Therefore, America would gain 138 percent more than it lost. Not acknowledged is the expansion of wetlands in the past few years because of the activities of beavers (some 200,000 acres in New York State alone).

Because the major news media perceive bad news as more newsworthy than good news, they uncritically report the liability or bad news side of the environmental world. Easterbrook (1995) gives many examples of the major media downplaying or simply not reporting environmental good news. For example (p. 640), he describes how William Reilly, EPA administrator, was frustrated with press coverage about the removal of lead pipes in municipal water systems. The press said that twenty-one years would be needed to remove the lead pipes, but said nothing about the 90 percent that would be removed in six years. Their handling of the news "bordered on intellectual dishonesty" in their eagerness "to convert good news into bad." Similarly (p. 643), in 1992 when America ceased dumping sewage into the oceans, the change "went entirely unremarked upon owing to its positive character." Wattenberg (1984) calls this the bad news bias.

Although huge amounts of good news are available, Gore, Browner, the Agricultural Lands Study, Tolman, Matschke, and the media in general choose to stress the largely anecdotal, liability side of the environmental ledger. Thus, environmental problems are exaggerated in the public's mind.

Being on the Side of Angels

The political Left hides its motives from the public by taking positions on the "side of the angels." The environmental movement has been such an angelic cause. The public was ready because as it became wealthier it expected a better environment and it could afford it. Before the so-called environmental movement was formalized, people were already instituting many beneficial changes. For example, improved sanitation, cleaner drinking water, expanding forests and wildlife, and reduced industrial air emissions were already well underway. The wave was forming and the deceivers caught it, took it for their own, and donned the cloak of environmental virtue.

The ploy was tried and true. Klehr et al. (1995) describe how the Communist Party, United States of America (CPUSA), contributed Americans to help in the Spanish civil war of the late 1930s. The recruits were never labeled Communists although the overwhelming majority (79.3%, p. 153) were either CPUSA members or in the Young Communist League. Instead, they were "fighters against fascism." They fought in such units as the Abraham Lincoln battalion, the George Washington battalion, or the John Brown Artillery battery (p. 152). Thus, they were firmly on the side of the angels even though they were largely Communists. However, as thoroughly documented by Klehr et al., their first loyalty was to the Soviet Union and the major purpose of the CPUSA was a conspiracy to overthrow American democracy.

Politically Correct Science

Politically correct science serves the purposes of the political Left. Following are three examples of politically correct science and their consequences. They all pertain to the Earth's atmosphere: ozone depletion, acid rain, and the greenhouse effect.

The Ozone-Ultraviolet Problem. An hypothesis usually presented to the public as fact is that halogen compounds, primarily chlorine from chlorofluorocarbon (CFC) refrigerants (freon), destroy ozone molecules and thin the atmospheric ozone layer. Thinning of the ozone layer theoretically lets in harmful wavelengths of ultraviolet light (UV-B), potentially increasing the risk of cancer in humans (see Maduro and Schauerhammer 1992). Scientists can easily check the accuracy of the idea by measuring incoming solar ultraviolet radiation at the Earth's surface. The National Cancer Institute (Scotto et al. 1988) made such measurements. They showed that, if anything, the intensity of the critical UV-B wavelengths over large areas is decreasing. In other words, actual measurements did not verify the theoretical idea. The U.S. federal government has now withdrawn funding for these stations. In effect, America's government has blocked the obvious reality check. Further, Scotto, "a world-renowned cancer expert, . . . no longer is receiving funding to travel to international conferences to present his findings" (Maduro and Schauerhammer 1992, 158).

Not learning anything from Scotto's situation about the importance of being politically correct, Dr. William Happer, a physicist and director of energy research at the Department of Energy, found out for himself "what happens to federal scientists who ask the wrong questions. He was fired" (Bailey 1993, 62). Happer's question: "Why not measure directly the thing that worries you that is UV-B at the surface, not just reduction in stratospheric ozone?" Happer said: "I was told that science was not going to intrude on policy" (Bailey 1993, 61). Politics again took precedence over facts. Having questioned the seriousness of Al Gore's ozone problem in testimony before the House Energy and Water Development Subcommittee, Happer was prematurely let go and is now back at Princeton University. The federal government censors research that can cause doubt about their politically inspired ozone idea.

(Interestingly, the ozone hole over the Antarctic was first observed in 1956 by G. M. B. Dobson, *before* CFC refrigerants could have had any effect [Bast et al. 1994, 68].)

The environmental community has also failed to describe the enormous economic and environmental implications of banning CFC refrigerants. The cost of refitting existing equipment or of replacing refrigeration equipment will be enormous for the developed world—trillions of dollars (Maduro and Schauerhammer 1992). For the Third World, which has trouble affording even existing equipment, it is even more serious. These nations already lose 50 percent or more of their produced food largely to spoilage. Hecht (1992) suggests that annual Third World death tolls could be in the 20 to 40 million range because of increased famine and disease due to lack of refrigeration. Also anything that increases food loss forces people to use yet more land to produce food they need. The stress on their natural environment, already severe, will increase. Additionally, lack of affordable refrigeration limits storage of temperature-sensitive medicine for immunization and treatment of diseases.

Bast et al. (1994, 79) summarize the CFC "problem" concisely: "If ever the environmental movement abandoned common sense, it did so in its campaign against CFC's."

The Acid Rain Obfuscation. Acid rain has theoretically caused acidity of New York's high Adirondack lakes. However, many pristine lakes were originally acidic. Then, with deforestation and burning of the slash in the late 1800s and early 1900s, water percolating through alkaline wood ash made many high country lakes alkaline. After water leached out the alkali and acidic conifers returned to the land, lakes again became acidic. The National Acid Precipitation and Pollutant study (NAPAP), prepared by a select group of scientists at Congress's request at a cost of $500 to $600 million, described this process. The NAPAP study was to help evaluate the Clean Air Act Amendments of 1990. Congress should have been elated to find that the expensive research they sponsored showed that they would not have to pass laws leading to even more expensive regulations. Instead, Congress ignored the findings of the NAPAP study, took the politically correct "scientific" position, and passed the law.

Senator John Glenn (D-Ohio) in frustration said, "We spend over $500 million on the most definitive study of acid precipitation that has ever been done in the history of the world and then we do not want to listen to what (the experts) say" (Bast et al. 1994, 81).

A member of the NAPAP scientific team, Dr. Edward Krug, insisted on complaining about Congress's action in speeches and in writing. His reward was loss of funds for research and an inability to get a new professorship at several universities. He now writes a newsletter aptly entitled *Environment Betrayed.*

The Greenhouse Effect—A Future Problem? Environmentalist leaders have replaced their old idea that human activities could lead to a new glacial age with the idea that human activities can lead to destructive heating of the Earth— the greenhouse effect. The so-called greenhouse effect results from an atmospheric buildup of certain gases, including carbon dioxide, in the atmosphere. Like glass in a greenhouse, these gases let wavelengths of visible light through to heat the Earth's surface. The rebounding wavelengths of heat energy are in the infrared range and do not readily escape through glass or through the greenhouse gases. Therefore, heating occurs.

Trouble is, scientists do not directly measure carbon dioxide in the atmosphere. They measure infrared absorption, and assume that differences in carbon dioxide content cause the changes. But other gases, far more common than carbon dioxide, are also infrared absorbents and are increasing (Janorowski et al. 1992). Further, scientists disagree whether heating of the Earth is good or bad. However, few would disagree that a new ice age covering the northern United States with thousands of feet of ice would be infinitely worse than some warming of the Earth.

Not discussed in the debate about the greenhouse effect is the fact that the "culprit," carbon dioxide, is *plant food.* According to Robinson (1994), "The concomitant benefits to the health of world vegetation from carbon dioxide release are documented in thousands of experimental studies" (see also Wittwer, 1992). The television documentary "The Greening of Planet Earth" (Archive Films, Ltd., sponsored by the Department of Agriculture and the Department of Energy) shows that the added carbon dioxide will increase crop yields by 50 percent or more, increase tree growth rates, and decrease water requirements for crops. As shown in chapter 2, increasing crop yields would indirectly increase forest cover and expand wildlife populations. Although some European television stations showed the documentary, the major TV networks in America have not. It is politically incorrect. In effect, the major media are censoring good news they do not want the public to hear.

Scientists disagree about whether the Earth is cooling or heating. A Gallup poll conducted on January 13, 1992, of members of the American Geophysical Union and the American Meteorological Society revealed that only 18 percent thought that some global warming may have occurred. Controversy is understandable because such measurements are notoriously difficult to make. The most reliable measurements (from satellites) do not verify the predicted temperature increases (Bast et al. 1994, 57). Instead, an atmospheric cooling trend appears to have occurred since 1987. *Reader's Digest* (Anon. 1994a, 132) printed the same temperature curves.

Taking a more historic view, Feng and Epstein (1994) dendrochronologically dated bristlecone pines and determined temperatures back 8,000 years using hydrogen isotopes. They concluded that for the past 6,800 years the Earth's atmospheric temperatures have been dropping. Their conclusion, they found, is consistent with scientific data gathered from ice cores and analyses of treeline fluctuations and pollen. They conclude, therefore, that the changes they observed are probably global. Further, Jaworowski et al. (1992, 4) conclude, based on studies of Arctic temperatures and increases in polar ice, that temperatures have been dropping for the past two decades. As Norwegians, Jaworowski et al. look favorably upon an increase in temperatures because it would extend their crop-growing season. Unfortunately, they conclude that increasing temperatures are less likely than cooling ones.

Concurring, the George C. Marshall Institute (1995), based partly on satellite data, concluded that during the past 16 years, global temperatures *cooled* at the rate of 0.06°C per decade (p. 19). They also found that Arctic temperatures cooled at the rate of 0.27°C per decade during the 40 years between 1950 and 1990.

Singer et al. (1991) and the George C. Marshall Institute (1995) conclude that environmentalists exaggerate the danger of global warming and that there is no need for a hasty political response. The article by Singer et al. is particularly significant because Revelle was a mentor of Vice President Gore and was quoted by Gore (1992, 4–6, 91) to document Gore's greenhouse warming concerns. With more recent data, Revelle, a scientist, changed his opinion. Gore, a politician, did not.

Finally, any attempt to reduce the carbon dioxide of the Earth's atmosphere could create major and costly changes in energy use. This is particularly a problem because "activists" have also blocked non-carbon dioxide producing atomic energy and hydropower projects over the world and are also against cold fusion power. It would seem that "activists" are simply against cheap energy. Expensive energy, however, is a huge problem for the Third World. Without cheap energy, human suffering will continue and developing nations will stress their forests, wildlife, and soil. *Cheap energy favors the environment.*

We see that actual measurements of UV-B and of historic temperatures show that the ozone and greenhouse problems may not exist. The NAPAP study shows that the acid rain problem is trivial. Says Princeton's Professor Happer, "With regard to global climate issues, we are experiencing politically correct science.

...Instead of policy being guided by factual information, the facts are being forced to fit the policy requirements of certain politicians, bureaucrats, and activists'' (Bailey 1993, 62). Yet some politicians, led by Al Gore, conclude that we already know enough and must act now. Gore concludes that we must censor any research that would question the currently politically correct ideas. Clearly, the Al Gores of this world, including their UN environmental counterpart, Maurice Strong, are willing to depress the whole world economy, to damage both the human and natural environments, to save us from UV-B, acid rain, and carbon dioxide. Yet they do not even know whether we are approaching another ice age (1970s idea), worldwide heating (1980s idea), or another ice age (1990s newest suggestion).

What the Public Should *Not* Know

Consistent with the bad news syndrome and politically correct science, major communications media have long decided what the public should *not* know. For example, they long resisted showing the documentary about the benefits of carbon dioxide.

One of the more astonishing phenomena in the history of human knowledge is that even with all the data about the environment available to everyone, the public is incredibly ignorant. We have shown that environmental ignorance increases with "education" and with exposure to communication media. Seitz (1990, 58) says: "mere facts cannot prevail over the raw semiotic power of so excellent a medium, even though its masters may be leading us into a future that may be beyond economic repair."

The major media have largely depicted the environmental debate as between only environmentalists and industry—the classic good guys versus bad guys. The major media do not show (1) that free market forces are the other side of the debate and that (2) many in industry and business actually do not like free markets because they increase competition. The free market side is strongly pro-consumer, not pro-business.

Systematically misinforming the public about environmental matters is part of a larger picture in which the major media for decades have hidden some facts from the public. "Public awareness of world events is largely the creation of the mass media" (Hollander 1994, 34). Hollander says (p. 30) that "There have been no television documentaries of the Gulag, not on public television, CNN or the networks. Russian television programs about these mass murders have not been shown on American television." (Some of these documentaries have appeared recently.)

What did they hide? Edwards (1994, 32) sums it up: "murder of several hundred thousand Don Cossacks in 1919, the starving to death of about five million Ukrainian peasants in 1932–1933, the extermination of perhaps 6.5 million Kulaks (well-off peasants) from 1930 to 1937, the execution of one million Party members in the Great Terror of 1937–1938, and the massacre of all Trotskyists in the Gulag.'' Rummel (1995, 4) estimates the total murders between 1917 and 1987 at 61,917,000. Additionally, Mao Tse-Tung killed 35,236,000 of his own people.

The media enthusiastically shows Adolf Hitler's atrocities ad infinitum (20,946,000 deaths according to Rummel 1995, 4). However, they rarely mention similar deeds by monsters of the Left, Joseph Stalin and Mao Tse-Tung.

For many years, the major media have shown only what the political Left wanted us to see. Environmentally, America's media have concentrated on news that makes America and its industrialization look bad by exaggerating environmental threats.

Guilt by Classification

America's public is not scientifically knowledgeable. It has been easy to deceive the public by first finding a substance that may be dangerous to humans. Regulators then classify as many other materials as possible with the harmful substance by showing a chemical similarity.

A classic example is asbestos regulation (National Institute for Occupational Safety and Health [NIOSH] and EPA). One type of asbestos, blue asbestos (crocidolite), is a potent carcinogen. Brown asbestos (anthophyllite asbestos) is evidently carcinogenic but nowhere near as deadly as crocidolite. The most common asbestos (95% of that used in America) is white asbestos (chrysotile). White asbestos is ubiquitous in California. Serpentine, the state rock, outcrops over two thousand square miles of the state and is virtually always rich in chrysotile asbestos. Yet Californians do not suffer from a cancer epidemic. Additionally, epidemiologists have found that people living among the piles of asbestos-bearing rock in Quebec's asbestos mining districts do not have increased rates of asbestos-related cancer.

However, America's regulators classify all types of asbestos as the same and treat them as though they were equally dangerous (contradicting their own data). Further, they redefined asbestos so it would include chemically similar minerals that were not asbestos at all. These were nonflexible, brittle counterparts. These counterparts do not cause cancer in any normal[2] exposures.

The regulatory agencies have always known these facts. Mineralogists from the United States Geological Survey and the United States Bureau of Mines, among others, described them. Only in the past few years have regulators admitted ''error''—well over $150 billion in asbestos remediation costs later.

Chlorine is another example. Chlorine gas is deadly to humans and some chlorine compounds are dangerous if taken internally. Some chlorine compounds may be carcinogenic to laboratory animals. The EPA seeks to ban many compounds simply because they contain chlorine. (They apparently do not include table salt and sea water.) Elimination of chlorine and chlorine compounds would cost American consumers about $91 billion annually, with no assurance that the substitutes would, themselves, be harmless (Bolch and Lyons 1994). Gribble

(1994) says that if the government bans the industrial use of chlorine and chlorine compounds, as proposed by the Clinton administration, the public would not have available over sixty pharmaceuticals containing chlorine. Chlorine compounds are used to treat depression, arthritis, fungal diseases, glaucoma, inflammation, psoriasis, allergies, infections, osteoporosis, ulcers, malaria, coronary disease, and cancer.

The guilt by classification ploy is an old idea.

"All Natural"

Decades of biased reporting have created a public chemiphobia about industrial chemicals. Some industries reinforce the chemiphobia by using such expressions as "all natural" or "no preservatives."

Many Americans now appear to believe that chemicals made by people are likely to be toxic or carcinogenic, but those made by nature are not. However, people now consume in food ten thousand times more natural carcinogens than industrial chemicals (Ames et al. 1990). Yet the public worries only about the latter and the EPA only regulates the latter. We show in chapter 11 that chemiphobia is catastrophic.

Synthetic Balancing

The practice of synthetic balancing is almost ubiquitous among those who wish to appear balanced. They show their balance or lack of bias by modifying their positions with a qualifying condition that they know will not be credible. Or the practice shows up as study committees on various controversial subjects with the committees weighted to produce a desired set of conclusions. It is common in newspaper articles that describe environmental "problems" in detail and then "balance" their reportage by quoting a representative of industry. The paper knows that the public will not believe industry's representative because he or she is an interested party.

A newspaper can achieve synthetic balance by showing that there is another side, but hiding it in the article. An article by William K. Stevens of the New York Times Service is classic. The article "Warning to UN on Pollution and Climate" appeared in the *International Herald Tribune* (September 22, 1994, 9). The use of the pejorative word "pollution" in the title sets the tone. The article describes the carbon dioxide buildup in the atmosphere, and an accompanying sketch shows smoking factory buildings surrounded by a deforested area. The subliminal association of industry and deforestation is undeniable. Stevens's politically correct position is quite clear. He quotes the Intergovernmental Panel on Climate Change (a weighted panel?), who said that the Earth's surface temperatures might rise by three to eight degrees Fahrenheit. Stevens shows his "balance" two-thirds of the way down the second column by saying the panel's conclusions have "been attacked by scientists who reached contrary conclusions." There is, of course, little doubt about Stevens's position and most people would probably not even see his "balancing" sentence. Stevens's article is consistent with Gore's admonition: the press should not give equal weight to conflicting scientific ideas if one idea (the preferred) is politically correct.

Speculations

The world has never suffered a shortage of environmental speculations. Environmental scientists in the 1970s speculated that the world would soon have a new ice age because of human activities. They replaced that speculation with the one that says the world will heat up because of human activities. The public appears to have accepted both speculations.

Perhaps the leading environmental speculator has been Dr. Paul Ehrlich of Stanford University. Ehrlich's scenario (Ehrlich 1970a, 1970b), articulated in the 1970s, ran as follows:

- The end of the whaling industry would come in 1973, the end of Peruvian anchovy fishing in 1975, and the disappearance of scores of other fisheries by 1977.
- The end of the oceans would occur in the summer of 1979 because of DDT poisoning.
- The green revolution would fail.
- Americans, by refusing to pay increased taxes, would be forced to close many schools.
- Water rationing would be required in 1,723 municipalities starting in 1974
- Air pollution would cause over 200,000 deaths in America in the early 1970s and Earth would become uninhabitable by 1990.
- In October 1973 the Department of Health, Education, and Welfare would announce that Americans born since 1946 (when DDT usage began) now have a life expectancy of only forty-nine years. Life expectancy would drop to forty-two years by 1980.
- In 1973 there would be general concern over the reduction of bird populations because of DDT.
- By September 1979 all important animal life in the sea would become extinct.
- Massive famine would occur in the 1980s.
- In about 900 years there could be 60 trillion people on Earth, about 100 persons per square yard of land and water (Ehrlich 1970b, 220).[3]

Ehrlich's ability to make incorrect predictions appears limitless. In the heady 1970s days of the early environmental movement almost any gloomy prediction would be seriously published. To question such speculations was to be antienvironmental—a major sin. This psychology still exists to varying degrees.

Public schools often teach such environmental speculations as facts. Children learn at an early age that the world, particularly the industrial world, has serious environmental problems. The problems, they learn, are largely the result of industry and technology. The National Education Association is responsible for much environmental miseducation (see chapter 1). London (1984, 157) of New York University says that of some thirty-one geography texts, almost half of those reviewed describe a possible catastrophic "future in developing and developed nations alike." Sewall (1994, A14), director of the American Textbook Council, quotes the 1985 edition of Todd and Curtis's *The American Nation:* "One 1982 report claimed that at least 140 species were vanishing each day! Activists are campaigning to slow this process and save at least some species from extinction." Considering the enormous expansion of so many wildlife populations in the United States and other industrial nations, this is rank speculation. Schools reinforce environmental fears and hysteria by giving credence to wild, unscientific speculations.

The Misquote

Information supplied in support of Senator Patrick Leahy's so-called Circle of Poison bill included this quotation: "Every year, the World Health Organization (WHO) estimates 220,000 people die of pesticide poisoning." Thanks to research by New York State Commissioner of Agriculture Richard McGuire (McGuire 1992), the actual quote taken from the WHO document is: "Of the more than 220,000 intentional and unintentional deaths from acute poisoning, suicide accounts for approximately 91 percent, occupational exposure for 6 percent and other causes, including food contamination, for 3 percent."

Sommers (1994, 30) quotes Gloria Steinem as saying that "in this country alone . . . about 150,000 females die of anorexia each year." Ann Landers used the number in a syndicated column in April 1992, and it has since been picked up in a college textbook. However, Dr. Diane Mickley of the Anorexia and Bulimia Association said that the original figure used in a 1985 newsletter was that there were from 150,000 to 200,000 *sufferers* of anorexia nervosa. The actual number of deaths probably averages less than 100 per year.

Misinterpreted Data

An exceedingly common practice is to misinterpret data to fit preconceived ideas. For example, a photograph in *The Living Wilderness* (Anon. 1990, 38) shows a concrete post in a New York City sewage plant. The post is badly deteriorating at its base. The Wilderness Society attributes the deterioration to acid rain. However, the deterioration is obviously the result of salt attack on a porous piece of bad concrete. The concrete on which the post sits is sound, although the supposed acid rain ponds on it and, therefore, it should be in much worse shape than the post.

Environmentalists have concluded that excessive UV-B (because of ozone depletion) causes inflamed eyes among sheep in Patagonia and New Zealand. The actual problem is conjunctivitis, an inflammation of the conjunctiva usually caused by an infection or allergy. Additionally, they attribute the death of frogs in Oregon to ozone depletion (Roberts 1994). Without evidence that the harmful rays are even increasing, the conclusions are meaningless.

Exaggeration of Risks

Exaggeration of risks, or seeing risks where there are none, has long been a mechanism for creating public fears.

An example of exaggeration of risks to nature is a children's book entitled the *Western Outdoor Environmental Guide—Coniferous Trees* (Hartsveldt 1971). It contains the following:

- Will there always be coniferous trees?

- We are losing more and more of our coniferous trees each year.

- Man is changing the environment in other ways, too.

- He pollutes clean air, water, and soil.

- This pollution destroys many coniferous trees.

- More people mean more airports, superhighways, garbage dumps, and houses.

- More people mean fewer coniferous trees.

- And with fewer trees, there are fewer plant and animal habitats.

- Man is the only animal that can control the environment. We must act quickly while we still have the chance.

Chapter 3 of this book shows how reality is just the opposite.

Berry (1990, 118) states: "The scale of the Third World urban growth is such that even if First World environmental impacts are significantly reduced, the reductions will be swamped by the increases occurring elsewhere. It is from the Third World's economic growth and urban concentration that the most serious regional threats to the global environment will come." He has exaggerated the problems of economic growth and urbanization. However, he is correct about reduction of First World environmental impacts (as shown in the early chapters of this book). In actuality, Third World nations need economic growth and urbanization before they can improve their human and natural environments as shown by statistical data in chapter 9. Although human health problems exist in the early phase of urbanization, as we have shown, the dispersed impact on the natural environment is beneficial.

Lies

Although lies are not necessary to confuse the public about environmental matters, environmentalists have used them extensively. Perhaps some of the best examples are from Rachel Carson's 1962 *Silent Spring,* the first major book causing public furor over industrial chemicals. An important thesis of the book is that industrial chemicals, particularly pesticides, have depleted much of America's bird populations. However, in the twenty years before Carson published her book, most bird populations had increased from ten to one hundred times (Whelan 1993, 107).

Carson was particularly concerned about one of America's most common birds, the robin. The alleged chemical culprit was DDT. Yet, during maximum use of DDT from 1941 to 1960, the robin population expanded 1138 percent, multiplying over 12 times, according to the Audubon Society's Christmas bird counts of 1941 and 1960.

The reality is that the improved habitat for many birds because of the increasing number of the nation's trees overwhelmingly counterbalanced any local problems caused by pesticides. As described in chapters 2, 3, and 4, pesticide use significantly contributes to high per acre agricultural productivity, so that pesticides bear much responsibility for expanded bird populations. *The effect of pesticide use is precisely the opposite of Rachel Carson's statements.*

Although Carson was obviously incorrect, Weizracker (1994) still states that agricultural chemicals are a major threat to wildlife. A big lie, repeated often enough, may sound like the truth.

London (1984) gives many examples of the lies found in textbooks:

From page 100: "It is possible that the buildup of carbon dioxide in the atmosphere may reduce the heat of the sun. That could mean the end of everything we value in modern civilization. . . . We are playing a game against our environment. The stakes are high—no less than survival of the human race. . . . do we have any 'plays' that nature cannot block? Can we ever win a game with our environment?"[4]

From page 108: "Every twenty-four hours more than 3,000 acres of green space are lost around this country. Every year this adds up to at least a million acres. . . . [I]ts place is being taken by housing, schools, business, industries, roads, highways. We need these, of course, but not all that are being built." Our chapter 3 shows that this statement is untrue. The textbooks may be politically correct, but they are lying to schoolchildren.

Industry is not blameless. WMX Technologies Inc., a waste disposal company, was still telling customers as recently as 1993: "This nation is quickly running out of places to dispose of trash" (Bailey 1995, A8). However, Bailey quotes a vice president of the company: "We never believed there was a disposal crisis." With a big assist from the Environmental Defense Fund and the EPA, polls show that "U.S. consumers rate trash the number 1 environmental problem and 77 percent think household recycling is the solution." Figures from

Bailey show that household trash is less than one percent of the total solid waste. On the radio, the EPA and the Environmental Defense Fund advertise the importance of recycling for the future of the Earth. They say nothing about the household cost in water, energy, and time to clean recycled items nor the costs for extra trucks and the energy needed for them. Finally, they say nothing about the extensive government subsidies needed to make the recycling "work" for many materials.

More subtly, the press is often guilty of lying in the sense that a reader is totally misled. Weaver (1994) describes how the press stages news, and how seemingly objective reporting, dispassionately written, can deceive the reader so that the net result is lying. For the sake of the story, newspaper and television reporters for years have misled the public. How else could the public be so poorly informed about environmental matters?

Politically Correct Language— From the Euphemistic to the Pejorative

To sway public opinion, leaders of the environmental Left have defined the language of the debate. A swamp becomes a wetland; a jungle becomes a tropical rainforest; the Indian becomes the Native American (naturally noble). The word "chemical" is synonymous with poison or carcinogen. And an industrial chemical is usually modified by the adjective "toxic." An air or water contaminant, especially a trace of an industrial chemical, is a "pollutant." A natural chemical is not. Natural is good. Industry is greedy, short-sighted, stupid. Greed and capitalism are synonymous. By implication, environmentalists are high-minded, never short-sighted or greedy. They think only of the public interest. The expression "free enterprise" is taboo; "capitalism" is preferred. In a socialistic society all people are working for the public interest. Competition is bad (it frustrates the less competitive).

Using the language of the environmental Left reinforces their positions. The debate is then in their terms.

Idealizations

Many environmental leaders idealize some aspects of the world, and idealizations influence many people. For example, they idealize primitive societies. They depict the American Indian as the ultimate environmentalist. They ignore his enormous influence on America's environment, despite his low numbers. They ignore his expansion of the prairies by fire and the slaughter of bison in drives (first observed by Lewis and Clark). They ignore his probable wiping out of many of America's large beasts. They ignore his extraordinarily inefficient use of land. Most environmentalists also ignore the cruelty of Indians to each other, including the frequent killing of unwanted girl babies.

A classic example of this idealization is the famous 1855 letter from Chief

Seattle of the Suquamish tribe to President Franklin Pierce. His "letter" became the basis for a best-selling children's book called *Brother Eagle, Sister Sky: A Message from Chief Seattle.* Gore (1992) quotes Chief Seattle, and one excerpt from his letter is on the base of the statue of Chief Seattle put up at the Seattle World's Fair site. In actuality, Ted Perry, a professor who now teaches at Middlebury College in Vermont, wrote Chief Seattle's letter for a TV program. Perry based the letter on an 1854 speech as recollected thirty-three years later by Dr. Henry Smith (Arnold and Gottlieb 1993, 40). The letter did not even accurately quote Smith. (The original research about the speech and the letter was by Rick Caldwell [1983] of the Seattle Museum of History and Industry.)

Moussalli (1994) quotes a 1990 article by Christopher Flavin of the Worldwatch Institute called "Bhutan, Paradise Preserved," comparing it to Shangri-La. Bhutan is a tiny mountain kingdom south of Tibet. This kingdom has a per capita annual GNP of $180. Bhutanese life expectancy is 49 years, and they have an infant mortality of 178 per 1,000 births. They have safe water for only 30 percent of the population and an illiteracy rate of 62 percent. Few people in industrialized nations would consider Bhutan to be Shangri La.

Idealizations have a curious and paradoxical result. Neither the idealists nor the public have bought the idealizations. There is no exodus from America to Bhutan, Uganda, Melanesia, or other more primitive areas. Any exodus is in the other direction. The idealists obviously do not believe their own idealizations.

Religious Legerdemain

Many of the environmentally concerned to whom this book is dedicated are quite religious. Many, however, have been environmentally deceived by the seductions of the various obfuscation mechanisms described in this and previous chapters. Through a sleight of hand, environmentalists have gotten the religious leadership to endorse and adopt a program that is pantheistic in its worship of Mother Earth, the goddess Gaia. Ernst (1994) calls the new god "resurrected Paganism."

The U.S. Catholic Conference, National Council of Churches, Coalition on the Environment and Jewish Life, and Evangelical Network are all participating in a program to "address the crisis of environmental justice . . . weaving together issues of environmental integrity and economic justice." The program to prepare and distribute material to churches and synagogues is funded by a $4.5 million contract with the Union of Concerned Scientists, an ultragreen organization.

In reality, the environmental Left, a group not noted for belief in God or sound science, has recruited major segments of the religious community. Many religious leaders fail to understand:

- Gaia is a pagan goddess.
- Worship of the "intrinsic value" of nature degrades humans.

- Most eco-socialists are on record as wanting to radically reduce the human population and promote programs that limit human potential for development.

- Recommended actions in this program endorse and promote socialist legislation. Most problems defined in the distributed literature are really nonproblems if examined in the light of true science.

- The current environmental programs are causing human misery on an unprecedented scale (see chapter 11). If adherents of these programs get their way, the misery will become worse, hardly compatible with church objectives or social justice.

Only sound science, not politically correct science or well meaning but scientifically illiterate theology, can appraise the risks and benefits of technological programs. Were these religious organizations even casually knowledgeable about environmental data, they would see major differences in published opinions. They would have been wise to seek review of their ideas by a prudent, informed third party, such as the National Academy of Science. Had they done so, they would not have distributed the recommendations as written.

Of course, not all the faithful have been deceived. For example, The *Mindszenty Report* by the Cardinal Mindszenty Foundation is extremely critical of environmentalism. An article by Father Sirica (1994) in the *Wall Street Journal* is similarly critical.

Environmental Awards

The political Left leadership has found a novel way to make even the most outlandish statements credible: give those who make such statements prestigious awards and media adulation. For example, according to Boland (1994, 1) of the Cardinal Mindszenty Foundation:

Ironically, the eco-radicals—even when caught falsifying data or proclaiming doom that fails to materialize—keep right on churning out junk science, collecting honors and accepting accolades from the adulating media. Take, for example, Dr. Paul Ehrlich, the bug-biologist-turned seer. In his 1968 book *"The Population Bomb"* he prophesied "hundreds of millions" would die in 1970 of starvation unless forced zero population growth were instituted worldwide. In 1969, he predicted that "hundreds of millions: would soon perish in smog disaster" in Los Angeles and New York. By 1979, Ehrlich warned, all the world's oceans would be dead of DDT poisoning. By 1980, U.S. life expectancy, he said, would drop to 42 years due to cancer epidemics. Wrong on all counts, yet Ehrlich has nonetheless been honored with a "genius grant" from the MacArthur Foundation, as well as the Swedish Academy's prestigious Crafoord Prize. He frequently appears as an "environmental expert" on NBC News' "Today" show—once forecasting melting northern polar ice might flood Washington, D.C., and most of the State of Florida.

Ehrlich was also wrong in a famous bet with Julian Simon that in ten years the price of five metals of Ehrlich's own choice would rise in constant dollars. It didn't happen.

Another example is Penti Linkola. Finland's intelligentsia have given Linkola, the Finn who advocates turning the clock back one hundred years, prestigious awards.

The philosophical component of the environmental Left has a different set of standards from normal people as evidenced by the accolades to Linkola and Ehrlich. Accuracy and common sense are obviously not requisites. However, what Linkola and Ehrlich have in common is that both have lauded causes dear to the intellectual Left. *The sole measure of their value is their potential impact on public opinion.*

DISCUSSION

Environmental conclusions are often apocryphal, often contradictory. Early predictions were of a new ice age caused by human activities. Later predictions were of a vast atmospheric overheating and consequent flooding of coastal areas. Predictions of general famine striking even America in the 1980s (see Ehrlich 1968) created fears among the more suggestible. Environmental leaders now tell us that CFC refrigerants, acid rain, pesticides, the gasoline engine, atomic power, hydropower, or the loss of species of plants, animals, or insects will do irrevocable harm to Earth. They also told us that Lake Erie is dead, DDT will destroy the birds, the oceans will die, etc., etc., etc. All predictions are negative; most were proved incorrect. The rest are highly controversial.

For some reason, continuously crying wolf has been successful. According to surveys, the public apparently believes that the environment is getting worse, that industry is primarily an environmental negative, that trivial amounts of chemicals are harmful. Wattenberg (1984, 221–22) calls the core beliefs DEM (Distilled Essence of Media). DEM is "the collective residue of a given story left behind by television and the print media." The just mentioned items are the DEM. The title of the article by Easterbrook (1990), "Everything You Know about the Environment Is Wrong," is an accurate description of the American public's state of knowledge. Wattenberg's book *The Good News Is the Bad News Is Wrong,* described the same problem in 1984.

The perspective of the obfuscators is stated by Paul Watson, founder of Greenpeace (Spencer et al. 1991, 174): "It doesn't matter what is true, it only matters what people believe is true." He calls Greenpeace a "myth-generating machine." Steven Schneider, a global warming advocate, makes a similar statement: "We have to offer up scary scenarios, make simplified, dramatic statements, and make little mention of any doubts we may have. Each of us has to decide what the right balance is between being effective and being honest" (ibid.).

Those who deceive about the environment want us to believe: (1) whatever happens, it will be catastrophic; (2) whatever happens, it will be the fault of humans; and (3) in any event, bigger government and more regulations are the answer.

Philosophically, the environmental obfuscation mechanisms of manufacturing, exaggerating, selecting, or otherwise stressing negative data are consistent with other efforts by the political Left. For example, the American History Standards and the National Standards for World History for grade schools and high schools by the National Standards Project at UCLA consistently stress negative data about American and Western history (Anon. 1994b). Great American and Western achievements are downplayed while the standards emphasize gender, race, and class oppression.

Both environmental negatives and much taught in America's education system stem from the political Left and are really attacks on Western civilization and America. For the political Left, the end justifies the means.

CONCLUSIONS

Public perceptions about the environment are largely incorrect. For decades the public has been systematically misinformed about environmental dangers. The mechanisms of misinformation include using anecdotal negatives, hiding unwanted news, blocking research that may lead to politically incorrect conclusions, lying, environmental speculations, misquoting, misinterpreting data, exaggerating risks, reclassifying substances, twisting language, idealizing the environmental, and religious legerdemain. The mechanisms described relate primarily to the environment; however, the Left counterculture uses the same mechanisms throughout the whole spectrum of conflict between political philosophies.

The consistent bias of sources of information from public school education, major communications media, and much of the federal government has created the education paradox: the more we are exposed to environmental "information" in America, the less we understand. It is better to be totally ignorant than to "know" only the environmental liabilities as portrayed by the political Left; for them, facts have politics. They ignore or hide facts that are "inconvenient." *The accuracy of data is irrelevant; political impact is the only measure of success.* Nothing shows this better than the awards and accolades given to Stanford's Professor Paul Ehrlich, who has a penchant for making inaccurate, wild predictions. The environmental Left has given him a "genius grant" from the MacArthur Foundation. Again, what is their standard of value? The standard certainly does not relate to accuracy or honesty. We observe that the obfuscation we have described is perfectly consistent with Cheney (1995) conclusions that for the Left: "There are no true stories, but only useful ones, no overarching principles, but only the interests of the moment" (p. 195), and that "Truth is something to be invented rather than pursued" (p. 17). Coffman (1994, 87) concludes about the environmental Left that: "Feelings *are* truth to mystic environmental leaders. Therefore, if they *feel* that Alar, acid rain, global warming, ozone depletion, and other catastrophes are destroying the earth, then they are.'' Whatever the motives, accuracy and honesty are not a part of them. The only real measure of effectiveness is political impact.

In a world where most people go to work every day to produce, sell, repair, or otherwise contribute to society's needs, the obfuscators are clearly counter-cultural. Facts are the basis of decisions for most people. The counterculture is bounded by no such restrictions. The environmental Left, led by the people quoted in chapter 1, has been remarkably successful. They have made large numbers of the very people who are responsible for the greatest environmental gains in human history see themselves as environmental culprits.

NOTES

1. Eleven federal agencies participated under the lead of the U.S. Department of Agriculture (USDA): the Council of Environmental Quality (CEQ), the Department of Commerce (DOC), the Department of Defense (DOD), the Department of Energy (DOE), the Department of Housing and Urban Development (DHUD), the Department of the Interior (DOI), the Department of State (DOS), the Environmental Protection Agency (EPA), the Water Resources Council (WRC), the Department of the Treasury, and the Department of Transportation (DOT).

2. Prolonged breathing of large quantities of any dust will cause lung problems, including cancer. For example, workers unprotected from dust in flour or rock milling operations are in danger.

3. We suggest that long before this would occur, the world would be overrun by oysters. After all, each female produces up to 125 million ova. The danger was first visualized by Dunn in 1934 in an essay written while in Roosevelt Grammar School, Burlingame, Calif.

4. This conclusion, stated so convincingly and forcefully, is precisely the opposite of current conclusions, also stated convincingly and forcefully. Whether the result will be heating or cooling, all environmental leaders agree it will be catastrophic.

REFERENCES

Ames, B. N., M. Profet, and L. S. Gold. 1990. Dietary pesticides (99.99% all natural). *Proceedings of the National Academy of Science* 87:7777–81.

Anon. 1990. What on Earth are we doing? *The Living Wilderness,* February–March.

———. 1992. Hiding good news. *Chicago Tribune,* June 25.

———. 1994a. Is the Earth really getting warmer? *Reader's Digest,* December, 132.

———. 1994b. McCarthy, Seneca Falls and history, review and outlook, editorial. *Wall Street Journal,* December 30, A6.

Arnold, R., and A. Gottlieb. 1993. *Trashing the Economy.* Bellevue, Wash.: Free Enterprise Press.

Bailey, J. 1995. Curbside recycling comforts the soul, but benefits are scant. *Wall Street Journal,* January 19, A1, A8.

Bailey, R. 1993. Political science. *Reason,* December, 61, 62.

Bandow, D., and I. Vasquez, eds. 1994. *Perpetuating Poverty.* Washington, D.C.: Cato Institute.

Banes, F. 1995. Can you trust those polls? *Reader's Digest,* July, 49–54.

Bast, J. L., P. J. Hill, and R. C. Rue. 1994. *Eco-Sanity.* Lanham, Md.: Madison Books.

Berry, B. J. L. 1990. Urbanization. In *The Earth as Transformed by Human Activity,* edited by B. L. Turner III et al. Cambridge: Cambridge University Press.

Bidinotto, R. J. 1990. Environmentalism: Freedom's foe for the 90's. *The Freeman,* November.

Boland, J. D. 1994. Environmentalism: Revolution in progress. *The Mindszenty Report* 36(6).

Bolch, B., and H. Lyons. 1994. Bad chemistry. *National Review,* September, 58–59.

Caldwell, R. 1983. The myth of Chief Seattle's environmental manifesto. Seattle Museum of History and Industry, unpublished report.

Carson, R. 1962. *Silent Spring.* New York: Houghton Mifflin.

Cheney, L. V. 1995. *Telling the Truth.* New York: Simon & Schuster.

Coffman, M. S. 1994. *Saviors of the Earth?* Chicago: Northfield Publishing.

DeBell, G., ed. 1970. *The Environmental Handbook.* New York: Ballantine Books.

Easterbrook, G. 1990. Everything you know about the environment is wrong. *The New Republic,* April 30, 14–27.

———. 1995. *A Moment on the Earth.* New York: Viking Penguin.

Edwards, L. 1994. In memory. *National Review,* May 2, 32–33.

Ehrlich, P. 1968. *The Population Bomb.* New York: Ballantine Books.

———. 1970a. Eco-catastrophe. In *The Environmental Handbook,* edited by G. DeBell. New York: Ballantine Books.

———. 1970b. Too many people. In *The Environmental Handbook,* edited by G. DeBell. New York: Ballantine Books.

Ernst, R. J. 1994. The real environmental crisis: Environmental law. *Imprimus* 25(5): 219–32.

Feng, X., and S. Epstein. 1994. Climatic implications of an 8000 year hydrogen isotope time series from bristlecone pine trees. *Science* 265: 1079–1081.

George C. Marshall Institute. 1995. *The Global Warming Experiment.* Washington, D.C.

Gore, A. 1992. *Earth in the Balance.* New York: Houghton Mifflin.

Gribble, G. W. 1994. Natural chlorine? You bet! *Priorities* 6(2): 9, 10, 11, 12.

Halls, L. K., ed. 1984. *White-Tailed Deer, Ecology and Management.* Harrisburg, Pa.: Stackpole Books.

Hartseveldt, R., et al. 1971. *Western Outdoor Environmental Guide, Coniferous.* San Francisco: Chevron Chemical Co.

Hecht, M. M. 1992. The death toll from environmental hoaxes. *21st Century,* Fall: 12, 13.

Hollander, P. 1994. Soviet terror, American amnesia. *National Review,* May 2, 28–39.

Janorowski, Z., T. V. Segalstad, and V. Hisdal. 1992. *Atomospheric CO_2 and Global Warming: A Critical Review.* 2nd ed. Oslo: Norsk Polarinstitute.

Klehr, H., J. E. Haynes, and F. I. Firson. 1995. *The Secret World of American Communism.* New Haven: Yale University Press.

Lilienfeld, R. M., and W. L. Rathje. 1995. Six enviro-myths. *New York Times,* January 21, op-ed.

London, H. I. 1984. *Why Are They Lying to Our Children?* New York: Stein and Day.

Maduro, R. A., and R. Schauerhammer. 1992. *The Holes in the Ozone Scare.* Washington, D.C.: 21st Century Science Associates.

Matschke, G. H., et al. 1984. Population influences. In *White-Tailed Deer, Ecology and Management,* edited by L. K. Halls. Harrisburg, Pa.: Stackpole Books.

McGuire, R. 1992. Economic priorities and the environmentalists. *Vital Speeches* 56(11): 329–33.

Moussalli, S. D. 1994. Worldwatch watch. *National Review,* April 18, 44–46, 60.

Roberts, P. C. 1994. Development planning in Latin America: The lifeblood of the mercantilist state. In *Perpetuating Poverty,* edited by D. Bandow and I. Vasquez. Washington, D.C.: Cato Institute.

Robinson, A. B. 1994. Radioactive coal. *Access to Energy* 22(3).

Rummel, R. J. 1995. *Death by Government.* 2nd ed. New Brunswick: Transaction.

Scotto, J., G. Cotton, F. Urback, D. Berger, and T. Fears. 1988. Biologically effective ultraviolet radiation in the United States, 1974–1985. *Science* 239:762–64.

Seitz, R. 1990. A war against fire. *The National Interest,* Summer.

Sewall, G. T. 1994. Triumph of the textbook trendiness. *Wall Street Journal,* March 1, A14.

Singer, S. F., R. Revelle, and C. Starr. 1991. *What to Do about Greenhouse Warming: Look Before You Leap.* Washington, D.C.: Cosmos Club.

Sirica, R. A. 1994. The false gods of Earth Day. *Wall Street Journal,* April 22, A12.

Sommers, C. H. 1994. Figuring out feminism. *National Review,* June 17, 30–31.

Spencer, L., et al. 1991. The not so peaceful world of Greenpeace. *Forbes,* November 11.

Stevens, W. K. 1994. Warning to UN on pollution and climate. *International Herald Tribune,* September 29, 9.

Tengs, T. O., et al. 1994. Five-hundred life-saving interventions and their cost-effectiveness. Working manuscript, Center for Risk Analysis, Harvard School of Public Health.

Tolman, J. 1994. Attack of the wetland enforcers. *Wall Street Journal,* July 18, A12.

Turner, B. L., III, et al., eds. 1990. *The Earth as Transformed by Human Activity.* Cambridge: Cambridge University Press.

U.S. Department of Agriculture. 1989. *The Second RCA Appraisal (Soil, Water, and Related Resources on Nonfederal Land in the United States).*

Wattenberg, B. J. 1984. The good news is the bad news is wrong. *Reader's Digest,* April, 101–231.

Weaver, P. H. 1994. The great pretenders. *Reason,* March, 27–33.

Weizracker, E. U. 1994. *Earth Politics.* London: Zed Books.

Whelan, E. M. 1993. *Toxic Terror: The Truth behind the Cancer Scares.* Buffalo, N.Y.: Prometheus Books.

Wittwer, S. H. 1992. Flower power, rising carbon dioxide is great for plants. *Policy Review,* Fall, 4–9.

CHAPTER 11

Regulations and Environmental Priorities

In this chapter, we evaluate some of America's current regulations of industrial chemicals to learn whether they produce significant cost-effective improvement in natural and human environments. Are they making the world greener? Do they help us live longer? Are they cost effective?

At their incipience, environmental regulations were in response to real problems. Raw sewage and many industrial wastes were being dumped into streams. In addition, particulates in air and some chemicals caused local health problems. The most serious problems were solved rather quickly. However, as major problems vanished, smaller and smaller problems were addressed. Major government regulatory agencies and environmental groups uncovered a continuous stream of increasingly smaller problems. The open-ended nature of environmental legislation made finding ever smaller problems easy. In fact, the open-endedness *encouraged* finding ever smaller problems. The absence of any economic analysis of risks versus benefits gave America no way of systematically evaluating environmental problems. Regulators failed to establish logical priorities. Warnings of the economic implications of excessive regulations of small problems came early.

Weinstein (1983, 221) says: "Failure [to spend our resources wisely] may result in lost opportunities to control the most dreaded diseases of our society." Efron (1984) thoroughly documented how America's regulatory agencies, in their efforts to survive, have deceived the American public and have caused enormous misallocations of wealth. After over ten years we ask: Have Weinstein's and Efron's warnings had any impact on America's regulatory agencies?

The answer is "no." In this chapter we show that one of the greatest threats to production of wealth is environmental regulations (see Arnold and Gottlieb 1993, among others). Environmental regulations have been very successful at shackling economic growth. However, most environmental improvement is the *result* of economic growth. Many regulations meant to improve the environment will ultimately be environmentally destructive because they slow economic growth. Roberts (1994, 14) points out that anticapital policies in the United States are looked upon favorably by "the old left that sees such policies as egalitarian, and the new left which sees them as pro-environmental because they stop economic growth."

RISK ASSESSMENT

In response to the obvious disorder in environmental priorities, the journal *Risk Analysis* was first published in 1980. Over the years, authors writing in this journal have used several methods of ranking risks. One of them is risk assessment. This is a method by which the number of deaths from various risks per 100,000 people per year are compared. The value of risk assessment is that it is a step toward establishing priorities: the more people at risk from a chemical or an activity, the more money should be spent to solve the problem.

We modify this method. We summarize the number of deaths per 100,000 per year from single risks and multiple risks and relate all risks to the EPA's so-called action level for controlling public exposure to industrial chemicals. The purpose of this approach is to show how money is *actually* being spent and relating this to how money *might* be spent.

Single Risks

Table 11.1 ranks annual fatality rates for some typical single risks in the order of their danger to Americans plus some risks of certain diseases worldwide. For comparison, we include the EPA's regulatory "action level" in this table. The action level is that concentration of a substance calculated as capable of killing an average of one person in 1,000,000 (10^{-6}) after a lifetime of 73 years of exposure. The concentration is usually extrapolated from data points derived from animal experiments using high concentrations of chemicals. Often the extrapolated concentration is controversial and on the low side—that is, *risks are exaggerated.* For analytical purposes, we assume the concentrations and risks are correct.

Kelly and Cardon (1994, 4) analyze the nature and origin of the one in a million risk level. They conclude: "The risk level of 10^{-6} is less than our current risk of background exposure to natural environmental contaminants or developing cancer from all causes by a factor of 1,000 to 100,000." That is, even if the extrapolated concentrations for substances are correct, the one in a million risk is trivial relative to many other common risks. We will show how trivial. (See also Jukes 1983.)

To make the EPA's risk level of one in 1,000,000 for 73 years' exposure compatible with the rate per 100,000, per year we first divide one by 73 (an average lifetime) to get risk per million people per year. The EPA risk level, therefore, becomes 0.014 deaths per 1,000,000 persons per year. We then divide 0.014 by 10 to get the risk of death per 100,000 per year. We evaluated all risks as multiples of

Table 11.1
Annual Single Risk Fatality Rates[1] as Related to EPA Action Level

Cause of Death	Rate per 100,000	Multiple of EPA's 0.0014 per 100,000[4]
Motorcycling	2000	1,428,570
Aerial acrobatics (plane)	500	357,140
Smoking	300	214,290
Heart disease	289	206,430
Dengue fever[2]	225	160,714
Cancer	201.7	144,070
Hang gliding	80	57,140
Cardiovascular disease	57.9	41,360
Pulmonary diseases	35.5	25,360
Pneumonia and influenza	31.3	22,360
Malaria (world)	28.3	20,210
Diabetes mellitus	19.5	13,930
Motor vehicles	18.5	13,210
Tuberculosis (world)	15.9	11,360
Measles (world)	15.9	11,360
Cholera (Peru 1991)	14.8	10,570
Suicide	12.3	8,790
AIDS (1990)	11.0	7,860
Homicide and legal intervention	10.2	7,290
Liver disease and cirrhosis	10.2	7,290
Kidney diseases	8.3	5,930
Septicemia	7.9	5,640
Prenatal-related condition	7.0	5,000
Atherosclerosis	6.6	4,710
Boating	5.0	3,570
Hunting	3.0	2,140
Fires	2.8	2,000
Drowning	2.1	1,500
Bicycling	1.0	710
4 tbs peanut butter per day	0.8	570
Firearms	0.6	430
Consuming Miami or New Orleans drinking water	0.1	70
Lightning	0.05	40
Asbestos in buildings[3]	0.008 to 0.012	7
EPA regulatory action level	0.0014[4]	1

Table 11.1 (Continued)

Cause of Death	Rate Per 100,000	Multiple of EPA's 0.0014 Per 100,000
Alar	about 0	—
DDT	about 0	—
Silica on beaches	about 0	—
Ethanol from baking bread	about 0	—
Cleaning chemicals from vents in air	about 0	—
Perfume factories, same rules as refineries	about 0	—
Gasoline fume collectors	about 0	—
Fumes off blacktop roads	about 0	—

[1]Crouch and Wilson (1982). Data are for the United States unless otherwise stated.
[2]After World Health Organization (1993).
[3]Health effects are not measurable, i.e., they are close to or equal to zero.
[4]See text for calculation of the 0.0014 per 100,000.

the EPA risk level by dividing the risk level by 0.0014. For example, heart disease causes 289 deaths per 100,000 people per year which, divided by 0.0014, is 206,430. An American is 206,430 times more likely to die of heart disease than from a chemical consumed at the EPA's regulatory level.

The value of the risk assessment technique is that by assessing and then ordering risks, a nation can plan expenditures to reduce human risks according to their relative danger. As Gold et al. (1992, 261) say: "it is not prudent to focus attention on possible hazards at the bottom of a ranking if the same methodology indicates numerous common human exposures with much greater possible hazards." In the case of heart disease, one might conclude that 206,430 times more money should be spent to understand and cure heart disease than to reduce exposure to a chemical at the EPA regulatory level. (For AIDS, the number is 7,860.)

The EPA bases its estimates of risk not on human epidemiological data, but on tumors developing in animals exposed to near toxic dosages of the substances. Federal policy says that if a substance (industrial only) administered to an animal (by inhalation, ingestion, or implantation) in *any* dosage over *any* period of time causes *any* tumor, that substance is a carcinogen. Whether the tumor is benign or malignant and whether humans have ever gotten cancer from that substance are not considered. In practice, there is no threshold below which a substance is declared to be noncarcinogenic. Therefore, the EPA (and other federal regulatory agencies) extrapolates the dosage at which the tumor developed to zero concentration, and calculates the concentration that would cause one cancer death per million assuming 73 years of exposure. Negative data are not acceptable; so, for example, the EPA may reject 1,000 tests that caused no

Table 11.2
Annual Fatality Rates: Multiple Risk Factors vs. EPA's Action-Level Risk

Cause of Death From Multiple Factors	Death Rate, 1990, per 100,000[1]	Multiple of EPA's 0.0014 per 100,000
Excess infant mortality, Afghanistan[2]	15,700	11,214,285
Excess infant mortality, average 36 poorest nations	9,300	6,642,857
Unnecessary disease deaths, worldwide (from Table 6.2)	700	500,000
Excess death rate, USA average[3]	300	214,286
Excess infant mortality, USA	300	210,000
Murder, Atlanta 1990	231	165,000
Murder, Medillin, Colombia 1992	200	142,857
Murder, Washington, D.C. 1990	1082	77,286
Murder, New York City 1990	97.8	69,857
All accidents, USA	37.3	26,643
Murder, USA	9.4	6,714

[1]Adapted from Wright 1994 unless otherwise noted.
[2]Excess infant mortality is the number above the 500 per 100,000 found in Finland and Japan.
[3]Excess death rates are defined as the number of deaths per year above 600 per 100,000 people which 25 nations have already reached. (Excess death rate, U.S. 900 minus 600 equals 300.)

tumors but accept one test in which a tumor develops. This is taken as evidence of potential carcinogenicity. (Not accepting information that is contradictory is consistent with other government policies and with Vice President Gore's *Earth in the Balance.* See chapter 12.)

Additionally, the EPA bases its regulation of pesticides in food on computer models, not on actual measurements. The EPA's "theoretical maximum residue contribution," on produce, for example, is 99,000 times higher for chlorothalonil than that actually measured by the Food and Drug Administration, 46,000 times higher for folpet, and 116,000 higher for captan (Gold et al. 1992). The actual intake of a chemical may represent a trivial risk. For example, the dietary intake of DDT by Americans before its ban in 1972 ranked in danger with the natural chemicals in two slices of white bread. It was much less dangerous than the natural chemicals in bacon, beer, potatoes, peanuts, plums, lettuce, carrots, celery, pears, and many other common foods, according to Gold et al. Clearly, many risks from which the EPA is protecting the public are very small or even nonexistent.

Multiple Risks

Table 11.2 is a summary of fatalities that have multiple causes in America and some other places. Two or more factors are responsible for death and,

Table 11.3
Risks Increasing the Chance of Death by One in a Million

Cause of Death	Health Effect
Smoking 1.4 cigarettes per day, 73 years	Cancer, heart disease
Drinking 1/2 liter of wine per day, 73 years	Cirrhosis of the liver
Living 2 days in New York or Boston	Air pollution
Living 2 months in Denver on vacation from N.Y.	Cancer caused by cosmic radiation
Living 2 months in average stone or brick buildings	Cancer caused by natural radioactivity
Traveling 6 minutes by canoe	Accident
Traveling 10 miles by bicycle	Accident
Traveling 300 miles by car	Accident
Flying 1000 miles by jet	Accident
Flying 8000 miles by jet	Cancer caused by cosmic radiation
One chest x-ray	Cancer caused by radiation
Drinking 30 12-oz. cans of diet soda	Cancer caused by saccharin
Eating 100 charcoal-broiled steaks	Cancer from benzopyrene

Note: EPA regulatory action risk level is one death per million human lifetimes of 73 years of exposure.
Source: Adapted from Crouch and Wilson 1982.

therefore, are not comparable to the death rates in table 11.1. Additionally, some deaths are from human activities not related to chemicals. For the United States, a person has 6,714 times greater risk of being murdered than dying from 73 years of exposure at EPA threshold levels. In such high-risk cities as Atlanta and Washington, D.C., the risk of being murdered is 165,000 and 77,286 times greater, respectively.

The infant mortality rate for Afghanistan is 15,700 per 100,000 births, which compares with 500 per 100,000 found in Finland and Japan. (Twenty-five nations are at 600 or less.) The 15,200 per 100,000 above the rate of 500 for Finland may be considered an "excess" mortality rate above what should be possible. This is 11,214,285 times higher than the EPA's threshold fatality level of 0.0014 per 100,000. Even in the United States, the excess infant mortality rate is 210,000 times greater than the EPA's 0.0014 per 100,000 action level risk. Should we spend more money on solving problems causing excess infant mortality and less on the EPA's idea of problems?

Public Accepted Risks

Table 11.3 summarizes some risks that increase the chance of death by one in a million. Most risks are well over 73 times greater than the EPA action level. The EPA's so-called action level is one death per million for 73 years of exposure. However, traveling 6 minutes by canoe is obviously far less than a lifetime of exposure. For 24 hours of canoeing, the chance of death increases to 240 per million people; for a year the number becomes 87,600 deaths per million; for 73 years the chance of death would be 6,394,800 per million, that is, 6,394,800 times the EPA's action level.

Similarly calculated, traveling 10 miles by bicycle carries a one in a million risk of death. If a cyclist covers 10 miles in 30 minutes, and this happens for 73 years, the rate is 12,790,000 times the EPA's action level.

Some risks, like 1.4 cigarettes, ½ liter of wine, and 4 tablespoons of peanut butter per day are comparable to EPA's action level of one per million for a lifetime. Other risks in table 11.3 lie somewhere between canoeing and the EPA's one in a million per lifetime risk.

This analysis shows that many Americans make choices that carry risks that vary from equal to the EPA's risk level to millions of times higher. The EPA is protecting Americans from risks that they not only are willing to take, but would probably not spend their own money to reduce. Should we, as a nation, be consistent and outlaw such dangerous pastimes as canoeing, bicycling, and living in Denver?

Some Further Implications of Risk Assessment

From tables 11.1, 11.2 and 11.3, we see that Americans and people in Third World nations live daily with risks far greater than the EPA's regulatory risk level. Additionally, Americans by lifestyle choice, take risks far greater than the risk level from which the EPA protects us.

Large Costs, Small Benefits. Too often, the amount of money expended to reduce risks is not proportional to the size of the risk. We might expect that a risk twice greater than another deserves twice as much money to alleviate. Is this the case? A further look at table 11.1 is enlightening. Billions of dollars (estimated from $150 billion to $200 billion; Bennett 1991) have been spent to remove asbestos from public buildings. The danger is close to the EPA's regulatory action level, an estimated 0.010 deaths per 100,000 per year (table 11.1). To spend a comparable amount of money for research on cancer, we might expect to spend 20,170 times the $160 billion (assumed from the above) or over $3,227,200 billion. This is 156 times of all the world's GNP or 573 times the United States' GNP. In actuality, medical research comes from profit, not gross. Assuming, therefore, that funding is derived from a 10 percent profit, the multiple to allow a comparable expenditure would be 1,560 times the world's annual GNP, a figure probably thousands of times over the total GNP produced in all the world's human history.

Looked at another way, had the money America spent to save 0.010 lives per 100,000 per year been spent on medical research to understand the causes and cures of cancer, could the nation have saved more lives? Perhaps even some people with cancer from asbestos exposure might have been saved. The consequence of the EPA's idea of saving us from cancer is, itself, an indirect cause of cancer fatalities: it diverts funds from cancer research.

Tengs et al. (1994) of the Harvard Center for Risk Analysis have analyzed the costs of saving a life and of saving a single life-year for 500 life-saving interventions. Consistently, they show that the most expensive interventions are those that come under the EPA. For example, the median cost of saving a life-year is $7,629,000 for the EPA. This is 86.7 times more than the same cost for the Occupational Safety and Health Administration (OSHA, $88,000), and 331.7 times higher than the cost for the Federal Aviation Administration (FAA, $23,000). The cost for saving a life-year for the environmental sector in general is $4,207,000 compared with $346,000 for the occupational sector. The cost is $19,000 for medicine, that is, it cost 221.4 times more to save one year of life with environmental regulations than as it does with medicine. The EPA's cost is 401.5 times that of medicine.

Tengs et al. also conclude that to save one life because of the ban of asbestos in diaphragms costs $15,546,543,284[1] or $1,434,478,118 for a life-year. The chloroform private well emission standard at 48 pulp mills costs $1,122,617,901,829 per life saved or $99,351,684,312 per life-year. For comparison, screening blood donors for HIV would cost $13,544 per life-year and the use of defibrillators in emergency vehicles for resuscitation after cardiac arrest cost $39, per life-year saved. And consider tuberculosis, which caused 2.5 million deaths worldwide in 1990. The cost of saving one life from tuberculosis in Tanzania: $10 (Anon. 1995, 81).

Wealth is squandered because the environmental regulatory agencies make decisions in a political environment, in a media environment. The most cost-effective decisions are virtually always made in an economic environment shielded from the regulatory and media spotlights.

Large Costs, Negative Benefits. Environmentalists and regulatory agencies have long criticized the use of pesticides in agriculture. Barrons' (1981) book, *Are Pesticides Really Necessary?,* was in response to environmentalist and government criticism of pesticide use. Some people fear even a single molecule of a pesticide. Yet, according to Case (1993, 6), "There is no evidence whatsoever that the approved, regulated use of pesticides has ever led to even one human death." Conversely, as we showed in chapters 2, 3, 4, and 6, not using pesticides could have an enormous negative influence on human health and could result in the destruction of much of our forests, wildlife, and soil. "One effect of EPA's concern with minuscule pesticide residues makes fruit and vegetables more expensive and thus serves to decrease consumption of foods that help to prevent cancer" (Gold et al. 1992, 261). "Since the risk of getting cancer from pesticides is relatively small and the risks of getting cancer from not eating enough fruits and vegetables is relatively large, pesticide bans probably cost more lives than they save" (Malkin 1994, 28). Again, the EPA's policies may indirectly increase the incidence of cancer.

Malkin also quotes a study by University of Southern California economist Ralph Keeney, who "estimated that every $7.25 million taken out of the economy through government regulations results in loss of one life." Keeney quantified for America the data we compiled in chapter 8 that related human health and longevity to wealth. However, the EPA's regulations save only one year of life per $7.6 million. The regulations are counterproductive.

The figures in tables 11.1, 11.2, and 11.3 suggest that a significant amount of the $800 billion to $1.656 trillion of American wealth spent annually on the "environment" (1990, $395 to $510 billion per year; Duesenberg 1994) would have far greater national benefit if it were spent somewhere other than on regulating chemicals at the EPA's level of risk. For example, some might be spent on increasing the number of police or on prisons to reduce the murder rate. Some could be spent for research on modifying American lifestyles to increase longevity. Monies could be effectively used to improve boat safety or could be spent on innumerable other activities that could save many more American lives than attempting to ameliorate the EPA's idea of danger. Making some funds available to Third World nations to provide clean water or indoor air would save millions of lives.

Some substances cause "risks" so far below the EPA's action level of 0.0014 deaths per 100,000 per year that the risks approach zero or may be zero. Some examples are at the bottom of table 11.1. According to Milloy et al. (1994, xiv), "given that many risks are unprovable, there is some probability that, in fact, they are zero." Alar (the apple growth regulator), DDT, ambient silica in beach sand, ethanol (produced by yeast chemistry in baking bread), and clothes cleaning chemicals vented into the air have never been known to cause human deaths at the low exposure conditions required by the EPA. Saving people from such unmeasurable risks might, of course, be prudent were it not for the high cost. Loss of wealth itself increases mortality rates.

The EPA regulates some chemicals that are necessary for human health. Zinc is such a substance. The EPA's regulation of zinc in mine effluent water stopped the zinc mining industry in Wisconsin and Illinois. However, at the EPA's acceptable concentration, *a person would have to drink 122.4 liters (32.34 gallons) of a mine's mill effluent water per day* to get the amount of zinc found in a common daily zinc dietary supplement pill.

The cost of EPA regulation of these substances at trivial levels is enormous. Alar cost the apple industry tens of millions of dollars, and controlling ethanol in a single bakery can cost $4.5 million for equipment installation and $2.5 million for annual maintenance (O'Brian 1994). These regulations result in high costs without measurable human benefits. As Milloy says: "It's insane that we're spending hundreds of billions of dollars chasing imagined risks" (Anon. 1994b, A28). Milloy is the senior author of the U.S. Department of Energy's *Choices in Risk Assessment*. The public always pays those costs in one form or another.

The EPA's policies are further questionable when we consider the cost of perfection. The cost of reducing the quantity of a "toxic" substance from, say, one part per million to one part per billion rises spectacularly. Not surprisingly, the cost of removing sulphur dioxide from West Virginia's Monongahela power plant is more than the cost of the original plant. The result is that more wealth is spent on less and less: as benefits decrease, costs rise. To a large extent this explains why the greatest expenditures for environmental improvement are found where the environmental problems are the least.

Regulatory Trends in Risk Assessment

The least costly and, for the most part, the earliest environmental regulations pertained to product and workplace safety. Gradually the regulations became more concerned with health. Coinciding with this change, costs rose spectacularly.

The Council on Environmental Quality (1991) summarized 56 regulations, starting in 1967 and ending in 1991, in terms of regulatory cost to save one human life. The cost per life saved ranges from $0.1 million to $5,700,000 million. For the first few years the average number of new regulations was less than one per year. Then the number rose to 4.0 per year for new regulations for 1983–1985, to 4.7 for 1986–1988, and to 5.0 for 1989–1991. The average annual cost per life saved was $36.0 million, $7,906 million, and $1,931,049 million (or almost $2 trillion), respectively. Thus, while the number of new regulations increased annually, the cost per life saved increased by 1,200 times from 1980–1982 to 1983–1985; by 220 times from 1983–1985 to 1986–1988; and by 244 times from 1986–1988 to 1989–1992. This is totally consistent with the trend of spending more and more on less and less. Is even the next step in the progression affordable?

Incidentally, the highest single cost per life saved, $5,700,000 million ($5.7 trillion), is for wood preservative chemicals. Wood preservative chemicals in general are responsible for an enormous reduction of pressure on America's forests and wildlife, a major conservation gain (see chapter 3). We quoted Barrons (1981, 60) as concluding that without wood preservatives America would need a forest twice the size of New England just to replace rotted wood in construction on a sustained basis. Is the EPA actually trying to make wood preservatives as expensive as possible? Is the EPA actually against increasing forest size and wildlife populations?

If the current trend toward regulating ever smaller amounts of substance or ever less dangerous substances continues, regulation will jeopardize the economy of the United States (see Arnold and Gottlieb 1993). Yet the EPA and other regulatory agencies want the trend to continue. As O'Brian (1994, A21) says: "States and EPA are going after relatively minor polluters because regulators have already achieved the biggest and easiest pollution reduction." That ever more trivial amounts of substances are regulated is a natural bureaucratic progression, a progression that neither the United States nor the human and natural environments of the world can tolerate for long. As Barro (1994, A14) says: "We would be in serious trouble if we spent liberally and took restrictive action in every area in which a semi-respectable theory of health risk has been advanced but has not been shown scientifically to be significant. In no time at all, imaginative environmentalists would exhaust the entire gross national product on activities with low or negative social rates of return.''

Under Clinton, the tendency to regulate to ever less continues. For example, the administration has decreed that benefits from a pesticide will not be considered during a product's approval process (Hurst 1994). The administration has institutionalized censorship according to Warren and Jones (1995). Under Bill Clinton, federal regulatory agencies in 1994 had 128,566 regulation writers. Plans for 1996 call for 130,929 regulation writers at an estimated cost of $15.6 billion. Clearly, downsizing regulations is not part of the Clinton–Gore plans.

WARPED PRIORITIES AND ENVIRONMENTAL COUNTERPRODUCTIVITY

Topsy-turvy priorities have thrown "the environment" into major economic conflict with all other government programs. Hence, government is not environmentally monolithic. The United States Bureau of Mines and the United States Geological Survey, for example, have been highly critical of asbestos and other mineral regulations for over fifteen years (for example, Ross 1994; Wilson et al. 1994). The United States Department of Energy has been very critical of EPA regulations in general, echoing many of the criticisms made in this book (Milloy et al. 1994; Parker et al. 1994).

However, most critically, environmental regulations conflict with the production of wealth, a *huge environmental negative,* because money spent on the environment rarely produces national wealth. Poverty creates the greatest environmental problems. Unrealistic environmental regulations, by squandering capital, can only make us poorer.

We see the greatest environmental sins as impeding the production of wealth, squandering wealth, and harming the natural environment. As shown in chapters 2 and 3, wealth has contributed to our enormously expanded forests of the past seventy years or so—an area of forest covering a land mass the size of all the lands of Vermont, Rhode Island, Massachusetts, New York, Pennsylvania, New Jersey, Maryland, Virginia, and North Carolina. Our wealth and agricultural technology, based on USDA predictions, give us optimism that forest expansion will continue to increase by tens of millions more acres to comprise a potential area of total new forest equivalent to the size of the eastern third of the nation. We look at the human environment and see that wealth creates environmental improvement in terms of human health, longevity, and decreasing birthrates (chapter 9).

The environmental importance of wealth is undeniable. Yet current regulations impede the production of wealth and squander accumulated wealth. Warped priorities produce counterproductive regulations.

America's lack of information about carcinogens consumed daily is also a result of warped priorities. Many common foods contain natural toxins and carcinogens. For example, potatoes contain amylase inhibitor, arsenic, chaconine, isoflavones, nitrate, oxalic acid, and solanine; celery contains nitrate and psoralens; carrots contain carotatoxin, myristicin, isoflavones, and nitrate; and broccoli contains allyl isothiocyanate, glucosinolates, goitrin, and nitrate (Heinz 1991, 132). All these natural chemicals are toxic or carcinogenic (as defined by tests on animals) and most occur in far larger quantities than a comparable amount of industrial chemicals allowable in food by the EPA. The total of such natural chemicals in our daily diets is about 10,000 times that allowed by the EPA for industrial chemicals (Ames 1990; Ames et al. 1987; Ames et al. 1990). As Ames (1990, 4) says: "We've set up tremendously strict standards on manmade things and completely ignored the natural world. We can sell celery full of carcinogens—as long as they are 'natural' nobody cares." Logically, someone should inform us of the point at which consumption of celery (or basil or beer or potatoes or steak or almost any food or drink) is dangerous to our health.

It is safe to say that if a chemical company manufactured the above foods, the EPA would have banned them long ago. Because they are natural, regulators ignore them. Logic, however, would suggest that we should spend ten thousand times more money studying and regulating natural toxins and carcinogens than industrial ones. The opposite is more likely true. Again, priorities are upside down.

Looked at another way, based on bad science, bad economics, and a lack of risk assessment analyses, we spend $111 million to prevent one premature death from asbestos; $168 million for benzene; $653 million per life saved for removal of traces of 1,2 dichloropropane from drinking water; $4.2 billion per life saved from hazardous waste from landfills; $86 billion for formaldehyde; $92.1 billion for atrazine alachlor in drinking water; and $5.7 trillion for wood preserving chemicals (Anon. 1994a; Loeb and Taboas 1994). Meanwhile the far more abundant natural carcinogens in food are virtually ignored.

How Did We Get off Track?

The principle that money spent to reduce risk should bear some relationship to the amount of risk is simple enough. People of normal common sense apply the principle every day of their lives. How did the U.S. government regulators get so out of touch with risk reality, so out of touch with how ordinary people think? For answers, let's look at what regulation of chemicals actually does.

From economic risk analysis, it is clear that most of America's current environmental regulation of chemicals cannot be justified by improvements in either human health or the natural environment. Moghissi (1994, 39) says: "The opposition by environmental advocacy groups to risk assessment (comparative risk assessment and cost-benefit analysis as expressed by them) is surprising. It must be concluded that their opposition was guided by objectives other than protection of human health and the environment." Although we continue to live longer, environmental regulations have virtually nothing to do with longevity.

What other objectives do excessive regulations serve? Perhaps we can learn if we look at the following effects of exaggerated risks and of resulting regulations:

- Exaggerating risks leads to the public contributing more funds to environmental societies.

- Regulations perpetuate a bureaucracy that can survive *only* by regulating continuously smaller risks.

- Regulations evolve from a stream of legislation. The legislation, in turn, has assured reelection of legislators (so long as the public is kept ignorant of their real motives).

- Excessive regulations financially benefit some in the private sector such as trial lawyers, environmental consulting firms, and remediation companies.

- Excessive regulations control vast components of society and, therefore, are compatible with the beliefs of those who see more government as answering all problems.

- Excessive regulations hamper the industrial system and the creation of wealth, and can drive the whole economy backward. This is compatible with the stated wishes of leftist environmentalists such as Gore, Strong, and Ehrlich.

Excessive environmental regulations might produce benefits for government and left causes. However, they are not in the long-term interests of the American people.

THE THIRD WORLD,
AND AMERICA'S ENVIRONMENTAL PRIORITIES

America probably cannot afford its current environmental regulations. For Third World nations, America's regulations are a disaster. They divert both wealth and energy from solving human environmental problems thousands to millions of times more serious than those addressed by America's environmental regulators. Were but 10 percent of the wealth America spends on "improving our environment" diverted to solving Third World environmental problems—those on the Shumburo list of chapter 7—the world would be greener, wildlife less endangered, erosion decreased, and humanity better off. In the context that a few cents' worth of vitamin A would save half the children who die in India, the enormous wealth America spends to solve "problems" with Alar, asbestos, dioxin, or acid rain looks pretty silly. This 10 percent, possibly a "mere" $165 billion, could be far more beneficial to the world's environment than all the other wealth spent by Americans to improve "the environment" as defined by America's government regulators.

The United States Agency for International Development (USAID) imposes America's regulations on Third World nations by requiring, as a stipulation to obtaining funds, that they must agree to abide by EPA dictates. Sometimes,

American regulatory agencies have not even imposed these regulations in the United States.

The following examples illustrate what happens when low-risk substances are banned from use in Third World nations:

- Methyl bromide, which protects grains from fungi and pests, has been banned through USAID. This reduces available food at a time when many African nations are less able to feed themselves. Spoilage and rodents destroy over 50 percent of the grains in some nations. Thus, those nations need 50 percent more land for grain production. This, in turn, needlessly stresses wildlife, forests, and humans.

- Similarly, because of USAID requirements the use of asbestos has been banned in many developing nations (including the relatively benign chrysotile asbestos, the most common variety). Chrysotile occurs in Uganda and other East African nations. The nations could make asbestos-cement pipes from local materials, which they can afford. However, because of the bans, they have to use meager hard currency to purchase plastic or metal pipes. This prevents Uganda from piping abundant high-quality water throughout the nation from such sources as Lakes Victoria and Albert, the White Nile River, and plentiful supplies of groundwater at shallow depths. The ban is irrational because (1) over four hundred thousand miles of asbestos-cement pipe have long existed in the United States with *no* demonstrated cancer risk; (2) Californians, with two thousand square miles of chrysotile asbestos-bearing serpentine (their state rock), have had most of their water supplies loaded for years with millions to billions of fibers of chrysotile asbestos per liter of water, according to the EPA's own data; (3) the EPA states that there is no health risk in ingesting chrysotile (EPA, 1991) and, specifically (EPA 1989), that the use of asbestos-cement pipe should not be stopped. Flooding California rivers distribute asbestos-rich waters. Californians wash clothes, water lawns, and bathe in water loaded with chrysotile fibers. Yet California has no cancer epidemic. Blocking the use of chrysotile asbestos by Ugandans when its use could save many lives by helping distribute clean water makes no practical sense.

- Based on EPA ideas, Peru stopped chlorinating its water supplies in 1991. From January 23, 1991 to September 1, 1994, cholera caused a reported 1,041,422 people to get sick and 9,642 deaths in South and Central America (Communicable Disease Center 1995; see also Anderson 1991). The EPA, has now released disinfection byproducts rules that will effectively end chlorination in America (Anon. 1996, 20). It also continues to exert pressure against the use of most other chlorine-bearing compounds (Smith, 1994). The EPA's bureaucracy seems incapable of distinguishing between the remote possibility of a problem that could *conceivably* cause concern *somewhere* to *someone,* and the very real and severe problems that go with banning many useful substances.

- DDT is a very practical insecticide for Third World use because it is inexpensive and a single application can last for six months or more. It has been used by many Third World nations to control malarial mosquitos and disease-carrying flies. According to Edwards (1981), the medical director of the World Health Organization wrote that DDT ''has killed more insects and saved more people than any other substance.'' Edwards adds that ''The National Academy of Sciences estimated that as of 1971 DDT has prevented 500 million deaths (human) that otherwise would have been inevitable.'' Further, the World Health Organization (1979, 20) states that DDT has a ''safety record, never matched by any other insecticide used in anti-malarial campaigns'' and could find no examples of death from it. Finally, Albert Schweitzer considered DDT to be one of the greatest health benefits for the poor of Africa.

What happens when people use DDT? India was able to reduce malaria from 75 million to less than 5 million cases from 1953–1962. Average life expectancy increased from 32 years to 47 years (Jukes 1986). This is about 3 billion years of human life (Robinson 1994). In 1948, before DDT use, Ceylon (now Sri Lanka) had 2,800,000 cases of malaria. The number of cases dropped to a low of 17 in 1963 during DDT use. After ending DDT use, Ceylon reported 2,500,000 cases of malaria by 1969 (Whelan 1985, 69). Zanzibar (off the east coast of Africa) reduced malaria incidence from 70 percent of their population in 1958 to under 5 percent in 1964, thanks to DDT. After suspension of its use the rate rose to 50 percent to 60 percent by 1984 (Bast et al. 1994, 100).

How much is DDT currently being used? Here, we find contradictions and a knowledge gap. Some DDT is used, according to Dr. Thomas Jukes, an authority on DDT. Brazil and Indonesia manufacture and use DDT. However, Drogin (1992) says that WHO decided in 1969 to abandon their effort to control malaria. Table 6.2 tells us that DDT must not be in general use, because diseases caused by such insect vectors as flies, mosquitoes, and fleas still kill millions of people annually in Third World nations. And, in 1984, ''An estimated three million Africans, a third of them children, died of malaria'' (Bast et al. 1994, 100). Hecht (1992), quoting entomologist J. Gordon Edwards, says that ''100 million deaths per year were caused directly or indirectly by the antipesticide activities of the U.S. environmental groups.'' Drogin (1992) says that malaria is increasing worldwide and that ''More than 1 million people—mostly children under 5— die each year from a disease [malaria] that is both curable and preventable.'' Why isn't DDT used more?

Personal conversations with health officials in Zambia, Senegal, and Uganda from 1985 to 1993 tell us that availability of USAID funds is contingent on nonuse of DDT along with many other useful chemicals (see also Kinney 1994). Drogin (1992) says that DDT is not used in the Solomon Islands to control malaria due to environmental damage and high costs. The bottom line is that DDT, perhaps the single most useful public health chemical ever invented, is not in general use. From table 6.2 we see that about 900 million cases of insect-related diseases occur worldwide with about 14 million deaths, annually. Additionally, of the 10 to 20 million deaths of children caused by diarrhea, an unknown number is from transmission of disease by flies, mostly picked up from human feces. The annual deaths from DDT-controllable diseases may well approach 20 million people. For the past twenty years, the total deaths that could have been prevented through DDT use must be well into the hundreds of millions.

Is this genocide? If so, America's leftist Liability Culture leaders may rank well ahead of the other great killer leftist societies—the Soviet Union (61.911 million deaths) and China (35.236 million deaths) (Rummel 1995). Rummel's murder tolls are caused by governments, in all cases by dictatorial regimes. In contrast, deaths from Liability Culture policies do not spring from a dictatorial government, but from Left-controlled shadow-government bureaucracies in America. Certainly, Americans have never voted to conduct genocide on the "little brown people" of the world (see Van den Bosch quote in chapter 1). Most Americans are not even aware of the part the Liability Culture may have played in producing human misery on a massive, unheard of scale.

Blocking the use of DDT has its origins in leftist political maneuvering. The EPA's decision to stop DDT use in the United States was a "political" decision by EPA administrator William Ruckelshaus. He overrode the recommendation of his own hearing examiner, Edmund Sweeney. The initial impetus for the drive against DDT was by Rachel Carson, who said DDT would deplete America's bird populations. However, during the maximum use of DDT in America, the populations of most common birds increased by a factor of 10 to over 100 because of habitat improvement (Whelan 1993, 107). We showed in chapters 3 and 4 that the total impact of pesticide use in general is environmentally very beneficial because it allows us to use less land for agriculture. Therefore, our forests have expanded as have the wildlife within them. Carson's major conclusions were incorrect. Paradoxically, Rachel Carson, who was largely responsible for the ban, dedicated her book to Albert Schweitzer, who clearly saw DDT's life-saving potential for Third World people. Based on false data and bad science driven by the environmental Left, the Liability Culture banned DDT use in America.

Knowledge of the worldwide human implications of a ban on DDT was not lacking. White-Stevens (1978) says: "they [DDT and its analogues] were unceremoniously and irresponsibly banned. . . . It was predicted at the height of the controversy that such ill-considered and unjustifiable legislation would be tantamount to genocide on a scale which would dwarf the murderous roles of Hitler, Stalin and Ghengis Kahn combined. Hundreds of millions of defenseless, innocent human beings would perish." Edwards (1981) quoted a British scientist as saying in 1980 that "If the pressure groups had succeeded, if there had been a world ban on DDT, *Silent Spring* would now be killing more people in a single year than Hitler killed in his whole holocaust." Has it happened as predicted? Apparently so. America's political Left has—typically of the Left—apparently placed politics above all, in this case above compassion for humanity. Edwards (1992) stated that one of the goals of the eco-industry is "decimation of humans in the Third World countries by any means possible" (see also Hecht 1992). In addition, what is occurring is consistent with statements in chapter 1 made by such environmental leaders as Stewart, Brand, Prince Phillip, David Foreman, *Earth First! Newsletter,* Van den Bosch, David Graber, Paul W. Taylor, and Charles Wurster. But then most of the casualties are just Van den

Bosch's "little brown people" (chapter 1) out of sight on other continents. The political Left protects people of color in America while apparently killing them elsewhere.

In chapters 2 through 6, we showed that regulations are *not* responsible for most of the great environmental benefits from industrialization. Above all, *our regulations will not solve a single problem on the Shumburo list* (chapter 7). Applying industrial nations' pollution control standards to developing nations is both absurd and cruel. Trying to save poor people by regulating dangers that may cause death for 0.0014 people per 100,000 per year is not relevant to nations whose populations have an average longevity of only 35 to 50 years. The people are clearly dying from much more serious problems.

A comparison of annual death rates per 100,000 for the major industrial nations with the death rates for some developing nations shows vast differences. For industrial nations, the average death rate is about 1,000 per 100,000 per year; for all African nations, it is 4,300 per 100,000 per year, with Malawi the highest at 5,500 (Wright 1994). The excess death rate[2] for the Africans is 2,357,140 times the EPA's action level for regulating chemicals; for Malawi it is 3,214,290 times. Political stability, safe food and water, technology, sanitation, wealth, and affordable health care combine to produce the low death rates for industrial nations. Such rates should be possible for Africans also. Instead, the average death rate for Africa is 3,300 per 100,000 people per year above what should be possible. The excess deaths are largely caused by environmental problems on the Shumburo list. The particularly high disease rates result from uncontrolled insect vectors in combination with particulate-rich indoor air, fecal-contaminated waters, and poor nutrition (see chapter 6). Even if Africans were to be "saved" from all the dangers on the U.S. list of environmental hazards, their death rate would be the same.

Mahdi Shumburo said it quite clearly: "There is a paint factory outside Addis Ababa and it probably contaminates the local water. However, people are sick and dying of so many other things that it is difficult to know if the paint factory is an environmental problem" (personal communication).

CONCLUSIONS

The data summarized in this chapter are consistent with Abelson (1994, 1507), editor of *Science,* who says: "The current mode of extrapolating high-dose to low-dose effects is erroneous for both chemicals and radiation. Safe levels of exposure exist. The public has been needlessly frightened and deceived, and hundreds of billions of dollars wasted." Agreeing, Ames (1994), the authority on cancer from the University of California, says: "Huge expenditures of money and effort on tiny hypothetical risks does not improve public health. Rather, it diverts our resources from real human health hazards, and it hurts the economy." Kelly (1994) says: "Defining 'acceptable' risks is a first step on the road toward more rational federal regulations.'' From a legal perspective, Ernst (1994) says: ''The instances where environmental laws have led to incredible waste of resources are legion. The laws favor false crises instead of real environmental problems and even create greater problems than they were meant to eliminate.''

The 1990 Report of the Science Advisory Board, *Reducing Risk: Setting Priorities and Strategies for Environmental Protection,* says: ''There are heavy costs involved if society fails to set environmental priorities based on risk. If finite resources are expended on lower-priority problems at the expense of higher-priority risks, then society will face needlessly high risks. If priorities are established based on the greatest opportunities to reduce risk, total risks will be reduced in a more efficient way, lessening threats to both public health and local and global ecosystems.'' It is remarkable that such a statement has to be made. What this august body is really saying is that government regulatory bureaucracies should use the common sense that virtually every human routinely uses in daily life. Thus, most people do not put twenty-foot reinforced concrete roofs on their homes to protect themselves from meteorites or crashing airplanes; most people do not build a wall around their yards to protect themselves from a lion that might escape from a zoo. However, our regulatory bureaucracies routinely protect us from comparably remote dangers—and at enormous expense.

We have shown that expenditures to protect Americans from industrial chemicals *increase inversely proportional to the size of the need. The cost–benefit ratio is upside down.* As a benefit approaches zero (or is zero), the relative cost approaches infinity because dividing by zero *is* infinity. The cost–benefit ratios are also upside down on a worldwide basis. Easterbrook (1994, 61) says that ''a dollar spent protecting the environment will accomplish 10 times as much in the third world as in the first.'' America's regulatory community appears to be totally impermeable to criticisms that they are squandering wealth on environmental trivia.

Applying America's regulations about pesticides through USAID, in particular DDT, has probably cost hundreds of millions of lives and unimaginable human misery worldwide. America's nihilistic political Left of the Liability Culture must bear major responsibility for these deaths. So must America. Yet the decision to ban DDT in America was ''political'' according to Ruckelshaus who made the decision. Science was ignored; leftist propaganda was accepted.

We cannot justify most environmental regulations on the basis of increased human longevity or improvement in the natural environment. We conclude that the purposes of environmental regulations are more related to the needs of leftist bureaucrats and politicians, and the stated wish by many environmentalist leaders to drive civilizations and the economy backward.

- We suggest that the most pretentious spending during all history could well be what America now spends on environmental trivia.

- Had the system been developed for the specific purpose of squandering America's wealth or impeding its production, we could not have designed it better.
- If America's environmental regulations had the specific intent of destroying the human and natural environments of Third World nations, we could not have done better.
- The exaggeration of environmental risks by America's regulatory community is absolutely consistent with the examples of similar exaggerations in chapter 10. Virtually all exaggerations are in the same direction and stem from the same philosophy. *Scare the public green.* Scare the public into supporting their economic, philosophical, and political power.

The enormous waste of wealth is consistent with statements by the nihilistic Left of the Liability Culture. They have stated directly or by implication that they would like to dismantle the wealth-creating machinery, that is, modern industry. Remember Gore's "industrial civilizations' terrible onslaught against the natural world" and similar quotes in chapter 1?

Finally, the legislation and regulations are open-ended. An end point has never been officially defined for any regulations. Sowell (1995, 102) states the problem clearly: "even the most beneficial principle will become harmful if carried far enough." We can, therefore, continue infinitely to regulate less and less at ever greater cost. The willingness of the regulatory community to do precisely this has been amply demonstrated. As conditions now exist, the end point will occur only when there is no wealth left. Then most of the wishes of the environmental Left leaders as expressed in chapter 1 will come true.

NOTES

1. Carrying out these calculations to a single dollar is mathematically incorrect because the last nine numbers are not significant. A better, more accurate number would be $15.5 billion.
2. Actual death rate less the death rate achievable were they industrialized.

REFERENCES

Abelson, P. H. 1993. Pesticides and food. *Science* 259: 1235.
———. 1994. Risk assessment of low-level exposures. *Science* 265: 1507.
Ames, B. N. 1990. Carcinogens reconsidered. *Free Perspectives* 13(4): 3–4.
———. 1994. Science and the environment. *Environmental Solutions* (Newsletter published by Gelman Sciences): 1, 7.
Ames, B. N., R. Magaw, and L. S. Gold. 1987. Ranking possible carcinogenic hazards. *Science* 236: 271–72.
Ames, B. N., M. Profet, and L. S. Gold, 1990. Dietary pesticides (99.99% all natural). *Proceedings of the National Academy of Sciences* 87: 7777–81.
Anderson, W. 1991. Cholera epidemic traced to risk miscalculation. *Nature* 354: 225.
Anon. 1994a. Public nuisance no. 1. *Detroit News,* May 20.

————. 1994b. Rethinking risk. *Wall Street Journal,* December 6, A28.

————. 1995. Tuberculosis joins the DOTS. *The Economist,* May 20–26, 81.

————. 1996. Safety for EPA. *National Review* March 11, XLVIII, 4:20.

Arnold, R., and A. Gottlieb. 1993. *Trashing the Economy.* Bellevue, Wash.: Free Enterprise Press.

Bandow, D., and I. Vasquez, eds. 1994. *Perpetuating Poverty.* Washington, D.C.: Cato Institute.

Barro, R. J. 1994. Send regulations up in smoke. *Wall Street Journal,* June 3, A14.

Barrons, K. 1981. *Are Pesticides Really Necessary?* Chicago: Regnery Gateway.

Bast, J. L., P. J. Hill, and R. C. Rue. 1994. *Eco-Sanity, A Common-sense Guide to Environmentalism.* Lanham, Md.: Madison Books.

Bennett, M. J. 1991. *The Asbestos Racket.* Bellevue, Wash.: Free Enterprise Press.

Carson, R. 1962. *Silent Spring.* New York: Houghton Mifflin.

Case, A. G. 1993. Extreme responses to environmental risk. *Priorities,* Fall–Winter, 36–37.

Commoner, B. 1995. Prevention is the best pollution Rx. *Newsday,* April 21.

Communicable Disease Center. 1995. *Morbidity and Mortality Weekly Report,* March 24.

Crouch, E. L., and R. Wilson. 1982. *Risk/Benefit Analysis.* Cambridge: Balinger.

Drogin, B. 1992. Malaria worsening worldwide despite efforts. *Dallas Morning News,* August 1.

Duesenberg, R. W. 1994. Economic liberties and the law, *Imprimus* 23(4).

Easterbrook, G. 1994. Forget PCB's, radon, Alar (the world's greatest dangers are dung, smoke and dirty water). *New York Times Magazine,* September 11, 60–63.

Edwards, J. G. 1981. *Silent Spring—Broken Spring.* Louisville, Ky.: National Council for Environmental Balance.

————. 1983. Banned DDT. *Fusion,* May–June, 37–44.

————. 1992. Remarks by J. Gordon Edwards, San Jose State University, to DDT Press Conference, National Press Club, May 21.

Efron, E. 1984. *The Apocalyptics, Cancer and the Big Lie.* New York: Simon and Schuster.

Environmental Protection Agency. 1989. *U.S. Federal Register,* July 12, 29497.

————. 1991. EPA regulates new group of drinking water contaminants. *Environmental News,* January 7.

Ernst. R. J. 1994. The real environmental crisis: Environmental law. *Imprimus* 25(5).

Gold, L. S., T. H. Stone, B. R. Stern, N. B. Manley, and B. N. Ames. 1992. Rodent carcinogens: Setting priorities. *Science* 258: 261.

Gore, A. 1992. *Earth in the Balance.* New York: Houghton Mifflin.

Hecht, M. M. 1992. The death toll from environmental hoaxes. *21st Century Science,* Fall, 13.

Heinz, A. 1991. *Issues in Nutrition.* New York: American Council on Science and Health.

Hurst, B. 1994. Some thoughts from a Missouri farm. *Wall Street Journal,* February 15, A15.

Jukes, T. H. 1983. Chasing a receding zero: Impact of the zero threshold concept on actions of regulatory officials. *Journal of the American College of Toxicology* 22(3): 147–60.

————. 1986. The tragedy of DDT. *Fusion,* July–August, 5–7.

————. 1992. Environmental hoaxes kill. *21st Century Science and Technology,* Fall, 11–18.

Kelly, K. A. 1994. The myth of 10^{-6} as a definition of acceptable risk. Paper presented at Air and Waste Management Association: 4th annual meeting, Vancouver, B.C.

Kelly, K. A., and N. C. Cardon. 1994. The myth of 10^{-6} as a definition of acceptable risk. *EPA Watch* 4(1): 4–8.

Kinney, J. E. 1994. U.S. bullied others into banning DDT. *Wall Street Journal*, May 25. Letter to the editor.

Loeb, A. P., and A. L. Taboas. 1994. Principles of a multimedia, risk-based, market-driven environmental approach. *Technology: Journal of the Franklin Institute* 331A: 279–94.

Maddox, J. 1972. *The Doomsday Syndrome: An Attack on Pessimism.* New York: Mc-Graw-Hill.

Malkin, J. 1994. How the U.S. wastes its preventive health dollars. *Priorities* 6(4): 27–28.

Milloy, S. J., P. S. Aycock, and J. E. Johnston. 1994. *Choices in Risk Assessment.* Washington, D.C.: Sandia National Laboratories and U.S. Department of Energy.

Moghissi, A. A. 1994. Risk analysis: An attempt to standardize the process and its applications. *Technology: Journal of the Franklin Institute* 331A: 29–40.

O'Brian, B. 1994. An illegal pleasure: The smell in the air of bread being baked. *Wall Street Journal*, April 23, A1.

Parker, F. L., et al. 1994. *Building Consensus through Risk Assessment and Management.* Washington, D.C.: National Research Council, National Academy Press.

Roberts, P. C. 1994. Development planning in Latin America: The lifeblood of the mercantilist state. In *Perpetuating Poverty,* edited by D. Bandow and I. Vasquez. Washington, D.C.: Cato Institute.

Ross, M. 1994. *The New Idria Serpentinite of California: A Toxic Rock?* Abstract, Department of Geology, Texas A and M, April 22.

Rummel, R. J. 1995. *Death by Government.* 2nd ed. New Brunswick, N.J.: Transaction

Smith, K. 1994. The media's war on essential chemicals: Targeting chlorine. *Priorities* 6(1): 6–11.

Sowell, T. 1994. When courts make the law. *Albany Times Union,* August 31, A12.

———. 1995. *The Vision of the Anointed.* New York: Basic Books.

Tengs, T. O., et al. 1994. Five-hundred life-saving interventions and their cost-effectiveness. Draft of working manuscript, July 7, Harvard Center for Risk Analysis.

Warren, M., and B. Jones. 1995. *Downsizing the Number of Federal Regulators.* St. Louis: Center for Study of American Business.

Weinstein, M. C. 1983. Cost-effective priorities for cancer prevention. *Science* 221: 17–23.

Whelan, E. M. 1985. *Toxic Terror.* Ottawa, Ill.: Jameson Books.

———. 1993. *Toxic Terror: The Truth behind the Cancer Scares.* Buffalo, N.Y.: Prometheus Books.

White-Stevens, R. H. 1978. *Coercive Utopians Unleash Insect-Vectored Diseases on Man.* Louisville, Ky.: National Council for Environmental Balance.

Wilson, R., A. M. Langer, R. P. Nolan, J. B. L. Gee, and M. Ross. 1994. Asbestos in New York City school buildings—public policy: Is there a scientific basis? *Regulatory Toxicology and Pharmacology* 20: 1–9.

World Health Organization. 1979. *DDT and Its Derivatives.* Environmental Health Criteria 9, Geneva.

———. 1993. *Tropical Disease Research Progress, 1991–1992.* Geneva: United Nations.

Wright, J. W. 1994. *The Universal Almanac.* Kansas City: Andrews and McMeel.

CHAPTER 12

The Cultural-Environmental War

A cultural-environmental war is raging. The outcome of this war will decide the future of both humanity and nature. Yet humanity is confused, largely because of the mechanisms described in chapters 10 and 11. Historically, the environmental conflict in America and other industrial democracies has had environmentalists (good guys) on one side, industry (bad guys) on the other. Chapter 7 showed that the American public believes this is the conflict. Arnold (1987) describes the nature of the war between environmentalists and industry. However, what was true in 1987 is only partially true now. With the death of communism and with socialism having doubtful viability, the nature of the conflict has changed. Still, the environmental war, as it always has been, is part of a much larger philosophical conflict, a cultural war.

The war has a curious aspect. Sowell (1994, A12) says: ''One of the reasons why one side has been winning the cultural wars around the country is that most people on the other side seem to be unaware that a war is going on.'' We suggest that even those who are aware of a conflict may not know who the foes really are.

We have a problem naming the sides of the cultural war so as to define their common threads, while assuring that we do not exclude some critical elements. More important, we do not wish to offend the probable majority of environmentalists who may be quite innocent, merely misled. We are also fearful of describing motives, because motives are highly variable. For example, many people who support one side may not subscribe to all the core philosophies of that side. Yet we must give the sides names, and we must ascribe some motives. Without names, discussions are unwieldy. Without some motivational analysis, nothing makes sense. So, with apologies, we plunge ahead.

We see the conflict as between a Liability Culture and an Asset Culture. The Liability Culture sees its economic, philosophical, religious, or political interests tied to the liability side of the environmental ledger. The group is heterogeneous.

For example, the political Left is a major part of the Liability Culture. Most examples of the causes of public confusion detailed in chapter 10 spring from the Liability Culture's political Left. However, many businesspeople who are not leftists are firmly in the Liability Culture corner. They are simply making a buck.

The Asset Culture considers the liability side, but they are more attuned to the asset side of the environmental ledger. This culture consists largely of doers. Doers have created most of the great environmental assets we now enjoy, along with some of the liabilities. They are not very good philosophers. Most are so busy competing in the marketplace that they have little or no time to debate with the Liability Culture. So the doers shrug their shoulders at the strings attached by the Liability Culture and keep on doing. Most of the members of the Asset Culture are not really part of the cultural debate, although they are very much in the war. They are probably the majority.

Free marketers, libertarians, and conservatives, for the most part, are the philosophical component of the Asset Culture. They are the Asset Culture's conscience and articulate its rationale. They are critical of the majority in the Asset Culture because they believe they should wake up. They are highly critical of the negativity of the Liability Culture. They do what they can to snip the strings that the Liability Culture attaches to the Asset Culture.

A major problem with the Asset Culture is that it primarily fights the Liability Culture by showing the extraordinary inefficiencies of the Liability Culture's regulations. The Asset Culture does not seem to understand the enormous environmental benefits for which the Asset Culture itself is responsible. Chapters 2 through 6 described these benefits and their causes. In addition, the Asset Culture does not seem to understand the enormous counterproductivity of the Liability Culture in its own terms of reference. So the Asset Culture moves onward not fully understanding its own worth. To a surprising degree, it appears to accept the evaluations of its critics.

While the doers are trying to go full speed ahead, the Liability Culture is trying to go full speed backward. This is the conflict.

The people of the philosophical core of the Liability Culture are the same as in the 1960s. However, some of their philosophies have changed to fit modern realities. The philosophical leaders of the Liability Culture present facts selectively based on political preconceptions. The deceptions of chapter 10 are theirs. So also are the exaggerations of chapter 11. Bailey (1993, 62) says: "Instead of policy being guided by factual information, the facts are being forced to fit the policy requirements of certain politicians, bureaucrats and activists." Whatever the details of their philosophies, they believe that increasing regulations and big government will produce the results they want. Expanding government in America and supporting even the United Nations' ineptitudes are results of their beliefs.

The free marketers, the Asset Culture's conscience, are apolitical in the sense that they base their views about the environment on science and valid statistics.

Facts are the basis for conclusions and political decisions instead of vice versa. They are primarily free market proponents who favor less government. Many are libertarian or political conservatives. Currently, the free market side has the upper hand, at least in the political arena. However, the Liability Culture is powerful, tenacious, and patient. The war is far from over (see chapter 13).

Industry, the sleeping Gulliver, is on the sidelines of the war. Industry as a whole so lacks understanding of the real conflict that it gives far more financial support to its enemies than to its friends (Maduro and Schauerhammer 1992b; Arnold and Gottlieb 1993).

THE LIABILITY CULTURE

The first and most important step toward improving the world's environment is to assure that educational institutions and the major media inform the industrial nations' people about environmental matters in a balanced way. This is not easy because the forces arrayed against balance are powerful. These forces include political, bureaucratic, educational, and industrial components. Their goals include power, wealth, and political or religious influence. Their success depends on the public being continuously uninformed or misinformed about environmental matters. They are the Liability Culture. Many believe they benefit from public hysteria and therefore, do what they can to perpetuate it or do little to dispel it. The Liability Culture has multiple motivating philosophies, which vary from honest concern to simple self-interest.

The "Good" People

Most of the people within the Liability Culture's ranks are the "good people," who, Reisman (1992) says, are basic to any "ism." They are part of the "concerned" to whom this book is dedicated; they are also the deceived. They are good because they are honestly concerned. They are deceived because the environmental Left has sold them the liability side of the environmental ledger. We are certain that they are totally unaware of many implications of the core philosophies of the Liability Culture's political Left. Our certainty is based on our judgment that most people are not suicidal. Because the "good people" do not direct the Liability Culture's agenda, we do not discuss them further.

The Academic and Other Leftist Theorists

The philosophies driving the Liability Culture have largely originated in academia. In this section, we discuss at length these philosophies and their implications. They have an enormous impact on the world's human and natural environments. The number of people at the philosophical heart of environmentalism (academics, politicians, and environmental society leaders) is small. Coffman (1994, 77, 98) estimates that they represent only about 5 percent of environmentalists. "Yet they have had a profound effect on America's environmental policy" (p. 78).

College protesters of the 1960s are sometimes credited with starting the conflict. In actuality, however, the real conflict is far older. Karl Marx in the early to mid-1800s supplied some of the philosophical base. The philosophical conflict about forms of government became intense around the world in the early 1900s when Lenin came to power in Russia. Interchanges between American and Russian academics were common (Klehr et al. 1995). The 1960s were the years when forces of the Left first had high visibility and major influence on public policy. The 1960s saw the rise of America's counterculture. We include it in the Liability Culture. Their basic environmental question was: *Why didn't you make the world perfect for us?*

The philosophical leftist core is centered in, but is not restricted to, academia. It consists partly of state-of-mind Communists (Bethell, 1995); some are Socialists; Efron (1984) calls them the "coercive utopians"; Sowell calls them "the anointed." Some appropriately call themselves Neo-Luddites or Neo-Luddita (see chapter 1). Sympathetic politicians for public record may call themselves simply Democrats or Republicans, or, less likely, liberals. None would call themselves Communists or Socialists, for that would be politically suicidal. All see big government as the answer to their version of the world's problems; all have a vision for the future of humans.

The visions of the leftist counterculture evolved through the years. Initially, intellectual idealists visualized a socialist or communist utopia. To achieve that end, they had to discredit free enterprise, democracy, and Western ideals along with the industry that thrived in the system. They used the environment as one mechanism to attack democracy. According to Swogger (1992, 7): "Marxists emphasized its [science and progress] dark side under capitalism." Then, with the failure of communism and socialism, their socialistic utopian ideal no longer made sense. The intellectual idealists then substituted the concept of ecological utopia in which humankind lives "sustainably," close to, and in harmony with, nature. Leguery-Feilleux (1995, 4) relates happiness in eco-topia not to income or things but to "good friends, appreciation of music, the arts, reading or finding fulfillment through spiritual, religious or aesthetic experience."[1] Socialists became eco-socialists.

According to Rubin (1994, 5), "dreams of socialist utopia, in which resources are managed by government to maximize the good of humanity, give way to dreams of ecological utopia, in which resources are managed by government to maximize the good of all life on earth."

Philosophies evolve. Most of the original Left are no longer idealistic. They are disillusioned. They long ago rejected Judeo-Christian religion; reality shattered their dream about a utopia of the Left; they rejected the disciplines of science, markets, and public opinion. Additionally, many have found that primitive people, including the American Indian, were never the idealized ecologists they imagined (see chapter 2). For example, Coffman (1994, 91) says that the

Mayan civilization west of Mexico City from 1,200 years ago until the arrival of the white man caused annual erosion rates of over "eighty-five tons per acre." Currently the erosion rate is about two and a half. Somewhat similarly, Graber (1959) remarks about the Third World's "suicidal consumption of landscape" (which we also observed in chapter 2). Many better-informed leftists now realize that the eco-socialist ideal of returning to the land to live in a more primitive state makes little sense. Again disillusionment.

Reisman (1992, 349) analyzes the philosophies that currently motivate many leftist intellectuals. He argues that to a large extent, their leaders' views are products of a mix of contaminating philosophies. Besides Marxism, he lists other related intellectual "toxins" such as "racism, nationalism, and feminism; and cultural relativism, determinism, logical positivism, existentialism, linguistic analysis, behaviorism, Freudianism, Keynesianism, and more." He says: "These intellectual toxins can be seen bobbing up and down in the intellectual mainstream." In one way or another, they all stress the liability side of the environment and Western culture.

According to Robert Bidinoto (quoted in Arnold and Gottlieb 1993, 272), "Environmentalism represents a now-denuded Marxism, stripped of all its tenets, desperately clutching its last fig leaf of mindless egalitarianism. As such, it is a purely negative, contentious 'ism.' It is the final rallying point for nihilistic drifters and collectivist dreamers, who are united, not by ideas, but by a hostility toward human thought; not by values, but by an aversion for human aspirations; not by some utopian vision of society, but by a profound alienation from human society."

As suggested by Reisman (1992), a world helped by the political Left (the philosophical heart of the Liability Culture) is akin to a patient going to a doctor who wants him dead or who is on the side of the disease. Reisman (p. 345) says: "All of the insanities of the environmental movement become intelligible when one grasps the nature of the destructive nature behind them. They are not uttered in the interest of man's life and well-being, but for the purpose of leading him to self-destruction." Reisman (p. 338) says that the current doctrines of the Left are rationalized by "the doctrine of intrinsic value of nature," which is a "negation of human values."

Bidinoto and Reisman both conclude that the environmental Left is motivated by something other than improving the environment. Key words are hostility, aversion, alienation, self-destruction, destructive nature, and insanities. Additionally, Moghissi (1994, 39) wondering about the opposition of environmentalists to economic risk analyses says: "their opposition was guided by objectives other than protection of human health and the environment." Finally, Coffman (1994, 114) concludes that "Most environmental leaders are not interested in finding better management tools" and that "environmental protection is not the real goal. The real goal is to obstruct all growth and development" (p. 116). The statements quoted in chapter 1 from leading members of the environmental Left are consistent with Bidinoto's, Reisman's, Moghissi's, and

Coffman's conclusions. We conclude that the total impact of the philosophies, legislation, regulations, and administrative actions driven by the environmental Left is to create enormous human hardship and to destroy much of the world's soil, forests, and wildlife (see chapters 2–6 and 12–13). The reason is quite clear: *virtually all major improvements in the human environment, all reductions in soil erosion, and all increases in forest and wildlife in the world are the results of technology, growth, and development—the very things the environmental Left so hates.*

The doctrines of the environmental Left are part of a larger philosophical picture. Kagan (1994, A12) says "Nihilism rejects any objective basis for society and its morality, the very concept of objectivity, even the possibility of communication itself, and a vulgar form of nihilism has a remarkable influence in our education system today." Teaching only the liability side of the environmental ledger in schools and colleges is consistent with teaching only the liability side of Western culture.

What are the ideologies that the environmental Left wishes to impose? After all, even history's most recent monsters—Hitler, Stalin, and Mao—offered people something, flawed though their offerings were. Does the environmental Left offer the public socialism, communism, or even fascism? Coffman (1994) suggests that what we call the environmental Left offers a new religion that glorifies nature and deprecates humans. "It is based on pseudo science" (p. 121). Many of its components spring from socialist ideas.

So, what do they really offer? Based on statements quoted in chapter 1 and on the environmental impacts of their activities they offer the following. *We seek to destroy the industrial system, democracy, and Western culture as now known. We will tolerate only politically correct science, only politically correct media.* We do not know whether any of these Neo-Luddites are astute enough to add, *we will also destroy the world's forests and much of its wildlife and soil* (see our chapter 13).

The absolutely fatal flaw in the environmental Left's perspective—the fatal flaw in Gore's book—is that it sees only the negatives of modern civilizations. Therefore, the Left cannot learn from the successes that have occurred. Because they see only the liability side of everything, they offer society nothing. No progress of any sort has ever resulted from negativism. Robinson (1994, 1) says of the leftist countercultural educational elite, the philosophical core of the Liability Culture: "Their values are inverted from ours. The things we see as advances, they see as destabilizing."

The only reason the environmental Left has credibility is that it has the support of so much of the educational area and is reported on uncritically by the major media. The environmental Left cannot state its true beliefs to the public. However, their own statements (chapter 1) and the results of their activities make their positions clear. According to Sowell (1995b, A10), "What we have . . . is a whole class of people dedicated to imposing their ideologies on others and too contemptuous of the society in which they live to feel any need to be honest about what they are doing." We believe that a fully informed public would relegate the concepts of the environmental Left to the junk pile of history's failures.

Private Environmental Societies and Clubs

We group the leaders of the most prominent environmental organizations within the Liability Culture's forces. Many of their leaders share the academic leftists' views. For example, Lichter (1995) reports a survey of the views of one hundred senior staffers and boards of directors of such environmental organizations as the Sierra Club, The Environmental Defense Fund, and the Natural Resources Defense Council. The survey showed:

- Most favor saving endangered species regardless of cost.
- Most would not compensate landowners when their land loses value because of endangered species.
- Most (93%) support Bill Clinton.
- Most see industry as the primary cause of cancer.
- Most favor keeping the Delaney Clause.

Their views were counter to those of the public for the first three items and counter to the view of knowledgeable scientists for the last two. Clearly the leaders of most environmental organizations are firmly within the political Left. Others' opinions do not shake their beliefs. Nor do facts.

Stevens (1995) describes the classic downside position of environmentalists. Although they now acknowledge reforestation of much of the East, they complain of "fragmentation of forest landscape" by development. Yet the loss of so many miles of no-longer-used rural roads in much of the East is precisely in the opposite direction. And Lovejoy (also quoted in our chapter 4) complains that biodiversity trends are "negative." Our data show the opposite. According to Stevens, they complain that "while there may be more trees, many are smaller." Of course that is the case. All trees start small. Further, the prevalence of smaller, new-growth trees, grasses, and forbs is precisely why there is abundant wildlife (see chapter 4). These groups belittle or ignore environmental gains, largely believing the environmental tenet that things can only get worse (Easterbrook 1995, 11).

With the benefits of industrialization reflected in enormous environmental gains, one might naively conclude environmental organizations would be elated. For example, the Audubon Society is well aware of the increased populations of many birds since the 1800s and that many species of birds formerly absent or rare are now abundant in the Midwest (see, for example, the 1992 article in *Audubon* by Welsch). The Wilderness Society, the Nature Conservancy, the World Resources Institute, the World Wildlife Fund, Conservation International,

Defenders of Wildlife, and the Fund for Animals should also be elated at the benefits to nature that have resulted from industrialization. Logically, they should encourage industrial development. After all, wildlife are most diverse and abundant in large areas of such highly developed states as New Jersey, Pennsylvania, New York, and Michigan. Further, development in small areas (cities) is usually more than matched by *dedevelopment* in other far larger areas (see chapters 2 and 3). Yet most environmental organizations are staunchly anti-industry, antidevelopment, and antiurbanization. This is even more surprising when one realizes that fully half the funding for environmental organizations comes directly from industry or industrial foundations (see Arnold and Gottlieb 1993, among others).

Some of the negativity of environmental organizations makes more sense if we realize their leaders' future is dependent on an uninformed or misinformed public. After all, who would contribute to environmentalists' coffers if there were few environmental problems? They cannot even stress the gains for which they are responsible. Their fear: to show how they have reduced auto emissions in the Los Angeles Basin by 90 percent, to show that America's air and waters are vastly cleaner than a few decades ago could lead to the conclusion that they are no longer needed. Perhaps the objectives Moghissi (1994) wondered about are more related to survival of their organizations and leftist philosophy than to the environment.

Communications Media

An indispensable frontline force of the Liability Culture has been the major communications media. Environmental organizations and environmentalists could have little impact without the cooperation of the major media, primarily television and some big newspapers. The moviemakers have also contributed. That the media have, long before Gore, been deaf to good environmental news is obvious. As Lichter (1995, A10) says, "And environmentalists have gotten a lot of help from journalists who regard them as upholders of the planet's interest, as against private interests who would despoil the earth for their personal or private profit." The position is typical of the Left. In addition, when major media interview environmentalists, those quoted in chapter 1 are high on their list of acceptable "experts." The result is widespread ignorance of the public about environmental assets created by industry, wealth, and free enterprise. Wattenberg's (1984a) "The Good News Is the Bad News Is Wrong" and Easterbrook's (1990) "Everything You Know about the Environment Is Wrong" are both intended to counteract the consistently negative view of the environment that the public sees in the major media.

Resistance to informing the public about environmental gains that Americans enjoy will be very difficult to overcome. The negative makes news. In addition, according to Wattenberg (1984b, 375), the media's "liberal bias is not conspiratorial. They're only telling the truth as they see it."

Environmental Authors

A vast literature describing the harm industry and humans are doing to the environment has been essential for the Liability Culture. Authors of this literature are academics, politicians, professional environmentalists, and professional writers. The best known early author was George Perkins Marsh (1864, 1874), who described worldwide influences of man on the environment. Other early authors were Muir (1913) and Leopold (1949). More recent examples are Carson (1962), Ehrlich (1968), Meadows et al. (1972), Lovins (1977), and Chivian (1993). These are but a few examples of a vast literature. The character of the literature has evolved from essentially apolitical to strongly political.

Predominant environmental literature of the past few decades has the following characteristics:

- It points out problems, many of which are anecdotal.
- In the early years, environmental literature usually blamed industry for problems.
- Currently, it describes environmental problems as both people-caused and industry-caused.
- It is short on practical answers.
- Most authors are from the political Left.

In addition, little politically correct environmental literature reaches peer-reviewed scientific journals. Scientists, particularly in recent years, have become better at recognizing research that produces only politically correct results. However, good sound research, carefully done and carefully checked, can always get into the literature no matter what the conclusions.

Teachers

Children learn environmental misconceptions early in school. Schools teach few of the facts summarized in this book. Instead, students learn about the severity of environmental problems, the liability side of the environmental ledger.

Kwong (1995, 155) summarizes the problem: "(1) children are being scared into becoming environmental activists, (2) there is widespread misinformation in materials aimed at children, (3) children are being taught *what* to think, rather than *how* to think, (4) children are taught that human beings are evil, (5) children are feeling helpless and pessimistic about their future on earth, and (6) environmental education is being used to undermine the simple joys of childhood." Teaching children the hopeless, bleak views of the academic Left is a potential tragedy. Our children are being used as pawns in a cultural war.

Part of the problem is the Left orientation of the National Education Association (NEA). Part of the problem is teacher ignorance. The failure to educate involves more than the environment. Scholastic Aptitude Test averages have dropped about 5 percent for mathematics and 12 percent for verbal skills since the 1950s. Simultaneously, the cost of education per student has risen about 250 percent in constant dollars. Children who lack the mental discipline imposed by a rigorous education are far more susceptible to slanting in environmental matters. Thus, one byproduct of America's educational system is gullibility about the environment.

Government Regulators

Government regulatory agencies are largely part of the Liability Culture because they have a high stake in the public's environmental opinion. An environmentally motivated public increases their power and their budgets. Exaggerating environmental dangers is in their interest (see chapter 11). Minimizing environmental gains, including their own, keeps them in business.

Often, regulatory agencies work closely with private environmental organizations (Arnold and Gottlieb 1993). For example, the EPA cooperates with the Environmental Defense Fund in radio advertising about the importance of recycling for "saving the earth."

Finally, both government regulators and environmental organizations fight the use of economic analysis of risks when evaluating regulations. Common sense is against both their self-interests.

Legislatures

Most of America's legislators have been part of the Liability Culture. They have been overwhelmingly liberal, and many of their goals have been compatible with those of the environmental Left. In the past two decades, Congress has passed some three hundred laws meant to improve the environment (Arnold and Gottlieb 1993). For environmental advice, Congress has listened extensively to the leaders quoted in chapter 1. It should come as no surprise, therefore, that America's environmental regulations produce results that are compatible with the no-growth, antihuman ideas of the environmental Left. Legislators have been the Liability Culture's frontline troops, translating their philosophies into laws.

Environmentalist control of the liberal component of Congress is still strong. For example, "environmental lobbyists are so scared of risk-assessment that in March 1994, they issued a memo declaring they'd rather not pass any environmental bills this year than pass legislation carrying risk assessment language (or property rights language or unfunded mandates relief). That strategy has been carried out by House enforcer Henry Waxman who from his perch at the Energy and Commerce Committee has blocked House considerations" (*Wall Street Journal* editorial, September 15, 1994). The ability of America's environmentalists to influence Congress is considerable.

Finally, we note that legislators never campaign on a no-growth platform that puts nature ahead of people. They know that most people would not vote to destroy industry and Western values. So, instead, they "save the environment."

Politically Correct Scientists and Engineers

"Scientists" who are politically correct only draw conclusions that are acceptable to the political Left. Several examples are given in chapter 10. They have supplied the technical base for the Liability Culture. Politically correct science has the following characteristics:

- It serves a political purpose, currently the political Left.
- It asks only politically acceptable questions.
- It arrives only at politically acceptable conclusions.
- It massively misinforms the public.

Thom (1994, 78) exemplifies politically correct engineering. In the name of the American Association of Engineering Societies he says: "All the indicators—ozone, climate change, loss of biodiversity, population, acid rain—show that the contest between technology and nature has now reached an advanced and dangerous stage." Thom's list consists of politically correct environmental speculations that are highly questionable at best.

Industry

Although we paint a picture of industry as the enhancer of the environment, it is not because industry has tried to save the environment (nor do we see that as industry's purpose). Environmental improvement resulting from industry is almost inadvertent and sometimes has occurred in spite *of* industry.

Many industries support politically oriented environmental organizations and are important for the Liability Culture's forces. Maduro and Schauerhammer (1992b) and Arnold and Gottlieb (1993) point out that about half the $1.178 billion annual revenues for major environmental organizations in the United States come directly from industry or industrial foundations. Considering that the environmental movement is largely anti-industry, this may seem surprising. Even more surprising, environmental organizations that do *not* see industry as a major culprit have difficulty obtaining industrial financing and often barely survive. Industry contributes over three times as much money to the Liability Culture as it does to the Asset Culture's forces.

The seemingly anomalous industrial support of environmental organizations occurs for several reasons. Some industries contribute to environmental organizations to show that they are not antienvironment. Some in industry are leftists, so-called limousine liberals. And Klehr et al. (1995, 26–30) conclude that Armand Hammer of Occidental Petroleum was a Soviet agent.

Most large industries have extensive divisions devoted to solving legal and other problems associated with environmental regulations. Thus, within industry is a major segment that *benefits* from environmental regulations. The more severe and irrational the regulations, the more that segment gains. Obviously this group has a stake in maintaining public concern. Can their employers rely on such people to give valid advice regarding regulations, especially when reduced regulations could mean their jobs?

Some large companies support environmental organizations because environmental regulations are much harder on small companies. Small companies may either be forced out of business or forced to sell out to larger companies. Arnold and Gottlieb (1993, 594) say: "Large, well-capitalized companies attempt to destroy their medium and small competition by systematically supporting environmental groups that conceive, draft, lobby, and test in the courts new environmental laws so stringent that only large, well-capitalized companies can afford to comply." Similarly, an article entitled "Regulate Us, Please" published in *The Economist* (Anon. 1994) shows how some companies lobby for environmental standards that their competitors cannot meet. Some lobby for regulations that create a demand for their own products.

Clearly, many businesses do not like competition. Free enterprise and competition are more favorable to consumers then businesses. DiLorenzo et al. (1990) and Echard (1990) conclude that many large businesses favor socialism because they see it as a way of holding down competition. The major element many leading environmentalists and some large industries have in common is dislike of free enterprise.

Some industries reinforce the public's phobias and hysteria to sell their products. Every product advertised as "all natural," "no artificial preservatives," "no chemicals added," or "no artificial coloring" reinforces the perception among many people that "natural" chemicals are *by definition* good and manufactured chemicals are *by definition* bad. Thus, some industries reinforce the public's irrational chemiphobia to feather their own economic nests.

Similarly, Chrysler advertises its use of CFC-free refrigerants, saying: "The ozone layer has protected us for 1.5 billion years. It's time we returned the favor." The natural gas industry has reinforced the environmentally questionable Clean Air Act Amendments of 1990 by advertising that natural gas does not produce acid rain.

High energy prices, which oil companies like, help neither the world economy nor the world environment. Failing to develop atomic energy, making coal continuously more expensive, and blocking hydropower developments all contribute to high energy prices and help the oil companies. We do not know the extent that these factors account for major support of environmental organizations by such oil companies as Chevron, Standard (largely through Rockefeller funds), Mobil, Ashland, ARCO, AMOCO, Pennzoil, Halliburtan, and Shell.

To help industries with environmental regulations, a substantial compliance industry has developed. The *Environmental Business Review* places its 1992 gross revenue at $133.7 billion, one of the largest industries in the United States. The health of this industry is absolutely dependent on a never-ending stream of regulations.

The environmental consulting industry also benefits from strict regulations (Dunn Corporation was such a firm). This industry has two major components: those who work for potential plaintiffs in litigation and those who work for potential defendants (usually manufacturing industries). Those who work for plaintiffs often are political leftists. Those who work for defendants often are more to the political Right. However, whether working for plaintiffs or defendants, consultants gain economically from regulations or government-funded cleanup programs.

A natural question arises: If so many major industries fund the Liability Culture, do those industries actually control it? We suspect that some industries believe that they are in control. They are certainly able to control some activities of the Liability Culture leading to short-term profits. Yet the "Neo-Luddites" are in philosophical control. A major potential result of activities fostered by the environmental Left will be to destroy both industrial productivity and industrial markets. These results are compatible with quotes in chapter 1. Thus the industries that assume they control the Liability Culture will themselves be victims of the environmental Left. They may be funding their own demise.

Trial Lawyers

America's trial lawyers, as much as any other group, have benefited financially from environmental regulations that spring from the irrationalities of the Liability Culture. Lawyers, in a sense, benefit from the incompetence of lawyers. Ambiguous and poorly written laws (largely formulated by lawyers in legislatures) create enormous legal conflict. Thus, lawyers get rich. For example, in 1980 Congress established unlimited liability when it enacted Superfund, a law so open to bureaucratic involvement as to drastically hinder achieving its avowed objective of cleaning up 1,800 hazardous waste sites. Only about 200 sites have been cleaned up to specifications at the cost of $15 billion—10 times the original estimate to remediate all sites. At least one-third of that went to attorneys. The current estimate for the rest of the 1,300 sites is $90 to $350 billion. Cleanup of what are defined as "contaminated" sites would cost over $1 trillion—about 670 times the original cost estimate.

The United Nations

We are critical of various environmental-developmental policies of the UN. The actions and published materials of the environment and development component of the UN have placed it firmly in the corner of the Liability Culture. The 1987 "Brundtland report," *Our Common Future,* details that position. First, the UN accepts crisis conditions as fact. Second, the report assumes that only a

UN environmental bureaucracy can prevent the loss of the planet. Thus, the UN merely repeats the attack on modern industrial societies and sees big government as the only answer.

Rarely does the UN's environmental and development component suggest that any environmental benefits can occur without government help. The possibility that many environmental problems may solve themselves as the natural outgrowth of industrialization and wealth creation is not seriously considered.

Other parts of the UN, however, may have somewhat different perspectives. The Food and Agriculture Organization (FAO) and the World Health Organization (WHO) appear to have a more positive view of the world.

THE ASSET CULTURE

Within the past fifteen years or so, a substantial groundswell of opinion makers has been critical of environmentalism. Most are conservatives or libertarians; many are former leftists or environmentalists. This section describes some proponents of the Asset Culture side of the environmental war. We include in the Asset Culture all doers, all people who see environmental assets in addition to liabilities, and all who are philosophically antagonistic to the political Left. We believe, however, that many who are within the Asset Culture's ranks do not fully understand the complexities of the environment.

Literature

Conservative, libertarian, and generally market-oriented authors have written many articles and books describing the follies of environmentalism and the resulting public confusion and government overregulation. A group of women authors are standouts: Efron (1984), Whelan (1985, 1993), Ray (1990, 1993), and Maxey (1990). We add the libertarian, Ayn Rand, who, although not writing about the environment, describes much of the current conflict in *Atlas Shrugged* as well as in many articles. Some male authors who have written excellent relevant books are Maddox (1972), Weber (1979), Barrons (1978, 1981), Maurice and Smithson (1984), Wattenberg (1984b), Arnold (1987), Simon (1990), Brooks (1991), Anderson and Leal (1991), Maduro and Schauerhammer (1992a), Lehr (1992), Fumento (1993), Arnold and Gottlieb (1993), Coffman (1994), and Easterbrook (1995). Some authors are highly critical of various components of the Liability Culture. Others, while still critical, summarize much of the asset side of the environmental ledger. These include Barrons, Wattenberg, Simon, Coffman, and Easterbrook.

Major Media

On occasion, the major media have taken positions supporting the Asset Culture side. Largely concurring with the above authors, the *New York Times* published a series of articles (Schneider 1993; Specter 1993; and Brinkley 1993). These articles stress the absurdity of spending huge amounts of money on trivial environmental problems. Easterbrook's (1994) article in the *New York Times Magazine* is also a departure from usual policy. Until these landmark articles, the *New York Times* had usually aligned itself with the largely liberal environmental community.

Typical of these articles, Schneider (1993, 1) says: "many scientists, economists and government officials have reached the dismaying conclusion that much of America's environmental program has gone seriously awry. These experts say that in the last 15 years environmental policy has too often evolved largely in reaction to popular panics, not in response to sound scientific analyses of which environmental hazards present the greatest risk. As a result . . . billions of dollars are wasted each year in battling problems that are no longer considered especially dangerous, leaving little money for others that cause far more harm." Schneider further quotes Richard Morgenstern, acting administrator of the EPA for Policy and Evaluation, as saying: "We're now in a position of saying in quite a few of our programs, Oops, we made a mistake."

On April 21, 1994, ABC news aired a program hosted by John Stossel. He discussed Alar, asbestos, and other substances and showed how the United States is spending its wealth on the wrong things, because it is not using risk assessment analyses. Stossel also concluded that because regulations can make us poor, our poverty could wreck our environment.

The *New York Times* articles and the ABC news special represent a significant departure for the major media, dominated as it has been for decades by liberal environmental views.

Other Media

Some newspapers (*The Detroit News* and the *Washington Times* come to mind) have been critical of many aspects of the environmental movement as have many magazines, including *Reader's Digest, Forbes, Fortune, Newsweek,* and the *Atlantic.* Some conservative radio talk show hosts take positions critical of the environmental movement and the regulations it has spawned. Such critical analyses even ten years ago were very rare. Apparently, an increasing segment of the media is now fulfilling its major responsibility to the public: truly informing the people that two or more sides of controversial environmental issues exist.

Scientists

Many scientists are concerned about the negativity of environmentalism and its corruption of science (Fumento 1993, among others). The Heidelberg Appeal (Anon. 1992), signed by over four thousand world leaders, largely scientists (including eighty Nobel Prize winners), best expresses this concern. The document is remarkable because most scientists are reclusive purists. They are largely apolitical in their work and abhor preconceptions because of the blinding effects on research. It is the politicization (corruption, according to Efron 1984) of science by many environmental scientists that the mainstream scientific community now finds so objectionable. The following technical organizations and newsletters have a similar orientation to the Heidelberg Appeal:

- The Science and Environmental Project under the leadership of Dr. S. Fred Singer
- The American Council for Science and Health under Dr. Elizabeth Whelan
- The Political Economy Research Center under Terry L. Anderson (with authors that include Leal, Shaw, and Stroup)
- Foundation for Research on Economics and the Environment under Dr. John Baden
- *Environment Betrayed* newsletter by Dr. Ed Krug
- *Access to Energy,* a letter formerly by Dr. Petr Beckmann, now by Dr. Arthur B. Robinson

Legislators

Many legislators have become increasingly skeptical that America's environmental regulations are really beneficial. For example, Representative John Mica (R–Fla.) (1993, A16) says that many regulations "do not create tangible benefits and are strangling our economy and costing us jobs." He says that there is a strong movement in Congress to force the EPA to "analyze costs and benefits of imposing regulations." The Clinton administration's Vice President Al Gore and EPA Administrator Carol Browner are fighting the movement to improve environmental regulation by using economic risk assessment analyses. However, Representative Mica believes that most Americans and most members of Congress favor using economic risk assessment analyses.

The environmentally skeptical contingent of America's legislators have increased their strength by virtue of the 1994 shift of America's Congress toward more conservative and libertarian views.

Industry

We do not see industry as an active participant in the Asset Culture side of the environmental war. However, industries genuinely in favor of free enterprise (the majority, we feel) could more actively support free enterprise environmental thought than they currently do. We believe most people in industry are as environmentally confused as the public. Given the data, such as that in this book, more companies would probably support the Asset Culture side of environmental thought.

Figure 12.1
The Heidelberg Appeal

We want to make our full contribution to the preservation of our common heritage, the Earth.

We are however worried, at the dawn of the twenty-first century, at the emergence of an irrational ideology which is opposed to scientific and industrial progress and impedes economic and social development.

We contend that a Natural State, sometimes idealized by movements with a tendency to look toward the past, does not exist and has probably never existed since man's first appearance in the biosphere, insofar as humanity has always progressed by increasingly harnessing Nature to its needs and not the reverse.

We fully subscribe to the objectives of a scientific ecology for a universe whose resources must be taken stock of, monitored and preserved. But we herewith demand that this stock-taking, monitoring and preservation be founded on scientific criteria and not on irrational pre-conceptions.

We stress that many essential human activities are carried out either by manipulating hazardous substances or in their proximity, and that progress and development have always involved increasing control over hostile forces, to the benefit of mankind.

We therefore, consider that scientific ecology is no more than an extension of this continual progress toward the improved life of future generations.

We intend to assert science's responsibility and duties toward society as a whole. We do however, forewarn the authorities in charge of our planet's destiny against decisions which are supported by pseudo-scientific arguments of false and nonrelevant data.

We draw everybody's attention to the absolute necessity of helping poor countries attain a level of sustainable development which matches that of the rest of the planet, protecting them from troubles and dangers stemming from developed nations, and avoiding their entanglement in a web of unrealistic obligations which would compromise both their independence and their dignity.

The greatest evils which stalk our Earth are ignorance and oppression, and not Science, Technology and Industry whose instruments, when adequately managed, are indispensable tools of a future shaped by Humanity, by itself and for itself, overcoming major problems like overpopulation, starvation and worldwide diseases. (Anon. 1992)

We are critical of the way some industries relate to environmentalism as it has taken form. However, we believe far more industries than not are highly responsible and concerned with the public and national interest. For example, the privately financed American Society for Testing and Materials (ASTM) effectively controls product quality for virtually everything the public and industry consume. It also helps competitors enter markets. Another example of responsibility is the extensive industrial support for a handbook for mineral aggregates published by the National Stone Association (1992). While the handbook effectively contributes to improving production efficiency and product quality, it also increases competition by showing competitors how to operate effectively. Such a high level of public responsibility by industries is probably more the rule than the exception. This is logical because, by nature, people in business respond to public opinion. Those who are successful understand the needs of their customers.

IS THE LIABILITY CULTURE CONSPIRATORIAL?

In chapters 10 and 11, we discussed some methods that are used to deceive or otherwise mislead the public about the environment. We took all examples from Liability Culture practices. We know of no such examples from the Asset Culture. Now we ask, if the leaders of the Liability Culture routinely deceive, are they also conspiratorial? We define conspiracy as the act of joining in a secret agreement to do an unlawful or wrongful act or to use such a means to accomplish a lawful end. What are the motives of the leaders of the Liability Culture? What are the factions? What will happen if they win? Are they conspiratorial?

The evidence is overwhelming that improving the major components of the earth's human and natural environments is not a result of the programs of the leaders of the Liability Culture. For example, they:

- favor high energy prices, even though low energy prices would vastly improve the global environment;
- are against agricultural chemical technologies, even though these technologies clearly improve the environment;
- are causing food production to be needlessly low, even though they express fears about global starvation;
- are against such technologies as frozen foods, irradiation, and gene splicing, leading to higher food shelf life, even though these technologies reduce pressures on land;
- favor old forests, even though old forests contain a smaller volume and less diversity of wildlife than a mix of clearings and forests at various stages of growth;
- favor old forests in the West, even though their fate will always be to burn and forest fires are harder on the wildlife they "protect" than lumbering. Fires are also very costly to control;
- discourage or prevent the use of insecticides, such as DDT, even though they could lengthen millions of human lives;
- are causing premature deaths of millions of people of color in Third World nations, even though they presumably are "friends" of people of color in First World nations;
- are retarding the development of mineral and energy resources globally, even though they say they are concerned about depleting mineral and energy resources;
- systematically hinder the production of wealth, even though wealth and related

technology are responsible for the greatest human health and environmental gains in history.

Most of the Liability Culture's leaders appear to be far more interested in having (or inventing) problems than in solving them. Typically, Kaufman (1994, 78) describes Dr. Edward Krug's dismay that when he was instrumental in showing that acid rain was not a serious problem, environmentalists dumped on him like a "ton of bricks" instead of thanking him. Similarly, Easterbrook (1995, 634) describes how John Todd, an ecologist who runs the Earth Island Institute in Providence, Rhode Island, discovered that wastewater could be purified by a natural process. Instead of congratulating him, members of the green movement were mad because he was taking away a means to stop growth. In addition, the obvious first step toward solving any problem is defining it. But in chapter 10, we have shown that the Liability Culture's leaders, such as Al Gore and Carol Browner, try to prevent all relevant environmental data about pet problems from being compiled or presented. Uniformly, they favor counterproductive "solutions" that lead to more regulations at excessive costs.

Arnold and Gottlieb (1993), Coffman (1994), Kaufman (1994), Moghissi (1994), and Reisman (1992) all conclude that environmental leaders are not really interested in improving the environment. For example, Coffman (1994, 270) says: "Environmentalism isn't about good stewardship or conservation; it's about locking people out—a 'get out and keep out' philosophy that benefits no one including the environment." In addition, Kaufman (1994, 54) concludes "Turning social and environmental decisions over to the environmental movement or to the politicians in debt to the movement will have deadly results for both humanity and our environment." Arnold and Gottlieb (1993, 74) say that the lily-white leaders of environmentalism are "better educated people of ample money and liberal privilege who benefit from—and are totally oblivious to— all the productive resources and enterprises they try to destroy." Reisman (1992) puts it even more bluntly when he says that getting help from environmentalists is like going to a doctor who wants you dead. In fact, we conclude that the financial/philosophical core of the Liability Culture as a destructive environmental force potentially approaches the magnitude of the havoc that apparently was caused when earth was struck by the huge extraterrestrial object that ended the reign of dinosaurs at the end of the Cretaceous Period.

In other areas where the Leftist core of the Liability Culture significantly impacts human endeavors, the results are similarly counterproductive. For example:

- They have had decades of control over much of education in America. Result: student test scores have declined while costs have risen spectacularly. Their concern appears to be more about indoctrination than education.

- They have largely controlled social services for the poor. Result: they have expanded a dependent underclass that probably would have been better off had they received no help at all.

• They are exercising continually greater control over areas of science, particularly environmental "science." Result: many mainstream scientists and authors (for example, Fumento 1993) see their activities as a threat to science itself.

If the leaders of the Liability Culture are not improving the environment (or apparently anything else), what are their real motivations? In chapter 1, we quoted several of the Liability Culture's environmental leaders. Many, including Al Gore, see little they like in America, people, industry, or free enterprise. Obviously, they are trying to change the system. But to what, and why?

The conformity of concepts throughout the UN's environment and development documents, major newspapers, and the EPA is surprising and may appear to be conspiratorily coordinated. For example, we referred to an article in a San Jose newspaper saying, in effect, that California's EPA will use less science in its decisions and listen more to public opinion, a demand of the enviros; Gore said we should not wait for all scientific research to be completed because, he claims, the dangers are so great; and the Economic Commission for Europe (1992, 5) concluded that when seeking to preserve a species, "lack of scientific knowledge should not delay the implementation of the best measures to prevent its decline." In other words, the idea that science is not only too slow but is of increasingly lesser importance in our way of life is widespread. Is such lockstep conformity planned?

A coordinated environmental core is suggested by Maduro and Schauerhammer (1992b, 37) who say that Anglo-American blueblood elites "centered around the New York Council of Foreign Relations, the Trilateral Commission, the Aspen Institute, and a host of private family foundations" control the environmental movement. The overlap of leaders in these groups along with the Environmental Grantmakers Association (EGA), the Club of Rome, and the UN is astonishing. As an example, the Commission on Global Governance's book (1995) was financed by two trust funds of the UN Development Program, nine national governments, and several foundations, including the MacArthur Foundation, the Ford Foundation, and the Carnegie Corporation (*Eco-logic* staff 1996, 4). The two foundations are listed as members of EGA (Arnold and Gottlieb 1993, 600–601). Based on analysis of UN, Trilateral Commission, and related literature, the group is trying to create a leftist one-world government based on the UN and held together and motivated by the environment. Is this conspiratorial? We think not because their literature clearly describes what they are trying to achieve. The environmental justification is spurious, but the endpoint is not hidden. Or is it?

The Communist Party United States of America (CPUSA) was a conspiracy. CPUSA was initially financed shortly after World War I by the Soviet Union for the purpose of overthrowing or neutralizing the American political system (see Klehr et al. 1995). Agents of the Soviet Union even included such prominent industrialists as Armand Hammer and his father, Julian, who were money launderers according to Klehr et al. That conspiracy died with the disintegration of the Soviet Union.

However, much of its nonconspiratorial component is still in place. Bethell (1995, 35) says:

Moreover, those who were sympathetic to the Communist cause were quite willing to help without being paid, and could keep in touch with the vast community of progressives in the West by open communication—no risky codes or Soviet contacts needed. They needed no instructions. Gus Hall, head of the U.S. Communist Party, got it right when he observed that the number of enrolled Communists was small, but the number of "state-of-mind Communists" was large.

The state-of-mind Communist network of unpaid agents was long ago disillusioned with the Soviet Union. However, their critical view of the Western democracies, America in particular, remained intact; only the rationale changed. In some ways the current version of America's Marxists may be more powerful than ever although they may no longer consider themselves Marxist. For example, to a large extent, they have molded how we think of ourselves. We have largely accepted many of their perspectives, their politically correct vocabulary and their vision of environmental history and problems. Still, this is technically not subversive. However, the Communists and the environmental leaders are similar enough so that we cannot say there is no conspiracy.

What are the motives of the elite? Maurice Strong may give us some clues. He says (see chapter 1) that he would like to write a novel in which a small group of powerful people conspire to destroy industrialization and western cultures. Strong states: "We may get to the point where the only way of serving the world will be for the industrial civilization to collapse." (Kaufman 1994, 141). First, can this be done? We and others have shown that environmental regulations alone could well achieve the purposes described by Strong. However, Strong seems to be talking about some additional mechanism. Perhaps he sees a massive sell off of trillions of dollars of stock assets held by the Liability Culture's private financial backers. Could this lead to a devastating free fall of stock markets throughout the world? Or could they, through their extensive banking connections, create some other form of financial crisis? (For more about Strong, see *Eco-logic* staff [1995, 4–5].)

Presumably, the wealthy backers of the environmental movement are motivated by the wish to create a world government. However, several things obstruct achieving this ideal:

- *The environmental mismatch.* In chapters 7 and 11, we described the mismatch in environmental problems of the First World and Third World. Solving problems for one world will do nothing for the other. The Left gets around this mismatch by giving financial aid to current leaders of Third World nations. This wealth redistribution is consistent with Leftist philosophies. However, the predictable result has been that the politicians get rich and their nations go into debt. In a sense, Third World leaders are paid to cooperate with the environment and development component of the UN.

- *Religions.* The Left sees Christianity, Judaism, and Muhammadanism as obstacles because they place humans above nature. Therefore they substitute Gaia worship or eastern religions that glorify nature.

- *Science.* The Left sees science as an obstacle because the scientific method and objectivity in general may not lead to agreement with their political conclusions. Therefore, they attack science and substitute unscientific, politically correct environmental "science."

- *Business.* Classically the Left disparages business, industry, and the profit motive as greedy. However, business has another drawback: the method of making business decisions is based on objectivity. The Left distrusts this thought process. Therefore they are critical of business.

- *Education.* Well educated, technically competent, and objectively analytical people are not in the interest of the Left. Therefore, they have sought to change the education system to create ignorance.

- *Western culture.* The Left sees Western culture in general as against their political interests. Therefore they have for decades done what they can to change Western culture and its values.

The Left largely ignores two obstacles that assure that even if their efforts to establish a world government are successful, this government will fail.

- *UN government.* The Left may not appear to understand fully the incompetence of the UN. A world totally in control of a UN bureaucracy, even a benign one, would probably self-destruct.

- *The propaganda problem.* A fatal flaw in the whole Leftist effort is that it bases its activities on propaganda, not on facts. Objectivity and facts are requisite to solving any problem whatever.

The Left has worked for decades to remove the first six of the above obstacles. However, the latter two items doom their ideal world to failure. The bottom line is that the Left's beautiful ideal of one world based on leftist philosophies, a world without war, is probably impossible. (A world government based on democratic ideals may not be.)

In contrast to that ideal, what is actually occurring? The probable destruction of much of the natural environment and much of humanity is actually nihilistic. The neo-Luddites appear to be in philosophical control.

Perhaps the wealthy Left does not know the environmental implications of its activities. We have shown that one result of the education of Americans about environmental matters is that they become misinformed about the environment. Carrying this trend to its logical conclusion, we suggest that the most highly educated environmentally may be the most misinformed. In this scenario, the environmental destruction to which the wealthy Left contributes is an unintended consequence.

Misinformation and lack of internal critical review of their data and conclusions by Leftist academics are occupational hazards. For example, Cheney (1995, 203) is struck by "an amazing lack of thought to the consequences of what they are teaching." Similarly, only lack of information could cause Gore (1992, 3) to be so influenced by Carson's *Silent Spring*. We have shown that Carson's major conclusions about the threat of pesticides to bird life are precisely the opposite of reality. However, the people Gore respects or admires will not tell him this. Continual peer reinforcement of environmental negativity and decades of seeing only the downside of the world around them (mostly exaggerated or fictional) has led to massive misconceptions. This constant reinforcement could account for so many of the environmental leaders apparently believing their own propaganda. In fact, they may not even see it as propaganda. In Cheney's words, they are only "telling the truth."

Cheney (1995, 95) describes how some Leftist intellectuals who visualize a postmodern society see their role as being critics. However, they do not consider it their responsibility to show what form their postmodern society might take. Unfortunately, the leaders of the political Left rarely have to take responsibility or pay a price for their ideas or activities. The reason is that the political Left concentrates in insulated occupations such as academia (particularly in liberal arts), government (particularly in regulatory and policy-making areas), the arts, environmental societies, private grantmaking organizations, the world banking community, and the UN. People in most of these occupations are shielded from the severely disciplining conditions that exist in business, industry, or science (what academics like to call the "real world"). They can speculate endlessly and irresponsibly in their comfortable nests. Conversely, in the more disciplined fields, bad judgement or bad luck are usually harshly rewarded with failure. This harsh system has no rewards for good intentions not accompanied by good results. However, the Left may even reward people because of their good intentions, no matter how incompetent they may be. Theirs is not the real world.

Finally, if ignorance is a major problem, we offer this prayer: Forgive them, O Lord, for they know not what they do. Of course, we cannot know whether God (or Gaia) will actually forgive them. We suspect that only Lucifer, the god of nihilism, might be happy.

We have speculated about motives. However, we do not speculate about results. As Coffman (1994, 219) says: "What is certain, however, is that America has already moved far beyond the altruistic goal of merely having a clean environment." Speaking about a possible conspiracy, he adds: "The blatant deceit in declaring that environmental catastrophes exist is real. The Earth Summit and its goals are real. These men and their agendas are real. The power and influence they wield is real. The Legislation and regulations they have produced are real.

Real people are suffering as a consequence of these self-appointed leaders.''
We add that the hundreds of millions of dollars the wealthy Left annually pour
into Liability Culture causes are real. The millions of needless premature deaths
in Third World nations are real. The needless destruction of forests, wildlife,
and soils in Third World nations is real. What is also real is that the philosoph-
ical/financial core of the Liability Culture plays hard ball. The severe problems
they cause for the natural and human environments may be far less important
to them than achieving their goals.

If the financial Left elite are successful in their endeavors, the world will be
radically different. They would break down present governmental and societal
structures. This would be a prelude to creating a world government under the
UN or a similar organization (see Commission on Global Governance 1995 or
Gore 1992). Their government would be highly bureaucratic and would have
power over virtually all human activities. It would be Socialistic or Communis-
tic. Economic efficiency would decline. Civilization would regress. We do not
know if the financial elite see humanity as living in an Orwellian Dark Age.

However, many of the intellectual elite say that they would like to set humanity back to a new Stone Age. The nihilists or the Neo-Luddites appear to
have this goal. In any event, the bottom line result will be philosophically consistent with statements by Liability Culture's leaders quoted in chapter 1. Additionally, the result will be consistent with one purpose of the original Marxist
conspiracy: the United States would no longer be powerful, no longer be democratic.

Paradoxically, the Left will have achieved the conspiratorial purpose of the
no-longer-existent Soviet Union. They will have achieved this end largely
through environmental deception and through the use of enormous wealth and
political power. They will also have used much of the wealth America's Democracy has created to destroy Democracy. They will have turned Democracy
against itself. The reader can decide whether they are conspiratorial.

CONCLUSIONS

One side of the environmental war consists of individuals and organizations
who see their philosophical, political, or economic interests as furthered by more
environmental regulations and the implied big government. We categorize them
as the Liability Culture. Although small in numbers, the environmental Left is
a significant part of this culture. We divide them into three components. One
component visualizes a utopian world in which a beneficent government manages all resources for the good of humankind; a second component visualizes
an ecological utopia in which a beneficent world government manages all resources for the good of the whole Earth. A third group evolved from the first
two. Theirs may be the predominant philosophy. They are disillusioned utopians,
the Neo-Luddites, as some call themselves. Their drive may be mystic. They
may believe in Zen, Gaia, Theosophy or even Lucifer (see Coffman 1994). The

major preoccupation for the environmental Left is impeding the wealth-creating sector so they can remake the world. They consistently see and stress the liability side of the environmental ledger. They consistently ignore, deny, or minimize the value of the environmental assets that have resulted from industry, free enterprise, and democracy.

Many people in the Liability Culture see a misinformed or even hysterical public as in their own best philosophical, political, religious, or financial interests. Included in this group are many environmental organizations, some industries and old wealth foundations, most liberal politicians, some scientists and engineers, and some educators. "Facts" that are acceptable to this side must be politically correct. Alternatives are ridiculed.

Most industry and the working public are so busy "doing" that they have little time for philosophical discussions. While many are firmly within the Asset Culture, they may have little knowledge about the asset side of the environmental ledger. We suspect that most are nearly oblivious to the nature and significance of the cultural war that is raging. To a surprising degree, many people within the Asset Culture have accepted the assessment of them by the environmental Left, their implacable enemy.

The philosophical component of the Asset Culture consists of people who believe in Democracy and free markets. They are skeptical about the ability of government to handle complex problems efficiently. They favor less government. For them, facts have no politics.

NOTE

1. He gives no credit to the Asset Culture's doers who are needed to manufacture the equipment for playing the music, manufacture paper for books, or supply the comfortable surroundings for his elite pursuits.

REFERENCES

Anderson, T. L., and D. R. Leal. 1991. *Free Market Environmentalism.* Boulder: West-view.

Anon. 1992. Heidelberg Appeal to heads of state and governments. *Projections,* July 8, 121–22.

———. 1994. Regulate us please. *The Economist,* January 5, 69.

———. 1995. Still lost at Yale. *Wall Street Journal,* March 23, A14.

Arnold, R. 1987. *Ecology Wars.* Washington, D.C.: Free Enterprise Press.

Arnold, R., and A. Gottlieb. 1993. *Trashing the Economy.* Bellevue, Wash.: Free Enterprise Press.

Bailey, R. 1993. Political science. *Reason,* December, 61, 62.

Barrons, K. C. 1978. *The Food in Your Future.* New York: Van Nostrand Reinhold.

———. 1981. *Are Pesticides Really Necessary?* Chicago: Regnery Gateway.

Bethell, T. 1995. Patterns of conspiracy. *National Review,* August 28, 33–36.

Bidinotto, R. 1990. Environmentalism: Freedom's foe for the '90s. *The Freeman,* November.

Brinkley, J. 1993. Animal tests as risk clues: The best data may fall short. *New York Times,* March 23, A1.

Brooks, W. T. 1991. PCB, Like dioxin, another false alarm. *Detroit News.*

Carson, R. 1962. *Silent Spring.* New York: Houghton Mifflin.

Cheney, L. V. 1995. *Telling the Truth.* New York: Simon & Schuster.

Chivian, E., ed. 1993. *Critical Condition.* Cambridge: MIT Press.

Coffman, M. S. 1994. *Saviors of the Earth?* Chicago: Northfield Publishing.

Commission on Global Governance. 1995. *Our Global Neighborhood.* Oxford: Oxford University Press.

DiLorenzo, T. J., et al. 1990. *Patterns of Corporate Philanthropy.* Washington, D.C.: Capital Research Center.

Easterbrook, G. 1990. Everything you know about the environment is wrong. *The New Republic,* April 30, 26.

———. 1994. Forget PCB's, radon, alar (the world's greatest dangers are dung, smoke and dirty water). *New York Times Magazine,* September 11, 60–63.

———. 1995. *A Moment on the Earth.* New York: Viking Penguin.

Echard, J. K. 1990. *Protecting the Environment: Old Rhetoric, New Imperatives.* Washington, D.C.: Capital Research Center.

Eco-logic staff. 1995. Meet Maurice Strong. *Eco-logic,* November/December, 4–5.

———. 1996. Report of the Commission on Global Governance: *Our Global Neighborhood,* January/February, 4–10, 15–18.

Economic Commission for Europe. 1992. *Code of Practice for the Conservation of Threatened Animals and Plants.* New York: United Nations.

Efron, E. 1984. *The Apocalyptics, Cancer and the Big Lie.* New York: Simon and Schuster.

Ehrlich, P. 1968. *The Population Bomb.* New York: Ballantine Books.

Fumento, M. 1993. *Science under Seige.* New York: William Morrow.

Gore, A. 1992. *Earth in the Balance.* Boston, New York, London: Houghton Mifflin.

Graber, D. M. 1959. Book Review of W. McKibben's *The End of Nature, Los Angeles Times,* October 22, 9.

Kagan, D. 1994. Why Western history matters. *Wall Street Journal,* December 28, A12.

Kaufman, W. 1994. *No Turning Back.* New York: Basic Books.

Klehr, H., J. E. Haynes, and F. I. Firson. 1995. *The Secret World of American Communism.* New Haven: Yale University Press.

Kwong, J. 1995. Eco-kids: New automatons on the block. *The Freeman* 45(3): 155–59.

Leguery-Feilleux, J. R. 1995. European perspectives on the ecological crisis. *ITEST Bulletin* (winter): 3–5.

Lehr, J. H., ed. 1992. *Rational Readings on Environmental Concerns.* New York: Van Nostrand Reinhold.

Leopold, A. 1949. *A Sand County Almanac.* Oxford: Oxford University Press.

Lichter, S. R. 1995. Liberal greens, mainstream camouflage. *Wall Street Journal,* April 21, A10.

Lovins, A. B. 1977. *Soft Energy Paths toward a Durable Peace.* Cambridge, Mass.: Ballinger.

MacNeill, J., P. Winsemius, and T. Yakushiji. 1991. *Beyond Interdependence.* Oxford: Oxford University Press.

Maddox, J. 1972. *The Doomsday Syndrome: An Attack on Passimism.* New York: McGraw-Hill.

Maduro, R. A. and R. Schauerhammer. 1992a. *The Holes in the Ozone Scare.* Washington, D.C.: 21st Century Science Associates.

———. 1992b. Who owns the environmental movement? *21st Century Science and Technology,* Fall, 36–45.

Marsh, G. P. 1864. *Man and Nature; or Physical Geography as Modified by Human Action.* New York: Scribners.

———. 1874. *The Earth as Modified by Human Action.* New York: Scribner, Armstrong.

Maurice, C., and C. U. Smithson. 1984. *The Doomsday Myth.* Stanford: Stanford University Press.

Maxey, M. 1990. *Managing Environmental Risks: What Difference Does Ethics Make?* Center for the Study of American Business, Formal Publication No. 90, Washington University, May.

Meadows, D. H., D. L., Meadows, J. Randers, and W. W. Behrens, II. 1972. *The Limits to Growth.* New York: Universe Books.

Mica, J. L. 1993. Quantify EPA's damage. *Wall Street Journal,* February 24, A16.

Moghissi, A. A. 1994. Risk analysis: An attempt to standardize the process and its applications. *Technology: Journal of the Franklin Institute* (Philadelphia) 331A: 29–40.

Muir, J. 1913. *The Story of My Boyhood and Youth.* New York: Houghton Mifflin.

National Stone Association. 1992. *Aggregates Handbook.* Washington, D.C.: NSA.

Ray, D. L. 1990. *Trashing the Planet.* Washington, D.C.: Regnery Gateway.

———. 1993. *Environmental Overkill.* Washington, D.C.: Regnery Gateway.

Reisman, G. 1992. The Toxicity of environmentalism. *The Freeman,* 42(9): 336–50.

Robinson, A. B. 1994. Philosophy of death. *Access to Energy* 21(12): 1.

Rubin, C. T. 1994. Environmentalism as "everythingism." *PERC Reports* 12(4): 4–5.

Schneider, K. 1993. New view calls environmental policy misguided. *New York Times,* March 21, 1, 30.

Simon, J. L. 1990. *Population Matters.* New Brunswick: Transaction.

Sowell, T. 1994. When courts make the law. *Albany Times Union,* August 31, A12.

———. 1995a. *The Vision of the Anointed.* New York: Basic Books.

———. 1995b. Subsidizing the counterculture. *Albany Times Union,* January 27, A10.

Spector, M. 1993. Sea dumping ban: Good politics, but not necessarily good policy. *New York Times,* March 22.

Stevens, W. K. 1995. Earth Day at 25: How has nature fared? *New York Times,* April 17.

Swogger, G. 1992. Why emotions eclipse rational thinking about the environment. *Priorities,* Fall, 7–10.

United Nations. 1992. *Earth Summit Agenda 21.* New York: United Nations Reproduction Section.

Thom, D. 1994. Engineering to sustain the environment. In *The Role of Engineering in Sustainable Development,* edited by M. D. Ellis. Washington, D.C.: American Association of Engineering Societies.

Wattenberg, B. J. 1984a. The good news Is the bad news Is wrong. *Reader's Digest,* April, 101–231.

———. 1984b. *The Good News Is the Bad News Is Wrong.* New York: Simon & Schuster.

Weber, J. A. 1979. *Power Grab: The Conserver Cult and the Coming Catastrophe.* New Rochelle, N.Y.: Arlington House.

Welsch, R. 1992. A song for the pioneers. *Audubon,* November–December, 112–116.

Whelan, E. M. 1985. *Toxic Terror.* Ottawa, Ill.: Jameson Books.

———. 1993. *Toxic Terror: The Truth behind the Cancer Scare.* Buffalo, N.Y.: Prometheus Books.

Wilson, R., A. M. Langer, R. P. Nolan, J. B. L. Gee, and M. Ross. 1994. Asbestos in New York City public school buildings—public policy: Is there a scientific basis? *Regulatory Toxicology and Pharmacology* 20: 1–9.

World Commission on Development. 1987. *Our Common Future.* Oxford and New York: Oxford University Press.

PART IV

Toward a Better Environment

Conclusions

- Positive thinkers who are knowledgeable about both sides of the environmental ledger are requisite for long-term environmental improvement of the world. Such thinkers do not appear to be present within the Liability Culture.

- Major factors contributing to a better environment include industrialization, urbanization, the creation of new wealth, technology, cheap energy, mining, efficient agriculture and food handling, efficient transportation, and free enterprise. The Liability Culture's leaders seek downscaling, elimination, or severe regulation of all these contributions.

- First World nations *multiply* natural resources; Third World nations *consume* natural resources.

- Environmental regulations are not responsible for the most significant environmental gains; currently, most gains from regulations are out of proportion to cost.

- Thirty-one principles pertaining to environmental understanding or environmental improvement are listed in chapter 13. Given the data summarized here, the principles are obvious. Yet one would be hard put to find a single one of these principles acknowledged by a single UN agency, U.S. government regulatory arm, or private environmental organization.

- Most current environmental regulations are environmentally counterproductive for America.

- Environmental improvement has different definitions. Because the Liability Culture's leaders focus on the liability side of the environmental ledger, they see regulating human activity as improving the environment. Because we focus more on the asset side of the ledger, we see encouraging human productivity as improving both the human and natural environments.

- Improvement of the environments of the world requires neutralization of the negative forces of obfuscation and the elimination of excessive environmental regulations.

- Third World nations have all of the world's most serious human and natural environmental problems.

- Most governments of the Third World (like their industrial counterparts) impede environmental improvement.

- Third World nations can best improve their environments by creating a political environment that encourages human initiative and outside investment by multinational corporations.

- The Third World cannot improve its human and natural environments until it reduces tribal conflicts, corruption, and ignorance.

- Improving the health of Third World people is basic to economic efficiency.

- Giving loans to Third World governments has not and probably will not lead to environmental improvement in those nations.

- Imposing an industrial nation's environmental regulations on the Third World is counterproductive in both human and natural terms.

CHAPTER 13

Some Environmental Principles

Based on data presented in the first three parts of this book, we can now summarize principles that will help us better understand and improve the world's environments. Most of the principles are surprising. Conventional wisdom derived from mainstream environmental thought has largely reached opposite conclusions. The radically different conclusions result quite logically from stressing opposite sides of the environmental ledger. Stressing the liability side leads naturally to the conclusion that regulations are needed to solve all environmental problems. Stressing the asset side leads to the conclusion that expanding environmental assets is the best way to improve the environment. The first approach is negative, costly, and destructive. Its adherents have little confidence in people and favor big government. The second approach is positive, inexpensive, and constructive. Its adherents have faith in individuals and favor less government.

The principles relate to the world in general. They concern the world's forests and wildlife; improving agricultural efficiency and reducing soil erosion; improving water resources; improving the human environment in terms of health and life expectancy; and increasing the world's assets and total wealth. The principles will help people understand and improve the environments of First, Second, and Third World nations.

Some principles summarize the reasons for environmental gains now found in wealthy nations. Some relate to roadblocks to continuing improvement. Some are guidelines for the Third World for improving their human and natural environments. Widespread, dispersed environmental effects are the basis for most of the principles in this chapter. Others are management principles. At the end of each principle is a reference to the chapters in this book that give the data on which each principle is based. At the end of the chapter we analyze some of the reasons our principles are so at odds with conventional wisdom.

ENVIRONMENTAL PRINCIPLES

Principle 1. First World Nations Multiply Resources.

Industrial nations have already evolved past sustainability to resource multiplication. Industrialization and its technologies expand resources in several ways:

- Efficient use of agricultural and energy resources takes pressure off forest, wildlife, and soil resources, improving all three.
- By learning how to use organic and inorganic resources, industrial civilizations create resources.
- Through chemical technology, industrial civilizations actually create new resources.
- By continuously modifying plant and animal resources, industrial societies create their own biodiversity.
- By introducing foreign fauna and flora, industrial societies expand biological resources in many areas.

Expansion of resources is beyond sustainability. Sustainability is a second-best idea. (See chapter 9.)

Principle 2. Third World Nations Consume Inordinate Quantities of Natural Resources.

The Third World is consuming its forest, wildlife, and soil resources at what may be the greatest rate in history. Further, people of the Third World walk on mineral resources that they lack the knowledge, social structure, wealth, and infrastructure to develop. Such development could contribute to saving the natural resources they are depleting and could lead to the resource multiplication characteristic of First World nations. (See chapters 2, 3, and 4.)

Principle 3. Industrialization Improves the Environment.

Major industrial nations have expanded forests and wildlife while improving water resources, soil, and the human condition. Because no developing nations have a comparable record, this principle is almost a platitude.

Because industries often produce wastes, many environmentalists see industry only in terms of the problems it creates or can create (for example, Gore 1992; United Nations 1992). The use of anecdotal negatives can show many examples of imperfection. This approach causes the enormous benefits of industry's dispersed environmental effects to be so ignored and so little understood that some environmentalists have even called for deindustrialization of the West (for example, Manes [1990] and Linkola [Milbank 1994]). Yet deindustrialization would inevitably lead to a huge reversal of environmental gains. (See chapters 2, 3, 4, 5, 6, and 8.)

Principle 4. Urbanization Improves the Environment.

When people leave marginal farmlands and move to cities where industry is concentrated, lands rest. Thus, *development* of metropolitan areas results in *de-development* of rural areas. Revegetation occurs, wildlife repopulates, and soil erosion decreases. In addition, per capita energy use decreases. Highly rural Wyoming, for example, uses four times as much energy per capita as highly urbanized New York State (the nation's lowest). Wyoming's being highest in the lower forty-eight states energy consumption is partly because of high gasoline consumption and the high cost of heating individual homes. The temporary reversal in quality of the human environment that characterizes the first phase of urbanization is followed by general improvement when the APCGNP exceeds $3,000. (See chapter 9.)

Principle 5. Free Enterprise and Capitalism Improve the Environment.

By far, the best system for helping the industrialization process is free enterprise and capitalism. The most highly industrialized nations of the world all have free enterprise in common. Except for some oil-rich nations of the Middle East, the top twenty nations in per capita income are all democratic and industrial. All these nations have improved their natural environments. (See chapters 2, 3, and 4.)

Principle 6. Wealth Improves the Environment.

A good environment, both natural and human, is purchased. The most significant environmental progress results when people act on their own behalf in economically efficient systems. Were the people of any developing nation to suddenly become wealthy, an immediate effect would be for them to improve their environments. Human longevity would quickly increase. Reforestation, the first sign of reversal of natural environmental degradation, would occur. This reversal occurs when the APCGNP of a population is about $1,000 and is well on its way by the time it is $3,000.

Conversely, the natural and human environments of industrial nations can regress if they become poorer. Because wealth is directly related to industrial productivity, poverty would be one result of deindustrialization. (See chapter 8.)

Principle 7. Forest Fires and Logging Improve the Natural
Environment, Provided the Vegetative Cover is Reestablished.

Forest fires and lumbering increase the total volume of wildlife *provided the
land revegetates.* American Indians understood this principle very well.
Therefore, they regularly set fire to forests and prairies. Similarly, the Michigan
Department of Natural Resources intentionally clears some of the state's northern forests to increase the deer population. Michigan's deer population ranks
with that of Pennsylvania for number of deer per square mile.

Fighting forest fires in the western United States is one reason deer and elk
populations have not increased as much as they might have. The alternative to
letting fires rejuvenate forests is to let lumbering rejuvenate forests. Logging an
old forest is far less traumatic to both people and wildlife and is far less costly
than a forest fire. (See chapters 3 and 4.)

Principle 8. Advanced Technology Improves the Environment.

Technology is the basis of modern industrial societies, and therefore, most
technology has an environmentally beneficial effect. For example, Barrons
(1975) points out that were it not for wood preservatives, a forest twice the size
of New England would be needed to replace rotted wood on a sustained basis.
Food technology bears a major responsibility for America's new forests and
wildlife. The whole industrial system and the wealth it creates are based on such
technologies as medicine, agriculture, materials, science, and water management.
Without modern technology and its economic efficiency the industrial world
would not have its human and natural environmental gains. (See chapters 2, 3,
4, 5, and 6.)

Principle 9. Use of Mineral Fuels Improves the Environment.

Without exception, people of Third World nations are unable to afford sufficient fossil fuels. Therefore, they burn wood, crop residues, or dried animal
dung for energy. Their forests are shrinking, and their soils are deteriorating and
eroding. Even within industrial nations, high fuel prices can put pressure on the
natural environment to the extent that people tend to burn more wood for energy.
The energy crises of the 1970s resulted in over 50 percent of the wood cut in
the United States being used for energy.

Elimination of fossil fuels or the internal combustion engine, as has been
suggested by some environmentalists, would eliminate engine-powered farm
equipment; farmers would once again need to use draft animals. Large areas of
forestland and productive cropland would then revert to pasture. (See chapters
2, 3, and 4.)

Principle 10. The Mineral Industry Improves the Environment.

The dispersed impact of the mineral industry, including oil and gas, has been to greatly improve the environment. The widespread dispersed benefits from the mineral industry include high agricultural productivity, expanded forests, and increased wildlife populations. Tall buildings are built from mined materials such as the raw materials for steel and concrete. They allow people to concentrate their living and working areas. When people concentrate in cities, they occupy less land area. In addition, the mineral industry is responsible for much of America's wealth.

Environmental gains provided by the mineral industry have been beneficial to hundreds of millions of acres. Land disturbance by the mineral industry amounts to only 0.3 percent of the nation's land. About a third has been reclaimed. (See chapters 2, 3, 4, and 9.)

Principle 11. High Agricultural Productivity Improves the Natural Environment.

High per acre food productivity helps the environment by releasing land for other purposes. If America's current agricultural production per acre was the same as that of 1935 to 1940, the nation would need an additional area the size of all the land east of the Mississippi River plus Michigan to meet its food requirements (Borlaug 1993). Our new forests and expanded wildlife would be nonexistent. Regulation of agricultural chemicals on "environmental" grounds should be tempered by balancing any potential problems against the huge dispersed environmental benefits that result from high agricultural productivity per acre. For example, far from hurting wildlife, the total impact of pesticides has been to expand most wildlife populations that require trees for habitat. This should have been obvious even for the four decades before 1960 when Rachel Carson published *Silent Spring*. It is still obvious. (See chapters 2, 3, and 4.)

Principle 12. Efficient Food Handling, Processing, and Distribution Improve the Environment.

Almost as important as high agricultural productivity is efficient handling of agricultural products to ensure that the greatest quantity reaches the market in a usable condition. This was a glaring failure of the former Soviet Union, where 30 percent to 50 percent of some crops rotted before they got to the consumer. With such losses, from 30 percent to 50 percent more land is required to get the same amount of food to consumers.

Canning, sun drying, freeze drying, refrigerating, vacuum packing, irradiating, and efficient transportation are components of efficient food handling. Such efficiency contributes to the release of agricultural land to other uses.

Current concern over using CFC refrigerant should be balanced against the potential loss of wildlife habitats. The reduced use of refrigeration in Third World countries would result in more land being needed for agriculture to accommodate food spoilage. (See chapters 2, 3, 4, and 11.)

Principle 13. Efficient Transportation and Energy Distribution Improve the Environment.

As noted in principle 12, efficient transportation is critical for food distribution without spoilage. Almost as important is efficient energy distribution. Without power lines and pipelines, without highway, rail, and water transportation for sources of energy, Americans would be forced to rely on local sources of energy (usually wood). Efficient transportation of all goods is basic to the efficiency of the industrial systems. This leads to lower costs and increased production of wealth. (See chapters 2, 3, and 4.)

Principle 14. Industrialization Reduces the Rate of Population Growth.

The lowest rates of population growth are in industrial nations, and many of these populations are not replacing themselves. For the 27 most industrialized nations, the fertility rate per woman is 1.9 children. Even without industrialization, the greater use of contraceptive technology by developing nations' people has reduced the fertility rate from 6.1 to 3.9 babies per woman in 25 years, a drop of 36 percent. As nations industrialize and technology improves, world population should stabilize. (See chapter 8.)

Principle 15. Environmental Problems of the Wealthy are Usually Not Obvious; Problems of the Poor are Readily Visible.

In industrial nations, environmental water or air "problems" are usually measured in parts per million, parts per billion, or parts per trillion, and can only be detected by sophisticated modern analytical equipment. Most often the public has to be told that problems exist; that is, problems must be publicized through the media.

For Third World nations, problems are quite different. They are generally visible in every landscape and in the faces and bodies of the people. These problems often assail the nostrils, and many are a matter of life and death, as close as the next meal, the next drink of water, the next breath. (See chapter 7.)

Principle 16. The Most Dangerous Form of Water Pollution is Human Feces.

Third World nations usually cannot afford sewage collection systems or sewage treatment plants except in some cities. Most Second World nations cannot afford adequate sewage treatment plants. Their rivers and streams transport raw or inadequately treated sewage, and the water becomes a source of such diseases as dysentery, typhoid fever, and cholera. The number of people of Second and Third World nations who die from water-borne diseases is from 10 million to 20 million annually. Most are children. (See chapter 6.)

Principle 17. The Most Deadly Form of Air Pollution on Earth is Indoor Smoke Particulates in Third World Nations.

Particulates from inadequately vented indoor heating and cooking fires cause from one-quarter to one-third of all childhood mortality (about 4 million annually) plus contribute to the deaths of many adults. Death is largely from acute respiratory infections. (See chapter 6.)

Principle 18. Environmental Regulations of Wealthy Nations Cannot Generally be Applied to the Third World.

Industrial nations' regulations meant to save one life in a million applied to nations whose populations are under environmental stresses that may be thousands of times more severe are absurd. Application of such regulations can only hamper the wealth-creating process that is mandatory for Third World environmental improvement. Misapplied environmental regulations can lead to catastrophic results, in terms of both the human and the natural environments.

Finally, applying the EPA's regulations to developing nations has been enormously detrimental to the human environment. Millions of people have suffered or died because of restrictions on pesticide use, particularly DDT. In addition, blocking use of grain fungicides contributes to a loss of 50 percent or more of some nations' food. This, in turn, puts excessive pressure on their land resources. The largely hypothetical environmental gain from not using such chemicals does not approach compensating for the resulting human and natural environmental deterioration. (See chapters 2, 3, 4, 5, 6, and 10.)

Principle 19. Humanity's and Nature's Great Environmental Problems are Solved Without Government Regulations.

Reforestation, expanded wildlife populations, reduced soil erosion, expanded water resources, improved sanitation, disease control, reduced birthrates, and increased human longevity all occur as an inevitable fallout of increased wealth. The drive to leave a better world for one's children is probably universal and is a far more potent force for environmental improvement than regulations. One result of costly, oppressive regulation is to make a nation poorer, potentially reversing the enormous environmental gains that exist because of wealth. (See chapters 2, 3, 4, 9, 10, and 11.)

Principle 20. When Nations Solve Their Major Environmental Problems, They Find Ever Smaller Problems to Regulate.

Concern about ever smaller environmental problems is an inevitable result of the accumulation of wealth. The wealthy worry about things that seem silly to the poor. While we believe that excessive regulation causes exaggeration of minor problems, we also understand that part of the trend of regulating less and less is a natural result of increased wealth. Wealthy people expect more. Such expectations have made it easier for government to regulate negligible risks. (See chapter 7.)

Principle 21. Benefits From Many Environmental Regulations are out of Proportion to Cost.

Perfection commands a high price. When we use "one molecule of a carcinogen can kill you" and "one fiber of asbestos can kill you" as a basis for environmental regulations, we spend too much. Removal of the last increment of any contaminant is prohibitively expensive and provides the least environmental gain. Excessive regulations divert resources from achieving real human and natural environmental benefits for all nations. The open-ended nature of environmental laws encourage regulating less and less. (See chapters 10 and 11.)

Principle 22. Money Spent to Solve Many Environmental "Problems" Is Not Proportional to the Need.

This is a corollary to principle 21. Benefits achieved from removal of the last increment of a problem substance are so small as to be almost meaningless and, often, cannot even be measured. Huge amounts of money are spent solving very small environmental problems in wealthy nations. Further, even though most of America's wildlife are proliferating, America spends hundreds of millions of dollars to save rare species. Far more species are threatened in Third World nations. The same money spent in the Third World could have enormous environmental benefits for both the Third World and the world as a whole. (See chapter 11.)

Principle 23. Stressing the Negative or Liability Side of the Environmental Ledger Leads to Warped Priorities and Will Only Damage the Environment.

Warped national environmental priorities are almost wholly the result of stressing or inventing liabilities and hiding or ignoring environmental assets. For hard-core Liability Culturists, facts have politics, science has politics, and only those facts that conform to the political ideas of the Left are acceptable. Facts (or nonfacts) that reflect negatively on industry or free enterprise are politically correct. Al Gore's *Earth in the Balance* is a classic example of focusing on negatives, focusing on the politically correct. It is difficult to see how such negativity can result in benefits either for the environment or for the economy. (See chapters 10, 11, and 12.)

Principle 24. Many Environmental Programs Recommended by Private Environmental Organizations Adversely Affect the Environment.

Environmentally counterproductive regulations often begin with private environmental advocacy organizations. The environmental impact of most of America's private environmental organizations is largely counterproductive within the United States and is clearly counterproductive for the Third World. (See chapters 11 and 12.)

Principle 25. Environmental Entities, Whether Private or Government, Need Exaggerated Environmental Problems and a Hysterical Public to Survive.

A fully informed, nonhysterical public would not tolerate excessive environmental regulations nor would it contribute to the coffers of private environmental organizations. Survival of most environmental organizations is contingent on the public's seeing only one side of the environmental ledger. (See chapter 10.)

Principle 26. Government Regulations Meant to Solve Environmental Problems in the United States will Ultimately Create Enormous Environmental Problems for the United States.

Because most money currently spent on the environment in the United States addresses very minor problems on the American public's list, "solving" these problems is enormously costly with little real benefit. A major effect of such regulations is to drain the nation's wealth. Because most of America's huge environmental gains are the *result* of created wealth, America's current regulations can ultimately reverse environmental gains. In addition, regulations leading to eliminating many pesticides and to raising energy prices can only reverse environmental gains. (See chapters 2, 3, 4, 5, 6, 7, 10, and 11.)

Principle 27. Long Before Environmental Policies in the United States Adversely Impact America, the Environments of the Third World will be Negatively Affected.

Accelerating deterioration of environments in Third World nations is well documented. Much of this deterioration is the result of environmental policies in the United States. Policies that drive up the price of energy have already been enormously detrimental to developing nations. Further, the high cost of energy drives up the price of mineral fertilizer. This reduces agricultural production per acre (Bumb 1989). One result is to put more pressure on Third World forests and wildlife. (See chapters 4 and 11.)

Principle 28. Populations of all Species of Wildlife Cannot Increase Simultaneously.

Proliferation of woodland wildlife in America has been at the expense of grassland species. Thus, bison, meadowlark, and prairie dog populations, to name a few, have declined in the United States.

Concerns about single species have often led to regulations, laws, or other activities to protect them. Yet in case after case such protection is at the expense of other species or other components of the environment. For example, protection of seals and sea lions has depleted the steelhead population of the West Coast. Reduction of trapping of nutria and beavers in America and furry opossums in New Zealand has put stress on vegetation and undoubtedly on the other wildlife that use the same habitats. Saving large areas of old forest to "protect" the rare spotted owl in the northwestern United States is at the expense of deer and the other wildlife that thrive in regenerating forests.

There are few easy answers in the area of wildlife management, but management by the public or by the political process has rarely optimized conditions for wildlife. (See chapter 4.)

Principle 29. Nature is Cruel, and Humans Who Are Closest to Nature Are the Cruelest to Other Humans.

The tendency for many environmentalists to glorify nature masks the continuous cruelties of nature. The history of humanity and its changing technology has been the history of controlling nature's forces to shield people from those forces. People closest to the brutal forces of nature on a continuous basis—the more primitive—are usually cruelest both to their enemies and to their own people. (See chapter 1.)

Principle 30. The Single Major Obstacle to Improving the Environments of the World is The Left-Driven Liability Culture of the First World.

It is no surprise that the nihilistic philosophies of the Liability Culture have been harmful to industry, the wealth-creating process, and free enterprise. After all, the nihilistic leaders clearly state their ideas and purposes. However, because wealth is a major requisite for environmental improvement, a drag on wealth formation is environmentally harmful. Further, mainstream Liability Culture leaders are on record as being against agricultural chemicals, cheap energy, urbanization, the internal combustion engine, and technology. These are the very things that have so vastly improved the natural and human environments in the First World. In addition, the Liability Culture, by slowing development, blocking useful chemicals, and keeping energy prices high, has been devastating to the environment of the Third World in both human and natural terms. Worst, Liability Culture policies have shortened hundreds of millions of lives of Third World people. Most major environmental benefits have been derived from activities of the asset side of the environmental ledger, the side the Liability Culture tends to deprecate or ignore. (See chapters 1 and 11.)

DISCUSSION AND PRINCIPLE 31

Virtually every human activity we see as needed to improve the environment is opposed or not acknowledged by leftist environmentalists. In fact, most of the above principles are almost the exact opposite of what has become conventional environmental wisdom. However, understanding the above principles has the potential of helping solve all problems on the Shumburo list of chapter 7, plus continuing to improve the rest of the world.

That conclusions should be so different should not be surprising. We have intentionally stressed the asset side of the environmental ledger. We have learned by seeing and understanding gains. Our definition of environmental improvement pertains to expanding our environmental assets. As Reisman (1992, 341) says: "Production and economic activity are precisely the means by which man adapts his environment to himself and thereby improves it." Conversely, current conventional "wisdom" springs from the liability side of the environmental ledger. Environmental laws and current administration policy reject the asset side of the environmental ledger. By rejecting the asset side and the means for its attainment, the Liability Culture has not learned from experience. Environmental improvement from the Liability Culture perspective is attained only by reducing liabilities, that is, *regulations are seen as the road to environmental improvement. However, reducing liabilities will not increase environmental assets.* Similarly, solving all problems on the American public's and the EPA's liability lists will not solve any problems on the Shumburo list of chapter 7.

A paradox pertaining to our list of environmental principles is that Mahdi Mohammad Shumburo or even an uneducated Ethiopian could have written the above principles far better than most Americans. To a truly remarkable degree, consistent bias in America's educational system and major media has created an environmentally uninformed population.

Currently, the asset side continues to expand, at least in First World nations, even though the Liability Culture is slowing that expansion. We have argued that if we focus on liabilities, especially ever smaller liabilities or invented liabilities, our priorities become warped. This can lead, in a sense, *to the liability side of the environmental ledger consuming the asset side.* Consuming vast wealth to solve ever smaller environmental problems will jeopardize our ability to continue to expand our environmental assets.

America's Liability Culture has been remarkably successful in getting its candidates into political offices. This is possible because the environmental Left component of the Liability Culture has two faces: the *honest face* (their true beliefs presented in chapter 1) and the *political face* (presented by its political candidates). The Liability Culture has long known that it could never elect candidates who campaigned on their true beliefs. So their candidates wear their political face, the face on the "side of the angels" (described in chapter 10). The difference between what they say and what actually occurs is stark. (See chapter 11).

In other words, the political leaders of the Liability Culture are counterproductive in their own stated terms. Their activities are destructive of both the human and the natural environments even though their political arm says it wants to improve both. The bottom line result of all laws, regulations, and rules emanating from the politicians of the environmental Left component of the Liability Culture is to further the aims of the major leaders of the movement as quoted in chapter 1. Thus, when the public votes for the political Left it is actually voting against refrigeration, air conditioning, and automobiles and voting for the destruction of much of humanity. This discussion leads to:

Principle 31. Politicians from the environmental Left trumpet their environmental concerns. However, the laws and regulations they create are antienvironmental because they produce results that are consistent with the ideas of the philosophical leaders of the environmental Left as summarized in chapter 1. (See also chapters 10, 11, and 12.)

CONCLUSIONS

Most leaders of the Liability Culture probably do not seek environmental improvement but political power leading to political changes (in the name of environmental improvement). Their power is directed toward implementing a new Luddism. Therefore, we see reducing the power of the leaders of the Liability Culture as absolutely essential for improving the environment of the world for the sake of both humans and nature.

We have described the cultural and political conflict as between those who focus on liabilities and those who focus on assets. We have described the sides as the Asset Culture and the Liability Culture or, philosophically, the free marketers versus the political Left. We see most doers of the Asset Culture as so preoccupied with doing that they ignore many of the implications of activities of the Liability Culture. When the Left attaches impediments to their productivity, the doers first complain, then shrug, and finally keep on doing while accommodating to the imposed constraints. The conflict is similar to that described by Ayn Rand in *Atlas Shrugged.*

So the doers build automobiles, television sets, and satellites; they grow crops, mine minerals, repair cars, pump gasoline, and go to work every day trying to improve their world, trying to fill their obligations. These people build the nation's assets. Full speed ahead!

The intellectual Left of the Liability Culture questions almost all of this. *They point out the liability side of virtually every activity devoted to the creation of assets.* So they dig in their heels and try to restrain the doers. Full speed backward!

Yet the intellectual Left that supplies much of the philosophical drive for the Liability Culture overlooks one factor: they owe their very existence to the doers. The arts, the educational and government institutions, only became possible when humans did not have to spend all of their time just surviving. The great ancient cultural centers arose when doers figured out how one person could produce enough food for many people. Only then did intellectuals have the time to criticize the doers.

Currently, there are few great artists, philosophers, or scientists in Third World nations. The people must simply spend too much of their time surviving. The opportunity to intellectualize is a luxury that rests firmly on the shoulders of the doers of the Asset Culture.

In the long run, the best way the world's human and natural environments can improve is for this chapter's principles to become an integral part of the world's culture.

REFERENCES

Barrons, K. C. 1975. *The Food in Your Future.* New York: Van Nostrand Reinhold.

Borlaug, N. E. 1993. Foreword to E. M. Whelan, *Toxic Terror: The Truth behind the Cancer Scare.* Buffalo, N.Y.: Prometheus Books.

Bumb, B. 1989. *Global Fertilizer Perspective, 1960–1995.* Muscle Shoals, Ala.: International Fertilizer Development Center for Agency for International Development.

Carson, R. 1962. *Silent Spring.* New York: Houghton Mifflin.

Gore, A. 1992. *Earth in the Balance.* New York: Houghton Mifflin.

Manes, C. 1990. *Green Rage.* Boston: Little, Brown.

Milbank, D. 1994. In this solitude, a Finnish thinker posits cataclysms. *Wall Street Journal,* May 20, A1.

Reisman, G. 1992. The toxicity of environmentalism. *The Freeman,* September, 336–50.

United Nations. 1992. *Earth Summit Agenda 21, The United Nations Programme of Action from Rio.* New York: United Nations Department of Public Information.

Whelan, E. M. 1993. *Toxic Terror: The Truth behind the Cancer Scare.* Buffalo, N.Y.: Prometheus Books.

CHAPTER 14

Toward a Better World for Future Generations

How can we leave an improved world for the future? Before we answer this question, we must define a word. We think this is necessary because the philosophical component of the Liability Culture has so confused values that once seemed self-evident. We define as *bad* anything that needlessly shortens people's lives. We believe that destroying forests, wildlife, soil, and other natural resources is *bad*. Now we can discuss how to improve the world.

- The First World, as typified by America, must do two things: (1) replace the Liability Culture's negativity with positive forces; and (2) eliminate government hurdles that hinder First World growth.
- Both the First and Third Worlds must realize that the most significant environmental improvements are the result of human activities on the asset side of the environmental ledger.
- Third World nations must eliminate internal roadblocks to industrial development so they can encourage investment by multinational corporations (MNCs).
- The First World must eliminate roadblocks it places on Third World industrialization and health.
- Third World nations must realize that loans to their governments from multilateral banking institutions and the UN usually do not help them evolve from Third World status.

One serious limiting condition exists: a shortage of capital. Because of the commitment of financial resources to solve currently popular liability-side environmental concerns (e.g., global warming, acid rain, ozone depletion, and trivial quantities of industrial chemicals), the amount of accumulated new wealth is greatly diminished. A major consequence of liability activities is that they make less capital available for improving the world's environmental assets.

In this chapter we briefly summarize the orientation and activities that can lead to an improved world environment—both human and natural. It is essential that development of natural resources (the extractive industries) and the facilities to convert the materials into marketable products be developed. Only this approach can provide the wealth all nations need for improving the environment. Open market economies best produce wealth. Johnson and Sheehy (1995), after analyzing ten economic indicators for 101 countries, conclude:

- Countries with free economic systems enjoy the highest degree of economic development.

- Government spending and interference in the economy, even in developed nations, restrict economic freedom and can lead to recessions.

- Some First World countries have less economic freedom than some Second World countries. Such First World nations first accumulated wealth but then adopted regulations that reduced their capability to generate new wealth. Simultaneously, they committed accumulated wealth to government programs.

SOCIETAL EFFICIENCY AND WEALTH

Humanity's production of wealth is basic to the improvement of both human and natural environments. Within the context of this book, we investigate briefly some factors that allow humans to improve the asset side of the environmental ledger while controlling the liability side. The lessons are learned from observing the wealth-producing environment of the First World and comparing it with that of the Third World.

Currently, the mechanisms that limit the ability to create wealth in the First World are largely *self-imposed.* They take the form of laws and regulations meant to protect people from liabilities. Too often the liabilities envisioned are either trivial or nonexistent. The Third World cannot learn how to overcome their own environmental liabilities from the First World's Liability Culture intellectuals. As we showed in chapter 7, solving all the environmental "problems" the First World visualizes will not make the world any greener and, most important, will not solve any of the most significant Third World problems.

As we showed in chapter 6, environmental liabilities found in the Third World are severe and indisputable. Many of the obstacles to the production of wealth are *imposed by nature* (in contrast to the First World's self-imposed obstacles). However, the Third World can still learn from us—not by listening to our Liability Culture intellectuals, but by seeing what we actually did to improve our most important environmental assets and to decrease our significant environmental liabilities. In chapters 2 through 6, we described the mechanisms and we further analyzed them in chapters 7 through 9. What have we learned? What can the Third World learn from us? What steps are needed for the Third World to improve its human and natural environments?

Health

First World people are the world's healthiest. Stripping away the hypochondriacal concerns that somehow the leaders of the Liability Culture are able to make many people worry about (Nader's corporate cancer, for example), the bottom line is that we live continuously longer. The health of people in First World nations increased in spurts—first because of chlorination of drinking water; then because of refrigeration; and then because of immunization. Improving health continues. The Third World can learn from us.

In contrast with our longevity, Third World people lead short lives. Perhaps, just as bad, human productive efficiency is low because so many Third World people suffer from debilitating diseases. If we total the number of people on Earth who suffer from sicknesses imposed largely by their natural environment, we find that over 14 billion people suffer annually (see table 6.2). Since there are only about 5 billion to 6 billion people on Earth, obviously many people suffer from more than one disease in a year, either simultaneously or sequentially. The effects of these diseases range from bouts with malaria to blindness. The ability of Third World nations to produce wealth is severely impeded by the debilitating effects of disease. Improving the human environment is a first requisite for increasing wealth.

Other Societal Efficiencies

People in most Third World nations live in very inefficient societies. For example, when people spend hours a day finding wood or dried dung for fuel, carrying water from wells or water holes, and transporting produce or other goods on their backs or on pack animals, industrial efficiency is virtually impossible.

People in industrial nations, by contrast, have energy and water at their fingertips and efficient transportation is ubiquitous.

Toward Greater Efficiency

So far as health is concerned, people of the Third World are improving. The bottom line—longevity—is improving. Yet table 6.2 shows that they have a long way to go. The World Health Organization and private organizations through education and medical help have done well. Still we count hundreds of millions of needless deaths because DDT is not in general use. Improved living conditions, clean water, and insect disease vector control are all insufficient. Only healthy populations can be vigorous, productive populations.

Inexpensive energy, developed water resources, efficient transportation, control of insect vectors, and refrigeration are all requisite to human efficiency. However, the leaders of the Liability Culture are against cheap energy, have blocked the construction of dams all over the world, and laud the bicycle as "appropriate technology." They also bear responsibility for the death of over 9,600 people from cholera in Latin America when Peruvian health officials ceased using chlorine in drinking water. Clearly, the leaders of the Liability Culture are major obstacles to improving the productive efficiency of Third World people. Unless their power is reduced, the Third World will continue to face excessive health problems. In addition, their ability to produce wealth will be severely hampered.

TO CONTINUE IMPROVEMENT OF AMERICA'S ENVIRONMENTS

Although America has vastly improved its human and natural environments, it can do much better. For continued improvement, we visualize the following steps:

- The public must be constantly reminded that the environmental ledger has two sides. Our analysis of the largely ignored asset side of the ledger shows that the most significant improvements in the natural and human environments historically have been in the industrial nations. Most of that has been in the past seven decades. Industrialization, with all its highly publicized faults, has created humankind's greatest environmental successes. Liability-side regulations caused significant environmental improvements in early days of the environmental movement. However, current regulations are costly and are now environmentally counterproductive.

- America's government should not discourage production of wealth and should not discourage[1] technological change, especially in agriculture, energy, and materials research. Government programs that drain a nation's wealth should be eliminated. Government nondiscouragement should manifest itself as staying out of the way, allowing a market-oriented system to operate. For example, the food industry should be allowed to continue increasing quantities of food per acre, getting the maximum percentage to market, and reducing spoilage once within stores, homes, and restaurants. These things occur naturally in a market-oriented system. They will not occur if government regulations block what makes them possible.

- America must massively reduce environmental laws and resultant regulations pertaining to both humans and nature. Only then can America retain and expand its environmental gains, and continue to multiply its resources. Any remaining regulations should be kept only after rigorous economic and environmental risk assessment analyses. As part of such analyses, dispersed economic and conservation effects should never be ignored. The value of agricultural chemicals, for example, should be not only measured in economic terms, but in terms of their indirect widely dispersed effects on forests, wildlife, water resources, and soil erosion.

- America should not overlook the option of totally eliminating many regulatory agencies (especially the 130,000 regulation writers). After all, people and business entities are already liable for any damages they may inflict. Federal regulatory control is an incredibly expensive way to control the environment. Additionally, the regulatory agencies may be too contaminated with Liability Culturists to be effective or efficient.

- The concept of multiple resource management in which the use of one resource creates or enhances another should consciously be used. To date, resource multiplication has largely been an inadvertent spin-off of the efficiencies of industrialization. Farsighted technology could lead to more resource multiplication.

- Free enterprise should be enshrined as a way of life. Free people will not only create wealth; they will inevitably improve their human and natural environments. Free people will usually leave a better world for their children.

- Any management of the natural environment should be in the hands of trained professional soil, water, wildlife, and forest managers who have no political agenda except that they feel people are more important than nature. Both people and nature will then be better off.

Until the some three hundred environmental laws and the resultant regulations of the following types are reevaluated and many removed, the United States will continue to be an economic giant with its hands tied. Consider:

- The Clean Air Act Amendments of 1990. In chapter 11 we showed that Congress ignored the NAPAP report and passed the Clean Air Act Amendment of 1990. Congress also ignored the huge annual costs of compliance and the resultant increase in energy costs. Congress also ignored the huge dispersed benefit of over 140 million acres of new forest generated in part because of *low* energy prices. Increasing energy prices potentially jeopardize the new forests.

- The Delaney Clause of 1958 to the Food, Drug and Cosmetics Act. The Delaney Clause forbids the addition of animal carcinogens to the food supply. An animal carcinogen means any industrial substance which, when fed to or inserted into laboratory animals at near-toxic levels, causes tumors or cancers. Only the risk of industrial chemicals could be considered, not the offsetting benefits. Yet, as we have shown, the dispersed benefits from industrial chemicals include not only economic benefits but a multiplication of natural resources. Given current knowledge, the Delaney Clause is a dinosaur that controls too much of the nation's economy.

    The most devastating research showing the silliness of the Delaney Clause is by Dr. Bruce Ames and his associates at the University of California–Berkeley. Dr. Ames is a biochemist who developed the Ames test for studying the potential carcinogenicity of chemicals by using bacteria. Ames and his associates found there are some ten thousand times more *natural* carcinogens in the foods we eat than there are industrial chemicals (Ames et al. 1987, 1990; Gold et al. 1992). Yet very little research is done on natural carcinogens. In other words, *our priorities are upside down;* for optimal public health, we *should* spend ten thousand times more studying the effects of natural carcinogens than on the effects of industrial chemicals. However, the reverse is more likely true. Consequently, we do not know how much we can eat of the many carcinogen-containing foods such as basil, tomatoes, tea, peanut butter, and celery, before they endanger our health. Nor do we know enough about natural food chemicals that reduce cancer. "The long-lasting flap about the Delaney Clause and synthetic pesticides probably had the side effect of increasing cancer by diverting attention from the real factors causing the dreaded disease" (Abelson 1993, 1235).

- The Environmental Impact Statement (EIS). The EIS, as it has been used, is a way to block development. Usually, the EIS only considers local or anecdotal effects of an action. For example, a mining operation in southern New York was blocked because it would disturb the habitat of the timber rattlesnake. The EIS could not point out that the habitat of the timber rattlesnake has enormously expanded in New York State because of afforestation. Countless projects have been blocked or, at the very least, made much more expensive because of environmental analyses. However, builders have *always* been legally liable for any damage they cause. The EIS serves only to hinder development. As we have shown, without development America would regress environmentally.

- The Endangered Species Act (ESA) of 1972. Arnold and Gottlieb (1993, 16) describe the act as "the single most destructive economy trasher law on the books." The ESA does not require the federal government to analyze the ecological and economic impacts of the extinction of a species; that is, only one side of the environmental ledger can be considered. Yet, considering America's vastly increased forest cover and woodland wildlife, *we are already improving nature and protecting many species.* We are doing this without regulations because it is the natural result of industrialization.

  Protecting rare species is very costly. Keep in mind that through all of Earth's history virtually all species of life have either become extinct or evolved into something else. Are we actually blocking the natural laws of nature for many species? Do we want to spend $620,331,000 to save some very rare species of flora or fauna (Anon. 1994a, A14)? These costs do not include loss of land values and personal assets of people whose land is home to an endangered species (or even near an endangered species; Richardson and Ziebart 1994, 54, 55).

  Perhaps worse, endangered species have been used to block many economic activities. Reduction of economic activities usually has negative dispersed environmental impacts. One of these impacts would be to harm wildlife (see chapters 3 and 4).

  Fraud has been common. The snail darter, used to block the Tellico Dam, was found to be relatively common; and the northern spotted owl, used to block lumbering activities in the Northwest, was found to have a much broader habitat than just old forests (Easterbrook 1994, 22–23). The "protection" of the old forest habitat of the northern spotted owl is at the expense of most other types of wildlife because old forests have little on which most wildlife can subsist. Additionally, old forests are very flammable. When such old forests burn, as they inevitably will, what happens to the northern spotted owl? We suggest that fire is far more traumatic than lumbering. Fires are also very expensive.

  Finally, we should remember that primitive people were responsible for the destruction of perhaps thousands of species (see chapter 4 and Steadman 1995). It has only been the industrial societies in the past few decades that have ever been deeply concerned about the loss of species. However, that concern has been misdirected. Were saving species the primary motivation, we would have directed much of the hundreds of millions of dollars spent in America to Third World nations where far more species are in danger.

Reisman (1992, 349) recommends repealing "every law and regulation in any way tainted by the doctrine of intrinsic value [of nature], such as the Endangered Species Act."

- America should review curbside recycling of household trash. Bailey (1995, A1) says: "It costs residents and local governments hundreds of millions of dollars more than can be recouped by selling the sorted trash." Bailey measures costs in terms of capital expenditure for new trucks, added energy consumption, increased traffic, and air pollution. Initially, curbside recycling started in response to a supposed shortage of dump space. There is no such shortage. Typically, the EPA, which agrees that there is no shortage of dump capacity, continues to distribute materials warning of a shortage of capacity. Further, radio advertising sponsored by the EPA, the Environmental Defense Fund, and the Ad Council implies that, somehow, recycling will save the world. Like virtually all other government environmental programs, curbside recycling is enormously expensive. It is largely simply bad conservation.

- The burden of proof in environmental litigation should be the responsibility of the plaintiff as in criminal and other civil cases. The accused should be presumed innocent unless proven guilty.[2] Considering the huge environmental gains in the past seventy years in industrial nations, the presumption of environmental innocence is reasonable. An accused industry can then be relieved of the position of having to "prove" a negative. That industry has not been given the rights of others in courts of law is a masterpiece of leftist maneuvering. Finally, to reduce frivolous and often costly lawsuits, the loser should pay the costs of litigation.

- The environmental and economic prudence of government locking up vast acreages of land in wilderness areas should be reevaluated. The environmentalists' rationale is what Reisman (1992) has called "the intrinsic value of nature." Such withdrawals of land place nature above humans. This is compatible with some environmentalists' views in chapter 1. Yet, do we really want to block such human activities as lumbering, mining, energy development, recreation, or other economic activities? Preventing such activities is ultimately environmentally harmful. In most cases, America has looked at the point problems of economic activities and ignored the dispersed benefits.

All of the above and all of the programs discussed in chapters 11 and 12 have high costs and in most cases gain little or no value in return. Financial priorities as related to risk are precisely upside down. Current regulatory trends are suicidal. In the long run, only some components of the Liability Culture seem to gain. The reevaluation and modification or elimination of laws, regulations, and regulatory agencies are basic to improving America's environment.

TO IMPROVE THE THIRD WORLD'S ENVIRONMENTS

Third World nations are those in environmental Phase I in which human survival is the uppermost problem (see chapter 9). Third World nations are characterized by the highest birthrates, highest infant mortality, highest air particulate levels, lowest longevity, highest disease rates, poorest sanitation conditions, poorest water, and lowest education compared with other nations. Agriculture is the primary occupation and most live directly off the land. They are consuming their forests, wildlife, and soil (see chapters 2, 3, and 4). However, their natural environment cannot be significantly improved until their human environmental problems are solved. Maslow (1970, 3) defined the problem: "For our chronically and extremely hungry man, Utopia can be defined simply as a place where there is plenty of food. . . . Anything else will be defined as unimportant." To ask people who are often short of the barest necessities to conform to First World environmental regulations is both cruel and impractical.

Even without First World impracticalities, improvement is difficult because Third World societies are both highly corrupt and culturally divided. Their APCGNP is less than $1,000 (see chapter 8). The Third World's first economic-environmental goal is to increase APCGNP to the Second World level of $1,000 to $3,000.

Environmental improvement for the Third World first requires removing internal and external obstacles to development. To remove internal obstacles a nation *must truly want to develop.* The reason is that major and, often wrenching, societal changes will be required. Sometimes it will be necessary to change cultural patterns that are thousands of years old. Removing external obstacles requires the removal of Liability Culture influences from the UN, USAID, the World Bank, and other aid institutions.

Self-Administered Prescription for the Third World

Environmental improvement in Third World nations means they must go through a process similar to that which has led to environmental gains in industrial nations. We see no alternative. The major human problems must be solved before problems of the natural environment. This requires technology and the production of wealth. The wealth-producing process can be accelerated because the Third World can learn from us, using our newest and most efficient medical and industrial technologies—*provided we teach them.*

One of the fastest and least costly ways to jump start a Third World economy is to create a sociopolitical environment that favors the entry of multinational corporations (MNCs). MNCs

- will enter only if there is probability of profit
- pay their own way

- will not cause national debt
- will train local people
- will show how to compete in the world economy
- will leave much of their generated wealth in the hands of local people
- will not require a massive bureaucracy

The value of MNCs for developing nations has been described and analyzed extensively by Osterfeld (1994). Osterfeld also answers many criticisms of MNCs that emanate from the political Left. The arguments of the Left against MNCs are considerably weakened by the Left's own total lack of economic and developmental success.

To start the industrialization process, Third World governments should encourage (or at least not discourage) entrepreneurs and the creation of wealth. They should begin by:

- creating a political environment that allows free enterprise and encourages the entry of MNCs
- being politically stable enough so created wealth is reinvested back into the economy by those who create it
- reducing corruption to the extent that siphoned wealth is reinvested in the nation
- maintaining such infrastructure as health clinics, power, transportation, water supply, and sewage disposal
- reducing tribal animosities
- minimizing restrictions on the private sector
- educating children

Assuming that the industrialization process proceeds, the sequence of environmental phases for improving Third World nations should be:

- Improving the human environment. Without a better human environment, other environmental gains will not occur. The first wealth created by a rising Third World nation should go to improving the health of its people.
- Improving agriculture. Just as First World nations needed agricultural efficiency before they could improve their natural environments, so must Third World nations. They need to increase food production per unit of land. They need to deliver food products to markets with minimum spoilage. The latter needs sound transportation infrastructure, including all-weather farm-to-market roads, and viable vehicles, along with such techniques as modern food preservation and protection from fungi and rodents. These improvements take pressure off natural resources. Any land reform must contribute to achieving these goals.
- Improving the natural environment and expanding resources. These occur as a natural result of an improved human environment and more efficient agriculture. They continue as nations modernize.

An improving human environment and more efficient agriculture, while starting at somewhat different times, are largely synchronous and closely interrelated. The third phase starts later, probably only after a nation has reached Second World status (i.e., its APCGNP exceeds $1,000).

Uganda is an example of what is possible. Under the leadership of Henry Ssewannyana of the Foundation for African Development in Kampala, a program was initiated to promote the "new African village of the year 2000." This is a self-initiative at the local level that includes not only the financial but educational, health, and governing aspects of life. In the Masaka area, progress has been phenomenal in just five years. Despite severe loss of life from AIDS, there are new schools, increased crop production, improved farm roads, properly designed wells to provide clean water, education and sanitation improvement, and eradication of measles (a major killer of children in Africa). None of these programs resulted from international financial or environmental organizations.

Externally Administered Aid for the Third World

The transfer of health technology from First to Third World nations has already been of much value. Many Third World nations now have human life expectancies that are higher than America's in 1900, although the Third World has not caught up with other technologies used in America in 1900. Additionally, use of First World contraceptive technology has reduced birthrates in many areas.

However, helping the Third World achieve Second World economic status has been a more stubborn problem. According to Bandow and Vasquez (1994, 1): "Multilateral lending institutions have flooded the Third World with . . . nearly $300 billion" since the 1950s, yet there are "few, if any, cases in which their efforts have led to improved living standards." Johnson and Sheehy (1995, 7) state that America's economic assistance alone has been $257,356,600,000 by 1994, with another $13 billion in 1994. America's total assistance, including military, through 1994 is about half a trillion dollars. The failure of the world's multilateral lending institutions to benefit the Third World is largely a bureaucratic failure. The blame is with bureaucrats both within lending institutions and within the Third World itself.

UN, USAID, and World Bank aid often come with leftist strings attached, effectively hampering the wise use of the aid. *The Economist* says: "To build obstacles on the developing countries' path out of poverty would be the crime of the century." We agree when *The Economist* added, "Happily, it is preventable" (Anon. 1994b, 69). (Preventable, we suggest, if the Liability Culture does not win the environmental war.) As we have noted before, the First World also needs to remove obstacles it places in the way of improving health of Third World nations.

Few politicians—particularly those with socialistic beliefs—understand that "We should realize that real prosperity is created from the bottom up, not from government down. Wealth must be created, not redistributed'' (Bauman 1994). Yet, Roberts (1994, 147) observes that at a 1987 conference at Stanford University about the Latin American debt crisis, most participants from both North and South America were Marxists. There is no historic proof that Marxists understand the mechanisms for creation of wealth. Additionally, aid to the Third World, if controlled by the nihilists, who are against free enterprise and economic growth, is certainly of doubtful value. Advice from the political Left will rarely benefit Third World nations.

Simply transferring wealth from the First World to the Third World does not help. Such money too often enriches politicians and bureaucrats. They then transfer the money to investments or accounts outside their countries. Also, Third World nations could become a permanent world underclass that is discouraged from helping itself by becoming reliant on handouts from other nations.

The Third World can be helped by the First World by educating them how to help themselves. However, meaningful education will only come from people with a pro-free market orientation.

Can the UN Help?

The UN's plans for the world's environment have been promulgated in many documents. We refer in particular to *Agenda 21,* an outgrowth of the Rio de Janeiro meeting on environment and development. The Rio document is consistent with Ruddle and Rondinelli (1982), the World Commission on Environment and Development (1987), and the UN (1990, 1991).

These documents largely imply that rich nations got that way by exploiting poor nations. The World Commission and UN documents have several things in common. Much of the justification for the major changes that they recommend are the ''eco-catastrophes'' they visualize from acid rain, CFCs (ozone depletion), and the greenhouse effect (mainly from carbon dioxide buildup). Considering that all these problems are very speculative, one must automatically be suspicious of all of their data and conclusions. These UN documents—typical of America's Liability Culture—make no attempt at balance, selecting only the downside of each ''problem.'' For example, the fact that carbon dioxide is plant food and could help alleviate hunger by increasing crop yields is minimized. So is the fact that earth warming could allow crops to be grown in more northerly areas. The importance of inexpensive refrigeration for environmental improvement is not mentioned in the CFC discussions. Similarly, discussions of such farm chemicals as mineral fertilizers and pesticides say virtually nothing about the increases in crop yields that result. The importance of high crop yields to forests, wildlife, and soil is a correlation also not made.

The UN documents, in other words, mirror the perspectives of the leftists of America's Liability Culture. Their primary interest is to attack the industrialization process, particularly in Western nations. Attacking Western cultures is not necessarily the same as improving the environment; in fact, it is precisely the opposite.

The questions the public should ask are: Has the UN been so contaminated with anti-Western philosophies that it has no redeeming features? Can the UN say that it represents people of the Third World? Does it represent people of the First World? In fact, what is the real purpose of the UN as it now exists?

We do not see how the UN, as currently constituted, can be of help for the Third World. Some excerpts from the *Earth Summit Agenda 21* (United Nations 1992) show why.

- From the foreword by Maurice F. Strong: "Industrial countries continue to be addicted to the patterns of production and consumption that have so largely produced the major risks to the global environment." Also: "eco-revolution— essential—to a more secure, sustainable and equitable future."

  Both statements show that Strong ignores, minimizes, or does not know of the natural and human environmental gains in industrial nations. Does he really want the Third World to industrialize?

- From *Agenda* principle 15 (p. 10): "Where there are threats of serious or irreversible damage, lack of full scientific certainty shall not be used as a reason for postponing cost-effective measures to prevent environmental degradation."

  This means, for example, whether the Earth is cooling (the 1970s idea) or warming (the 1980s idea) or cooling (the most recent scientific research), most eco-socialists have decided that the politically correct position is that the Earth is heating. (Do we actually believe that a five-degree increase in temperature is a bigger problem than a thousand feet of ice?) Preventing the use of fossil fuel (along with hydropower and atomic power) can only increase the use of wood for fuel. The carbon dioxide from burning a tree is no different from the carbon dioxide produced by burning coal or oil. However, if a tree is not replaced, there is *less* plant growth to absorb carbon dioxide; that is, if there is a carbon dioxide problem it is exacerbated.

- From *Agenda* principle 17 (p. 10): "Environmental impact assessment, as a national instrument, shall be undertaken for proposed activities." This opens the door to blocking virtually any development. Even without official empowerment, some of America's environmental organizations have already blocked many foreign developments (particularly hydropower and mining).

- From p. 91: "Ensuring the sustainable management of all forest ecosystems and woodlands, through improved proper planning, management and timely implementation of silvicultural operations." We ask, planning by whom, managed by whom, implemented by whom? The UN plans to carry out its ideas through what would have to be a massive bureaucracy. On page 286, the UN is visualized as coordinating various existing agencies and making a new agency called "Development Watch" to be coordinated with Earthwatch. Is an efficient, flexible, and, above all, wise UN bureaucracy a possibility? Or is this a fantasy? None of this can give assurance to people of the Third World that the UN will do any more than place more obstacles in the way of their industrialization. They should be particularly concerned about their future because the world's two leading government environmentalists, Strong and Gore, see little benefit from industrial development.

The UN's Rio conferees saw more government (presumably leftist) at both the world and individual state levels as the best mechanism for "development." However, the writers of *Agenda 21* say little about the ability of free people to make decisions or about the creation of wealth. They say much about the redistribution of wealth, for example, "a substantial flow of new and additional financial resources to developing countries" (p. 15).

Incidentally, many Third World representatives at Rio approved the Strong–Gore proposed protocols. However, representatives of many Third World countries will readily agree to any proposals that promise funds to their countries because so much of the money finds its way into the pockets of bureaucrats and politicians.

We suggest that the UN's environmental and developmental components do not represent the needs of people of the world. They represent the Liability Culture and its destructive underlying Luddite philosophy. First World nations should either change the UN perspective or should consider abandoning the UN as a lost cause. In fairness to the UN, the World Health Organization and the Food and Agricultural Organization are in conflict with the environment and development component. The latter's policies are detrimental to both world health and the production of food.

Can America Help?

The UN and multilateral lending institutions, as currently constituted, are unlikely to help the Third World industrialize. What can America do on its own? In addition to removing obstacles to pesticide use, America can help in a surprising way: America can *look out for its own economic self-interest in energy.* A major setback for improving environments of Third World nations was the sharp increase in oil prices, starting in 1973–1975 when OPEC quadrupled oil prices to $12 a barrel. Then in 1978–1979 they managed to get oil prices to $35 a barrel. This caused an increase in oil costs for Africa from $1.4 billion in 1978 to $3.1 billion in 1980. Expensive fuel forced Third World people to use more biomass for energy (for more details, see also Dunn 1978, 1980). High energy costs also drove fertilizer prices sharply upward (Bumb 1989). Both results put added stress on Third World land, forests, and wildlife, along with their economic systems and their human environments. *The United States indirectly contributed to high energy prices and environmental stresses* by making itself vulnerable to oil price increases. It failed to develop many of its coal and oil resources and failed to properly develop atomic energy. Even now, development of much of America's energy resources is being blocked by environmentalists. It may not be coincidental that several members of the Environmental

Grantmakers Association owe their wealth to big oil companies that benefit from high energy prices. If the nation reverses the trend and drives energy prices downward, America could do more for the natural and human environments of the world than almost any other single activity. Also the United States would benefit. One of the largest single items in its balance-of-payment deficit is purchase of petroleum from the OPEC nations, some $30 billion annually. Additionally, relatively high use of wood for fuel in the United States (22% of the wood cut now, up to 55% in 1980 during the energy crisis) would probably be reduced. Unfortunately, the Clinton administration is on record as favoring higher energy prices for "environmental" reasons.

America can help in another way. Do not impose leftist, anti-industrial strings on aid to Third World nations. A recent example is from H.R. 5162, 1992, a bill authored by Representative Owens. It calls for all loans in the energy sector to Third World nations to be for "least cost" investment plans that "analyze end-use efficiency and nonconventional renewable energy applications, especially solar energy technologies" and provide "gradually [to] forgive those debts [obligations of the governments of developing counties] in return for adoption of sustainable development policies, such as programs of agrarian reform and energy conservation and dissemination of nonconventional, renewable energy technologies." The agrarian reform includes nonuse of commercial fertilizers and pesticides; the energy conservation emphasizes the use of nonmotorized transport, both road and rail. Such a policy would be suicidal for the natural environments as can be seen in chapters 2, 3, and 4. Further, applying America's environmental standards to Third World nations can only retard their development and, hence, damage their health and longevity. Chapter 12 showed that health problems of Third World nations can be millions of times more severe than America's. America's standards are simply not applicable to the Third World.

Environmental Impacts of Third World Industrialization

If American government and UN obstacles to development can be overcome, the industrialization process for the Third World can proceed. When wealth is created, the following environmental benefits *will occur naturally:*

- Continued improvement of health (better nutrition and personal hygiene, improvement of health clinics, treatment of drinking water and increased water storage, sewage collection, and sewage treatment)
- Reduced population growth
- Expansion of forest, wildlife, and soil resources

The above gains are the inevitable and largely spontaneous results of industrialization as have been demonstrated for all major industrial societies. Regulations, particularly stringent arbitrary regulations, are not required for these events to occur.

Finally, once major environmental improvements become a Third World reality, appropriate regulations controlling waste materials can be introduced because the people will expect more. However, the regulatory process must proceed cautiously. Any regulations should be made only after performing appropriate cost–benefit analyses within the framework of the appropriate risk assessment analyses, dispersed effects analyses, and public wishes for each nation.

Is all of this possible? We think so. Faiia (1991) puts it well: "We human beings have wonderful opportunities before us. We can assure that everyone has enough to eat and no one suffers unnecessarily. We can go beyond ideology and narrow self-interest. It just remains for us to do it." Faiia, no Pilgrim, speaks from two years' experience with the Peace Corps and thirteen years with CARE in such places as Bangladesh, Malaysia, Ethiopia, Somalia, Haiti, and Nepal. The answers to improving our world are around us and clearly visible to those capable of positive thinking—the problem solvers of the world.

Largely, our book is a warning about the danger of losing the environmental gains much of the world has enjoyed in recent decades. We seek to shine light into the dark corners of environmental ignorance. Environmental blindness can cause us to regress. Environmental regressions are a real danger. Some have occurred.

For example:

- America regressed during the high energy prices of the 1970s. Suddenly, wood was the fuel of choice for many people; about 55 percent of the wood cut in America was used for fuels. We started to lose our new forests. Fortunately, energy prices adjusted and our forests did not suffer excessively.

- Russia is seeing a sharp reduction in life expectancy, so that men now anticipate a life of less than sixty years (Spector 1995). Life expectancy this low is Third World class. Their wealth-creating machinery is in disarray, and their wealth decreases (see chapter 8).

- Some Third World nations are regressing as their agricultural sectors expand and their wealth decreases (see chapter 8). (This is the normal result of agriculturalization of a population.)

Those who want the world to revert to some previous state do not have far to go. After all, for thousands of years, humans have caused deterioration of the natural environment as the price of improvement in the human condition. Only in the past seventy years has humankind also been able to improve nature. Regression is easy. The normal situation has been environmental deterioration. If we continue to raise the price of energy and continue to hinder the wealth-creating machinery; if we continue to hamper or block the use of life-saving chemicals; and if we drive agricultural productivity backward, *societies will regress.* The nihilistic component of the Liability Culture will have "won." The natural environment will also deteriorate. Both humanity and nature will then pay the price of ignorance.

CONCLUSIONS

Improving the human and natural environments of the world is complex and requires education leading to the public's understanding of both the asset and liability sides of the environmental ledger. The people of First World nations will then understand the need to remove regulatory obstacles that impede further expansion of natural resources and continue to improve the human condition. All environmental regulations and federal withdrawals of wilderness lands should be reviewed—in particular, those laws that place the welfare of nature above the welfare of humans. The human and natural environmental benefits of all environmental regulatory agencies should be reviewed. We have shown that the environmental impact of America's current laws and regulations will ultimately be destructive of both the human and natural environments.

Improving the human and natural environments of the Third World requires removing their own obstacles to development plus reducing obstacles placed by leftist political forces of the First World. Their internal obstacles are corruption, ethnic conflicts, lack of education, and incompetent governments.

External obstacles are largely created by politicians and bureaucrats of the political Left who dominate world organizations. Environmental-developmental programs under multilateral lending institutions and the UN are more directed toward furthering leftist ideologies than toward development. Redistributing wealth and controlling free enterprise are not the same as improving the human and natural environments. Blocking the development of energy resources, manufacturing industries, mining, and agriculture is environmentally destructive. Given its head, the Liability Culture will destroy much of the earth's soil, forest, and wildlife resources plus much of humanity. Mechanisms to accomplish this destruction are in place in both the United Nations and America. The destruction could occur in America even if conservatives are in power if they allow the destructive mechanisms to function.

Are we already too late? Have we already done irreversible economic and environmental damage? We suspect not. Can the American public be educated with sufficient rapidity about dangers of the cultural war? Or will they again put the forces of Luddism into political control? If they do, will the environmental Left achieve its destructive goals? While this is possible, we are optimistic that the public and their political representatives will exercise sound judgment.

Ultimately, the answers to the world's great environmental problems will come from people living in political systems that encourage technology, industry, and entrepreneurship. The benefits will be the natural result of caring, responsible human beings trying to leave behind a better world for their children.

NOTES

1. We use the phrase "not discourage" in preference to "encourage" because too frequently government "encouragement" is counterproductive.

2. As of March 1995 President Clinton had moved to remove "the presumption of (environmental) guilt from small businesses" (Klein 1995). We see this as a small step in the right direction.

REFERENCES

Abelson, P. H. 1993. Pesticides and food. *Science* 259: 1235.

Ames, B. N., R. Magaw, and L. S. Gold. 1987. Ranking possible carcinogenic hazards. *Science* 236: 271–72.

Ames, B. N., M. Profet, and L. S. Gold. 1990. Dietary pesticides (99.99% all natural). *Proceedings of the National Academy of Sciences* 87: 7777–81.

Anon. 1994a. The endangered gremlins act. *Wall Street Journal,* June 3, A14.

———. 1994b. Economic survey. *The Economist,* January 5, 69.

Arnold, R., and A. Gottlieb. 1993. *Trashing the Economy.* Bellevue, Wash.: Free Enterprise Press.

Bailey, R. 1995. Curbside recycling comforts the soul, but benefits are scant. *Wall Street Journal,* January 19, A1, A8.

Bandow, D., and I. Vasquez, eds. 1994. *Perpetuating Poverty.* Washington, D.C.: Cato Institute.

Bauman, M. 1994. The dangerous Samaritans: How we unintentionally injure the poor. *Imprimis* 23(1).

Bumb, B. 1989. *Global Fertilizer Perspective, 1960–1995.* International Fertilizer Development Center for Agency for International Development.

Dunn, J. R. 1978. Back to the land: Environmental suicide. *Reason* 9(11): 16–20.

———. 1980. Energy and environmental responsibility—an alternate view. *EOS Transactions* 61(3):1.

Easterbrook, B. 1994. The birds: The spotted owl, an environmental parable. *The New Republic,* March, 20.

Faiia, S. 1992. Balancing logic and compassion. *Rensselaer Alumni Magazine* (June): 22–27.

Gold, L. S., T. H. Stone, B. R. Stern, N. B. Manley, and B. N. Ames. 1992. Rodent carcinogens: setting priorities. *Science* 258: 261.

Johnson, B. T., and T. P. Sheehy. 1995. *Index of Economic Freedom.* Washington, D.C.: Heritage Foundation.

Klein, J. 1995. The birth of common sense. *Newsweek,* March 27, 31.

Maslow, A. H. 1970. *Motivation and Personality.* 2nd ed. New York: Harper and Row.

Osterfeld, D. 1994. The liberating potential of multinational corporations. In *Perpetuating Poverty,* edited by D. Bandow and I. Vasquez. Washington, D.C.: Cato Institute.

Reisman, G. 1992. The toxicity of environmentalism. *The Freeman,* September, 336–50.

Richardson, C. E., and G. C. Ziebart. 1994. *Red Tape in America.* Washington, D.C.: Heritage Foundation.

Roberts, P. C. 1994. Development planning in Latin America: The lifeblood of the mercantilist state. In *Perpetuating Poverty,* edited by D. Bandow and I. Vasquez. Washington, D.C.: Cato Institute.

Ruddle, K., and D. A. Rondinelli. 1983. *Transforming Natural Resources for Human Development: A Resource System Framework for Development Policy.* Tokyo: The United Nations.

Spector, M. 1993. Sea dumping ban: Good politics, but not necessarily good policy. *New York Times,* March 22.

———. 1995. Russian health care in a dismally poor state. *Albany Times Union,* February 19, A24.

Steadman, D. W. 1995. Prehistoric extinctions of Pacific Island birds; biodiversity meets zooarcheology. *Science* 267:1123–31.

United Nations. 1990. *Global Outlook 2000.* New York: United Nations Publications.

———. 1991. *Population, Resources and the Environment.* New York: UN Fund For Population Activities.

———. 1992. *Earth Summit Agenda 21, The United Nations Programme of Action from Rio.* New York: United Nations Department of Public Information.

World Commission on Environment and Development. 1987. *Our Common Future.* New York: Oxford University Press.

Selected Bibliography

We divide the selected bibliography into two parts: Left-compatible (Liability Culture) and Conservative-compatible (Asset Culture). The books of the two listed have contrasting purposes.

LEFT-COMPATIBLE OR LIABILITY CULTURE BOOKS

The books on this list advance the aims of the leaders of the Liability Culture. The books create or are based on fears. Some of the books are the basis for most of America's environmental legislation of the past three to four decades. The current answers to the envisioned problems are to increase regulations, preferably administered by a worldwide organization such as the UN. The environment is visualized as the cohesive force for world governance.

Carson, R. 1962. *Silent Spring*. New York: Houghton.

Chivian, E., ed. 1993. *Critical Condition*. Cambridge: MIT Press.

Commission on Global Governance. 1995. *Our Global Neighborhood*. Oxford: Oxford University Press.

DeBell, G., ed. 1970. *The Environmental Handbook*. New York: Ballantine Books.

Ehrlich, P. 1968. *The Population Bomb*. New York: Ballantine Books.

Gore, A. 1972. *Earth in the Balance*. Boston, New York, and London: Houghton Mifflin.

Lovins, A. B. 1977. *Soft Paths Toward a Durable Peace*. Cambridge, Mass.: Ballinger.

Mac Neill, J., P. Winsemius, T. Yakushiji. 1991. *Beyond Interdependence*. Oxford: Oxford University Press.

Meadows, D. H., D. L. Meadows, J. Randers and W. W. Behrens, II. 1972. *The Limits to Growth*. New York: Universe Books.

United Nations. 1990. *Global Outlook 2000*. New York: United Nations Publications.

———. 1992. *Climate Change and Transnational Corporations*. New York: United Nations Publications.

———. 1992. *Earth Summit Agenda 21*. New York: United Nations Reproduction Section.

World Commission on Environment and Development. 1987. *Our Common Future*. Oxford and New York: Oxford University Press.

CONSERVATIVE-COMPATIBLE OR ASSET CULTURE BOOKS

The books on this list are meant to advance the causes of Democracy. All are critical of the political Left from Communists to Socialists to many Liberals. Many are primarily critiques of Leftist anti-technologic concepts and are reactions to what the authors see as excesses. Some are mainly analyses of the economic impacts of Leftist policies. Some are devoted to analyses of the personalities, motivations, financing, and political impacts of the core of the political Left. We are in general agreement with these books.

Arnold, R., and A. Gottlieb. 1993. *Trashing the Economy*. Bellevue, Wash.: Free Enterprise Press.

Bailey, R., ed. 1995. *The True State of the World*. New York: The Free Press.

Barrons, K. 1975. *The Food in Your Future*. New York: Van Nostrand Reinhold.

Cheney, L. V. 1995. *Telling the Truth*. New York: Simon and Schuster.

Coffman, M. S. 1994. *Saviors of the Earth?* Chicago: Northfield Publishing.

Easterbrook, G. 1995. *A Moment on the Earth*. New York: Viking Penguin.

Efron, E. 1984. *The Apocalyptics: Cancer and the Big Lie*. New York: Simon and Schuster.

Kaufman, W. 1994. *No Turning Back*. New York: Basic Books.

London, H. I. 1984. *Why Are they Lying to Our Children?* New York: Stein and Day.

Maduro, R. A., and R. Schauerhammer. 1992. *The Holes in the Ozone Scare*. Washington, D.C.: 21st Century Science Associates.

Ray, D. L. 1993. *Environmental Overkill*. Washington, D.C.: Regnery Gateway.

Sowell, T. 1995a. *The Vision of the Anointed*. New York: Basic Books.

Wattenberg, B. J. 1984. *The Good News Is the Bad News Is Wrong*. New York: Simon and Schuster.

Whelan, E. 1993. *Toxic Terror: The Truth Behind the Cancer Scare*. Buffalo, NY: Prometheus Books.

Index

About the Authors

JAMES R. DUNN is a geologic consultant to Behr Dolbear, New York City. For twenty years a professor of geology (including environmental geology) at Rensselaer Polytechnic Institute, he founded the Dunn Corporation in 1960, a geological consultancy that evolved into an environmental firm with more than 350 employees. Dr. Dunn has more than 140 publications to his credit and has served as president of the American Institute of Professional Geologists.

JOHN E. KINNEY, P.E. DEE, is a Registered Professional Environmental Engineering Consultant and a Diplomate, American Academy of Environmental Engineers. A consultant to government, industry, and civic organizations for many years, he has testified at several legislative and oversight hearings on water and natural resources and provided consulting service on various environmental problems in Africa. He is author of more than 200 papers on environmental issues as well as many presentations.